The
Heart
of the
Photograph

100 QUESTIONS
FOR MAKING STRONGER,
MORE EXPRESSIVE
PHOTOGRAPHS

David duChemin

rockynook

The Heart *of the* Photograph
100 QUESTIONS FOR MAKING
STRONGER, MORE EXPRESSIVE
PHOTOGRAPHS

David duChemin
www.davidduchemin.com

EDITOR Ted Waitt
PROJECT MANAGER Lisa Brazieal
MARKETING COORDINATOR Mercedes Murray
COPYEDITOR Cynthia Haynes
PROOFREADER Valerie Witte
INTERIOR LAYOUT Kim Scott, Bumpy Design
COVER PRODUCTION Kim Scott,
Bumpy Design
COVER PHOTOGRAPH David duChemin

ISBN 978-1-68198-545-9
1st Edition (1st printing, March 2020)
© 2020 David duChemin
All photographs © David duChemin

Rocky Nook Inc.
1010 B Street, Suite 350
San Rafael, CA 94901
USA
www.rockynook.com

Distributed in the UK and Europe
by Publishers Group UK
Distributed in the U.S. and all other
territories by Ingram Publisher
Services

LIBRARY OF CONGRESS CONTROL NUMBER
2019939057

This book is printed on acid-free paper.

Printed in Korea

Dedicated to the memory of my father,
Richard Eric Duchemin (1942–2018).

About the Author

DAVID DUCHEMIN IS A HUMANITARIAN and world photographer. He has photographed on all seven continents, looking for adventure and beauty along the way. He is the author of several books about the craft and art of photography, including *Within the Frame, Photographically Speaking, The Visual Toolbox*, and *The Soul of the Camera*. He is the accidental founder of CraftandVision.com—an online educational resource for photographers—and a passionate fan of the amateur.

David's work can be found online at DavidDuChemin.com, as can his blog and the growing community of photographers who read it.

Table of Contents

Always the beautiful
answer who asks
a more beautiful
question.

—E. E. CUMMINGS

Better Questions

ONCE YOU START READING, it won't take you long to see that the subtitle of this book is wildly misleading. There are *many* more than 100 questions in this book.

This is a book of questions, many of which are intentionally vague, questions to which you may never find one single answer, nor should you. But it is important that you ask them all the same, because it is the search for possible answers, with camera in hand, that will produce for you the best photographs of your life. By that, I mean the strongest pictures of the life you live, the experiences you have, the moments and people that stir your heart and give your life meaning. It is through questions, and your pursuit of the possibilities they represent to you if you'll look earnestly for the answers, that you can best learn this craft in the way you long to know it.

The path to intuition and instinct begins with intention. It begins with learning to see things and think about things in new ways.

Before you begin, I want to have a word together, as though we were sitting in a cafe somewhere in the world, sharing stories and a cup of tea or a glass of wine, and the subject came around to the way we learn our craft, which is not far off from what is really happening—me sitting here with my cup of coffee imagining what I would say to the person to whom I write this: you.

It would be very easy to read this book in one sitting, to blaze through it in search of a few spells or incantations that give you a nudge here or there, secrets that reveal to you some new insight that changes everything. They aren't here. But the keys are. The questions I pose, and others that will come to you as you read, are the keys. It is you asking them, chasing down answers of your own, and wrestling with them, often while shooting, that will open your mind to new directions and new understanding.

In reading this book, it would be easy to get overwhelmed. I imagine you cracking the spine and looking up, already defeated, and asking if I'm serious. Do I really expect you to ask every question in this book before you make a photograph? It's not possible. It's not realistic. It's probably not even humane!

Several years ago, someone wrote a criticism of my encouragement to photographers to be more intentional and thoughtful about their photographs. He wrote, "I didn't pick up a camera to think this hard." Perhaps this explains why so many photographs seem so unintentional and thoughtless, and why they lack any real impact. I think we can do better.

I think most photographers long to photograph intuitively, to be able to pick up the camera and respond with something like instinct, to see the lines, the light, the moment, and do something with them quickly enough that they make a photograph that engages us, stirs our emotions, or grabs our curiosity before that moment is gone forever. I think it's that longing for the ability to create intuitively that made my critic say what he did. He just wanted the process to be more like what Chilean photographer Sergio Larrain called "a state of grace" in making photographs. I do too.

But wishing and hoping are notoriously poor ways of achieving what we long for. The path to intuition and instinct begins with intention. It begins with learning to see things and think about things in new ways. It begins with internalizing techniques and creative possibilities, then making them our own. That's what learning is. And questions, as teachers as far back as Socrates and millennia of rabbis know, offer the best path toward that end. You don't need me to teach you. You need better questions so you can teach yourself.

So, before the coffee gets cold, here is my plea: don't get overwhelmed and start looking for shortcuts. Craft is a long game. Craft takes intentional focus, applied over time. For some of you, just the awareness of these questions will be a tremendous help and provide greater creative freedom. For others, you'll need to ask these questions many times—as you photograph, as you edit your photographs, and as you study the photographs of others—before they become your own. But as you get used to asking them, they will become more and more subconscious, the way your mother tongue did as it became more and more a part of you and required less and less conscious effort to recall the right words. That's when you'll begin to discover the intuitive or instinctive moments, the states of grace that come when you're in the moment—receptive, aware, and able, like a great musician, to improvise with the instrument in your hand.

There are a great many things that go into the making of a compelling photograph. What are those elements, and what do you do with them? What are the things to which we respond in an image, and how can we use them to make photographs that are not just good, but our own? Those are good questions. Let's see if we can find answers to them by asking a few more.

Don't get overwhelmed and start looking for shortcuts. Craft is a long game. Craft takes intentional focus, applied over time.

About the Photographs

There is a fairly recent convention in books about photography, particularly in how-to books, whereby the text is accompanied by illustrations, usually also with a description of camera settings, and sometimes with circles and arrows. In books concerned with the how-to, this can be a helpful approach. But this is not a how-to book. It's a why-to book. It's more concerned with learning to ask questions than it is with providing you the answers. The photographs in this book are my own recent answers to my own questions. You will make your own. But that doesn't mean they can't be helpful. If we ask the right questions, every photograph can teach us something. And questions abound in *The Heart of the Photograph.*

When I completed the first draft, it was suggested that we take all the images and pair them up with the concepts. Images where moments were important, for example, would accompany the chapter about the importance of well-considered moments. But the thing is, it's rare that an image succeeds because of one single device or technique; my "choice of moment" photograph also relied on my point of view, the light, my chosen aspect ratio, and whether or not I used colour well. It's a dance. It always has been and always will be. So when I assigned the images this way, it not only felt contrived, it felt like a random mishmash. Worse, the images stopped working together in the context for which I made them. As more and more I consider it important for my photographs to work in harmony with each other, this felt like a step in the wrong direction.

So I've grouped the images in the way I might choose to present them to the world, not to simplify them into one-dimensional educational tools. That does not mean they aren't an important part of the book. In fact, I think they are *more* powerfully educational this way because, if you engage with them, they will force you to ask questions in much the same way as I'm hoping to nudge you toward asking questions of the scenes you photograph.

I encourage you to use the photographs on these pages to give your reading some rhythm and create natural breaks, to look at them and perhaps find some spark of inspiration. But most importantly, I encourage you to *question* them: What are the lines doing in this image? What does the choice of framing or shutter speed, or moment, or the use of contrast or perspective, or any of the other questions raised in this book, contribute to this photograph? Forget for a moment whether you like or dislike the photograph; instead, ask what decisions I made to come to this final image, and what those decisions accomplish for you in your reaction to it.

Unlike many of my earlier books, you will not find creative exercises here, but perhaps you'll consider the images as one long educational through-line: one thread that urges you to specifically engage with what you see and try these questions on for size. When you begin to find your own answers to these questions, they will become part of your vocabulary, and they will quietly work their way into your own process of making photographs—a process that becomes more and more your own, and results in pictures that do the same.

PART ONE

A Good
Photograph?

Mastery of craft is necessary, but insufficient; it does not *necessarily* create a good photograph.

01
Is It Good?

AS ONE WHO MAKES PICTURES FOR A LIVING and teaches others to do so, I have long been preoccupied with what should be, one might think, a simple question: What makes a good photograph?

To hear popular photographic culture speak their answers to this question, we could be forgiven for thinking it is merely a matter of meeting a particular technical standard. When we first learn this craft, it's miracle enough that we can bring our skills to bear on the creation of a photograph that is focused and well-exposed. That becomes our first standard, and often, though expressed with more sophistication, our last. Our thoughts lean toward, "If only I could wrap my head around the complexities of the technique, or the understanding required to operate the camera in my hands, I will at last create a *good* photograph." I think we can do better.

I am not downplaying the need for that initial skill set, nor the pride that comes when we finally find our images focused and well-exposed more often than not. I am suggesting, however, that those skills are merely the price of admission; they are the foundation we build in order to move forward in this craft. Mastery of craft is necessary, but insufficient; it does not *necessarily* create a good photograph. And, to some extent, it must be acknowledged that good photographs can be made by anyone, by any means, depending on what "good" means to us.

Ask others what a good photograph is and you'll hear a variety of answers: A good photograph tells a story. A good photograph shows you something in a new way. A good photograph makes you feel something or ask questions or . . . Well, which one is it? Is it all of them? Must every image be evaluated in the same way?

Is there a more helpful question than "Is it good?" Might it instead be possible to reframe the question entirely?

I think it is, and I think this reframing is important. Because while the question "Is this a good photograph?" is next to impossible to answer objectively, it's undeniable that the drive to make photographs that are good, or strong, or that connect with us and our audience, is what pushes us to explore this craft and challenge ourselves both as artists and practitioners of craft. It is the connection to the human that is at the heart of this book.

This connection is important because it is we humans who decide why a photograph is made at all. It is we who read an image and respond to it on a dizzying number of levels. Was the photograph made to show you something specific, such as what a Blue-winged Teal looks like? Was it made to retain a memory of some fleeting moment? Was it made to tell a specific story, convey a certain feeling, or raise certain questions? Was it made to anger, arouse, or amuse?

I think it's time we photographers asked ourselves what it is we hope to accomplish with our work. And, in fact, it might be time to stop talking about "good" photographs entirely and find a better thing to pursue with our craft.

This book is, in part, an exploration of the search for that better thing, and before you roll your eyes at me, I ask you to trust me as I make this promise to you: this exploration will be deeply pragmatic. I have about as much interest in debating what art is as I do in arguing about how many angels can dance on the head of a pin. What I want to discuss is this: What makes a photograph that pleases us as its creator, and has any chance of creating a desired experience for others who will read that photograph?

To backtrack a little, when we ask about one of our photographs, "Is it good?" I wonder what we mean. It seems logical that at the very least we could revert to those first technical standards and ask, "Is it sharp? Is it well-exposed?" But what if sharpness is not the point? What if the best expression of this particular subject or moment is pure movement and blur, pure impression or abstraction? Asking if it is sharp is no more meaningful than asking if it is blue, unless sharp or blue is the point entirely.

And when we talk about exposure, we must admit that to be under- or over-exposed means to be "under" or "over" relative to . . . what? The meter on the camera? The camera has no idea what you want to accomplish with your photograph. The best it can tell you is how much light there is. Whether you want to expose for your shadows and allow parts of the image to go blinding white or expose for the highlights and allow the shadows to become black holes free from any detail is a matter of taste and intent. There is no room for what we "should" do in art, and frankly, less room for it in the craft and the technique than we like to imagine.

Every decision we make as photographers is relative not to what we *ought* to do (as outlined in your camera user manual or by your local camera club) but to what we desire to accomplish. This is where we get the first clue as to how we might start answering the question, "Is it good?" Perhaps we should first ask, "Does it accomplish what I hoped it would?"

If you are starting out and you create a sharp, well-exposed photograph, when before you had nothing but frustration, and you show me that photograph, I would have to be a monster to tell you it wasn't good. Is it good in the same way Ansel Adams might have meant good when looking at his own work? Is it good the way I think the work of Josef Koudelka is good? Probably not. But I think that has little to do with the work of Adams or Koudelka, or even you, and more to do with the standard against which we measure things. Sometimes the good photograph, at least in terms of our craft, is the one that represents growth, new mastery of technique, or next steps taken. In that instance, to strive for more and to skip the necessary lessons of the craft would sabotage the process of mastery. Sometimes the good photograph is the one that signals forward progress and is measurable only to you.

Humour me a moment and let me suggest that the language we use to talk about photographs is underdeveloped, and maybe, just maybe, the engines of popular photography culture (mostly the camera manufacturers because that's where the biggest money is) have a vested interest in keeping us talking about a "good" photograph in purely technical terms. Why? Because a target that never stops moving is a target we will continue to spend money to pursue. If the new standard of sharpness becomes the new standard of what is good, it's reasonable to believe we can spend our way to "goodness," which is absurd. A Leica does not a better photograph make.

Every decision we make as photographers is relative not to what we *ought* to do, but to what we desire to accomplish.

We must shift the language away from what is or is not good and instead talk about whether an image expresses our vision, satisfies us creatively, and creates a desired experience for the reader, and—importantly—we must talk about *how* it does this. There are many ways for an image to be "good," just as there are many ways an image might be "bad." If we can learn to talk about those things, we will be much closer to a conversation that is both meaningful and helpful, at least in terms of getting us to the second and much larger conversation in this book, which addresses this question: What are the things to which we respond in a photograph? If we can know that, then we are closer to being able to put those things into our photographs and choose from among them those that best do the job.

But wouldn't it be much easier if we created an objective standard or pretended one already existed? Of course it would. What freedom it would bring us to labour without the burden of following our vision (or having to identify it at all) and struggling to say the things we want to say, explore ideas we want to explore, and give the subject an expression that is most authentic to ourselves! Would it be easier? For the love of Ansel Adams and all the saints, yes! But would the results be good? Would they be authentic? Would they say anything new? Would they shock? Would they inform? Would they make us ask questions? Would they be any more than propaganda or imitations? Would they make us laugh or cry? Would they be the kinds of photographs we'd grab on the way out the door when the house is on fire?

If you're looking for more helpful questions, would those not be better questions to ask in order to explore and investigate our work? Wouldn't those questions help us to know if we're accomplishing something of any value?

They would. They are. That they exist at all is what pushes me to ask them and let them lead me, challenge me, and suggest new possibilities in my work. If my work is to be "good," it's more likely to become so by asking those more oblique questions than by asking merely, "Is it good?"

When I ask, "Is it good?" there are two immediate replies possible. Yes and No. Neither helps me do a better job of making photographs that are closer to my vision or doing what I hope for them to do. Yes, this is a book about what makes a photograph good, whatever that means. But this is the last time I will talk in those terms. I won't ask that question again. But I will ask questions that I think are stronger and more helpful, and I'll encourage you to do the same, in the hopes of helping us all move a little closer to stronger photographs.

An example of a stronger, more helpful question: Is this photograph dynamic? If dynamism is what you want, and the answer is yes, then you're on your way. If it's no, then at least there's a logical follow-up question: What might make it more dynamic? And now you've got some direction. If you know what you want to accomplish with your image, such as illustrating what a particular bird looks like, then asking, "Does this photograph clearly illustrate this particular bird?" is more helpful than asking if the photograph is "good." In fact, you might not want the image to be a straightforward illustration of the bird at all. You might be looking to create an interpretation of the bird in flight. Or it might be something more about colour and motion, and then that intention gives you your question: Does this photograph give that colour and motion their best expression? Whatever your answer, you'll use different tools to accomplish what you want to create, and different questions to evaluate the final image.

I'm not trying to be difficult. Lord knows I don't need a reputation as a trouble-maker. I just want to write about this craft I love in terms that actually help us learn and practice it with greater reward for ourselves and deeper connections and experiences for those who will read our images. If I get carried away, I hope you'll forgive me, knowing it's mostly just because I truly give a damn about this stuff and would rather trip over my opinions once in a while than play it safe with you or feed you platitudes.

I want this to be a truly human book, something that resonates with you and pushes you to make photographs that come from your deeper and more human places rather than merely from technical proficiency. To create this more human book means to be very human in the making of it, and that means risking the possibility that you disagree with me, which I welcome. Art is not about consensus. If this book prompts deeper questions to which you find different answers, then I've done something worthwhile.

What is most certainly true is that all writers write from their particular perspective, and I'm no exception. I can only write about what I know. This book, like my others before it, is not an attempt to write an encyclopedic and exhaustive coverage of the ideas within as much as it is an attempt to explore them, turn them over in our hands, and ask: How can they help us make our images stronger? Perhaps, too, these conversations will help us read photographs differently, and with that comes the possibility of seeing the world in different ways as well.

In the long list of elements and devices that make a photograph resonate with us, I will undoubtedly miss some, if not many. I will get some wrong. But I will try hard not to be prescriptive or absolute about any of it, because photography, like all art, is deeply human and subject to all the nuances, exceptions, what-ifs, and ragged edges that we ourselves are. I have learned to be very suspicious of anything prescriptive or absolute. What is important is not that we have an encyclopedia of these things but a conversation about them. We all approach this craft and art differently and for different reasons, but the basic conversation about what is within ourselves and the photographs we both make and find compelling is profoundly needed.

We all see the world in unique ways from those around us, and photography offers us the chance to both deepen that way of seeing and communicate or express it to others. Some see wonder, some injustice, some beauty. Some see questions and stories and new information. But the final photograph is a two-dimensional thing to which we respond, and it's the nature of that two-dimensional thing that we must explore if we're to make it a stronger vehicle for expression. God knows the camera won't automatically do that for us.

I'm quite sure there's nothing in these pages that hasn't been said before by other, and often wiser, voices. After all, nothing in the fundamentals of this craft is truly new. But I'm hoping to express these ideas in new ways. Perhaps more accessible ways. It's worth a reminder that it's not the newness of ideas that makes them valid, or important, or that impacts what our photographs become. It's what we do with those ideas. There is no magic button hidden in these pages, but if for you there is a new way of seeing, questioning, or approaching your craft in the pursuit of your art, then much magic lies ahead.

Get comfortable with
nuance and ambiguity.
Uncertainty isn't a
bad thing.

02
The Audience's Good

BECAUSE I TOLD YOU I WANTED TO ABANDON asking the "Is it good?" question, consider this your invitation to ask a different question: How will others experience this photograph? Since so many of us make photographs as a means of expression and in hopes that, through our images, others will see the world in new ways, it's a fair question. It also begs another: Does it even matter how others will experience this photograph? But we'll get to that in the next chapter.

First, let's acknowledge that when our images find an audience beyond ourselves, there is an alchemy that occurs; the photograph, previously just a two-dimensional image, becomes an experience when viewed, or read, by other people.

Those other people are among billions of people on this planet. More than likely (and certainly if the photograph finds its way to the internet), many of those people will be unknown to you. They will come from different cultures and, if your work has any longevity, from different times. They will bring with them a lifetime of experiences, influences, memories, tastes, and ways of understanding the world. This is true even for those close to you. Showing your photographs to your mother or your kids or a neighbour will result in experiences of those photographs that you would never be able to predict with any accuracy.

This is not a weakness of art. It is not a deficiency in your photograph. It is the alchemy that happens when your intent, expressed through your craft, becomes a photograph that is interpreted by that one singular person. You can choose to be uncomfortable with this chemistry and try your best to control it, but the results will likely be contrived and feel controlling, heavy-handed, or manipulative. Or you can embrace the mystery. It's probably healthy for artists to get comfortable with nuance and ambiguity. Uncertainty isn't a bad thing.

What is not healthy is to reconcile yourself to the idea that you can't control others' experiences of your photographs and, therefore, to conclude that your intent doesn't matter. To throw your hands in the air and say, "Why bother?" But that won't get you anywhere, and here's why: Your intent may not come through in an image the way you hoped it would, but it is still important to the creation of that image, to every choice you make from the moment you pick up the camera, to your framing and choice of lens and composition and every setting available to you, not to mention your choices in the edit and in any post-production you do. Your intent, or vision, matters every step of the way until that photograph or body of work is set down in front of an audience and you invite them to experience it on their own terms.

That experience is a mix of your many choices, what the photograph itself becomes, and the many different people who will read it. If that combination is not magic, it can certainly border on the mystical. And if not that, then at the very least it is unknown, unpredictable.

So why bother asking how others will experience my photograph at all? And if I do ask this question, where do I begin if I don't even know who those others are?

I took counselling courses in college, and one of the teacher's lessons that stuck with me was this: While we are all different, we are also all the same. In the particular lies the universal. And while there are few certainties, there are many commonalities. This is the beginning of empathy, and I want to argue that empathy is a powerful place from which to create and refine your photographs.

You can't know what others will think. Not for sure. But you can put yourself in their shoes and ask the question. "Will someone who isn't here in the moment and place in which I am making this photograph get a sense of what I am trying to show them? Are there elements I need to exclude to make that clearer? Are there elements I need to include or make prominent in the frame? What elements of the visual language could I include to increase the mood and make this scene a little less ambiguous (assuming clarity or a specific mood is important to me)?"

As with much of this book, it is not having the specific answers that will help you; it's asking the questions and looking for possibilities and that sweet spot where the subject gets its best expression—first for you, and then for your audience.

That last sentence is a loaded one. Momentarily setting aside the troubling term "best expression," let me quickly address the idea of an audience and suggest that we stop worrying so much about it, and why that's possible. This is a theory, so take it with a grain of salt. But here's my idea: If you make the work that is for you, work that you love, work that gives the subject its best expression (definitions to come, so stick with me), and work that is also empathetic, then it will draw an audience that responds to that work. Your work determines the audience. On some level, your audience self-selects based on what you make. If they don't get you or your work, they won't be your audience. So you don't have to consider them in what you make. You don't have to try to guess what they'll think or how they'll read it. It's about resonance. Your work either will or won't resonate with them. And if it does, and they become part of that group of people who want to listen to you through your work, that resonance will ensure a certain level of understanding because you're already on the same wavelength. If your audience is, on some level, like you, it will be easier to create work that resonates with them because you're first making it for you, and—to repeat—they are like you (as much as they are also very different).

Rather than asking if others will like or respond to my work, I make my photo-graphs for me. I am my own first audience. So then the question becomes: To what things within a photograph do we respond? Is there some kind of list of the photographic devices to which we are drawn? Authors have many literary devices that they use to accomplish certain things. Is it possible to begin explor-ing those photographic devices so we can be aware of them as tools, or elements, of visual language, and use them to give better expression to our subjects?

In *The Soul of the Camera*, the book that precedes this one, I suggested that if there is going to be soul or life in our images, then it is up to us to put it there. Really, I was suggesting that we ourselves are the soul of the camera and that we become much more aware of the role of the photographer in the making of pictures. Here I want to take that suggestion further and explore the idea that if our photographs are to give the best expression possible to their subjects and connect to others, and if they are to have a heartbeat of some kind with which we resonate, it's up to us to understand that and use every tool we can to make it happen. If *The Soul of the Camera* asked, "What is it within the photographer that makes possible the creation of a stronger photograph?" then *The Heart of the Photograph* asks, "What is it within the photograph itself that might make it stronger, more resonant, better experienced by the reader? What can we do to give the subject its best expression?"

Part Two explores what I mean by giving the subject its best expression, and Part Three, the bulk of this book, is about the tools we have to create that expression. Part Four wraps it up and brings it all together. But we're not there just yet, and before we head in that direction, we need to talk about you, the photographer.

You cannot know exactly how one person will read your image any more than you can know for sure how one person will take a joke or interpret a page from the Bible. If that one person (or many people) doesn't like your photograph, it is not necessarily an indication of whether your work is worthwhile, valuable, or even art, any more than the fact that many people don't like sushi or the paintings of Jackson Pollock disqualifies sushi as its own culinary art or the work of Pollock as worthy of consideration.

This is a conversation not about certainties but about possibilities, and to some extent, you must always embrace that mystery when you create any art at all—the possibility that you might be misunderstood, disliked, or just ignored. But remember, this whole conversation is about finding new ways to understand the possible reactions to a photograph in order to engage with those possibilities more playfully and more intentionally as you create art first for yourself and then for an audience that has chosen to experience your work because they resonate with it, and with you.

Nothing authentic
is ever made while
looking over our
shoulders at others.

03
The Photographer's Good

ACKNOWLEDGING THAT WE ALL MAKE PHOTOGRAPHS for different reasons and that one of those reasons might indeed be the acclaim of others or the communication of an idea to a broader audience (as in a commercial or advertising context), I want to take some time to explore the idea that the photographer, regardless of competing ideas, must be their first and most important audience. To put it another way, we must be the ones to determine why we make a photograph and whether that photograph succeeds at the purpose for which it was made. Even simpler, we alone must be the ones to decide if it is "good," though I'd still rather we avoid that word.

This is not a book about professional concerns, but even if you work in a commercial capacity or for someone else who calls the shots, if you are not a photographer with your own vision and voice, the only basis on which to hire you is your ability to use a camera. And if you've not yet discovered it, you'll soon have to wrestle with the reality that selling a commodity, such as the ability to use a camera, is no foundation on which to base a business as a photographer. If you want to succeed professionally and not compete with others in the race to the bottom, you must be a brand and sell your vision and your voice. That means making photographs that first please you—that are first faithful to your own perspective on the world, your own preferences, and your own willingness to find an audience that aligns with that. It is on that basis that creative directors and others will hire you, not on a willingness to compromise your own vision and voice to sell yourself as a mere camera operator.

If you want to please your audience and you don't want to compromise your vision, then the only way I can clearly see to do this is that you yourself become that first and most important audience. If not, you will spend the rest of your photograph-making days chasing thousands of moving targets, all with their own preferences and tastes, all willing to suggest that you should take a differ- ent direction in your work—that colour images would be better than the black and white work you love, that you should make portraits instead of landscapes, or that you should stop with those multiple-exposure photographs that they just don't understand. If you let the crowd decide, your work will never be sharp enough, happy enough, serious enough, or edgy enough. It'll be too playful, too sombre, too sentimental, too self-referential, or any other of a hundred charges that have more to do with the tastes of others than the work itself.

Does this mean we don't listen to others? Of course not. But we'd be wise to be very careful in choosing the voices we listen to, and even more cautious about what we do with the things those voices say and the changes they encourage us to make. If you're starting out, find people you can learn from, who do work you respect in a way you respect. Find people who will listen to your hopes for your photography and help you take the necessary next steps to create work that is faithful to those hopes, not merely a copy of themselves, of which the world has no need.

The question I encourage you to ask in this chapter is this: Is it mine? That is not an easy question to answer, and it's impossible if you don't first have a sense of what that means. Being introspective doesn't come easily to everyone. I think the more honestly you're willing to look at yourself and your desires, the stronger your photography will become. But if that's too tall an order for you, then consider asking more specific questions that can be more easily answered:

- What kind of photographs do you naturally gravitate toward? If you could only look at the work of ten other photographers for the next couple years, who would they be, and what is it about their work that so resonates with you?

- If you looked at the work of those ten photographers, would they share anything that indicates your own preferences? Do they all make black and white images? Do they explore certain common themes or subjects? Do you see similar things in the best of your own work, the photographs that most feel like your strongest images?

- If you look back at the photographs you've made over the last couple years, what common threads do you see in the best of that work?

- Are there themes or ideas you see repeated in your own work as you look back? Do they still feel relevant or important to you? Are there things left unsaid that you feel you need to explore or express?

Whatever you discover about yourself through the questions above, remember that your photographs provide a means to say something and that the big lack in photography is not better tools but something authentic to say. Something honest. That intent, that way of seeing the world, is what we so often call vision, and rather than writing more about the idea of vision, I'd like you to consider asking yourself a different question: What do I want to accomplish with this photograph?

Your answer to that question will be different from image to image, and it will be different from my answer. By now, I hope it's really clear how that reality means you are the one who must decide whether your image works or not. Should you let me see the photograph, I will decide whether it resonates with me, but that's a different question from whether it succeeds or is "good."

Several hundred words ago, I started using the phrase "a subject's best expression." I will expand more on that in the next chapter, but there's another question we need to ask: Who gets to decide what the best expression of a subject is? For that matter, who gets to decide what the true subject is? The blunt answer: *you*. You do. Only *you* get to decide what is important enough to direct your lens to. Only you get to decide what you want to say about that thing or that idea, and only you get to make the decisions that go into expressing your intent or vision about that subject.

That's what this book is about, and I will fight tooth and nail to have you get to the end with a renewed determination to make photographs that are unapologetically your own, that bring not just your technical choices to the creative process, but your soul, your curiosity, your emotions, and your opinions. Every photograph, it is said, looks both ways. It is my hope that you'll reveal yourself more and more in your photographs, and that your presence there—your own fingerprint—will become the scale on which you measure (at least at first) the success of your images.

What I am not making a case for in this book is a photographic free-for-all, where we just make what we want and thumb our nose at the harder stages of growth in our craft and as artists. I am not advocating a childish approach in which we never get past the anarchy of macaroni, glue, and glitter (though if that's what makes you happy, there are worse things in the world). I am making a case for knowing what you want to accomplish so you can choose the best tools and the strongest combination of techniques, and that you have a more realistic, and more human, means of evaluating the work you create.

I don't want to give you answers, which more often than not result in an adult version of paint-by-numbers. I want to give you questions that lead you to possibilities. I've given you some already, but now, in Part Three, I want to get even more specific and practical with those questions while reminding you that the answers will change as you evolve as a person and as your skills develop. And though you remain open to a world of influence, the answers will always come best from yourself. Nothing authentic is ever made while looking over our shoulders at others.

Next spread: Lalibela, Ethiopia, 2017

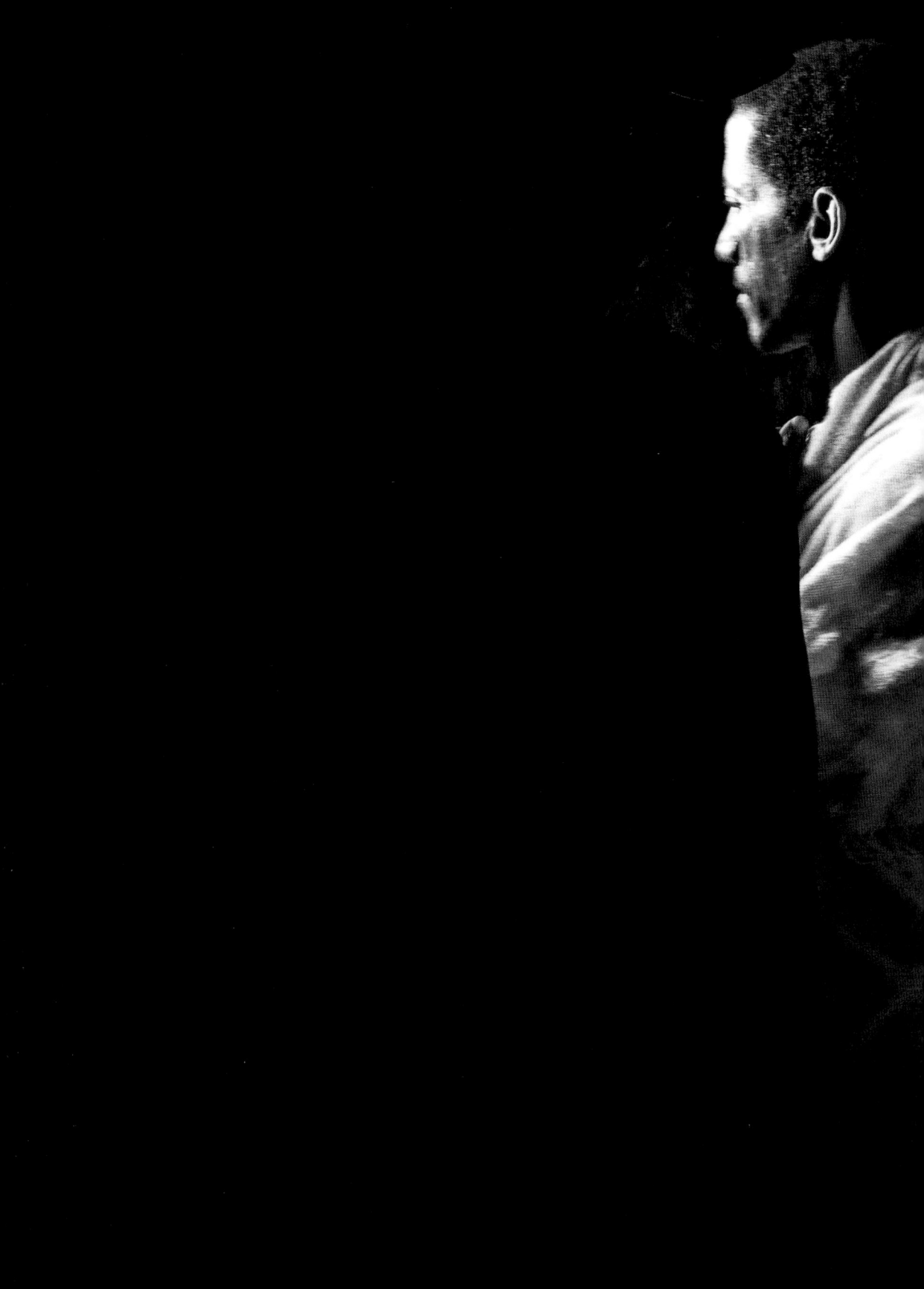

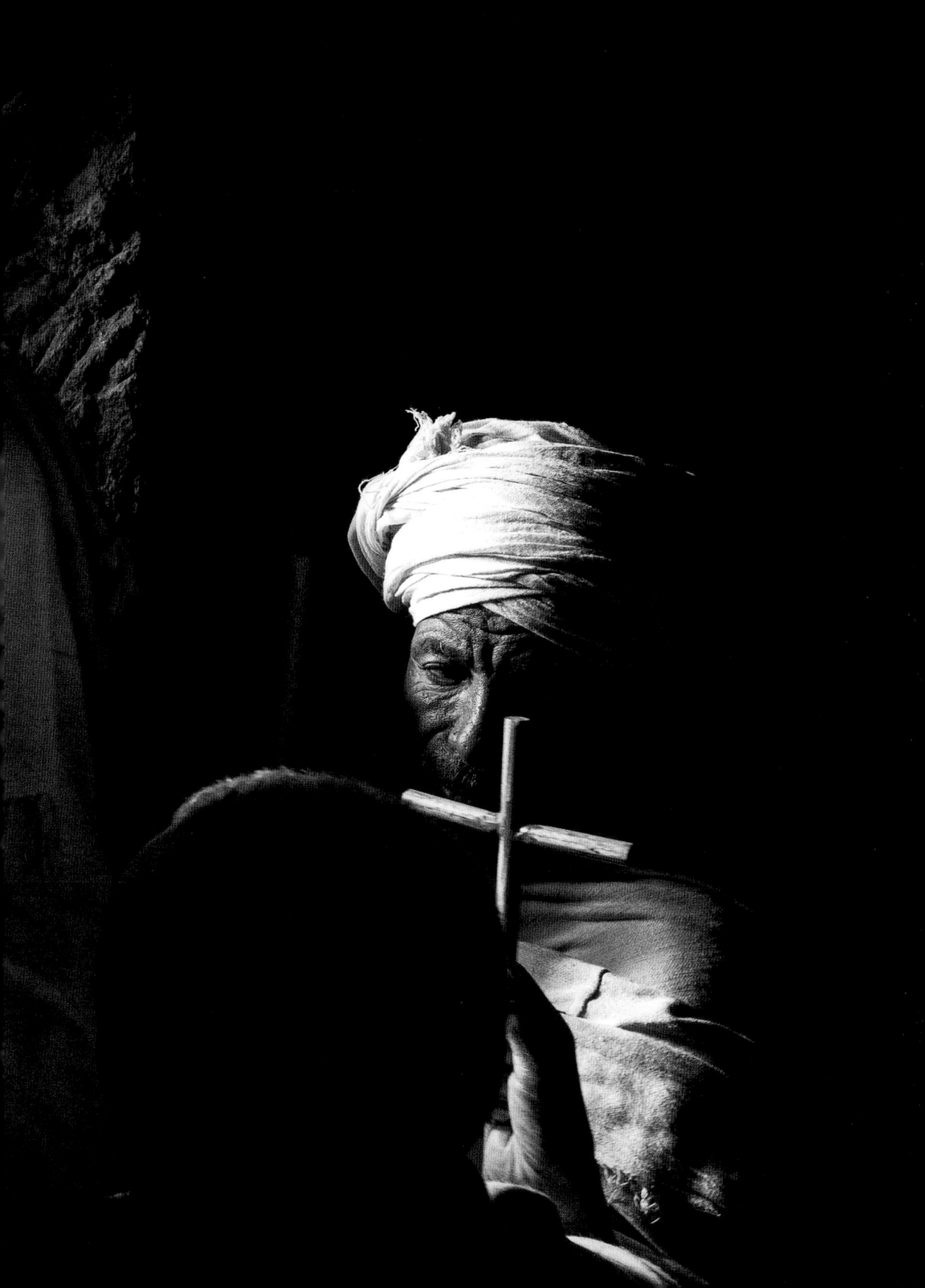

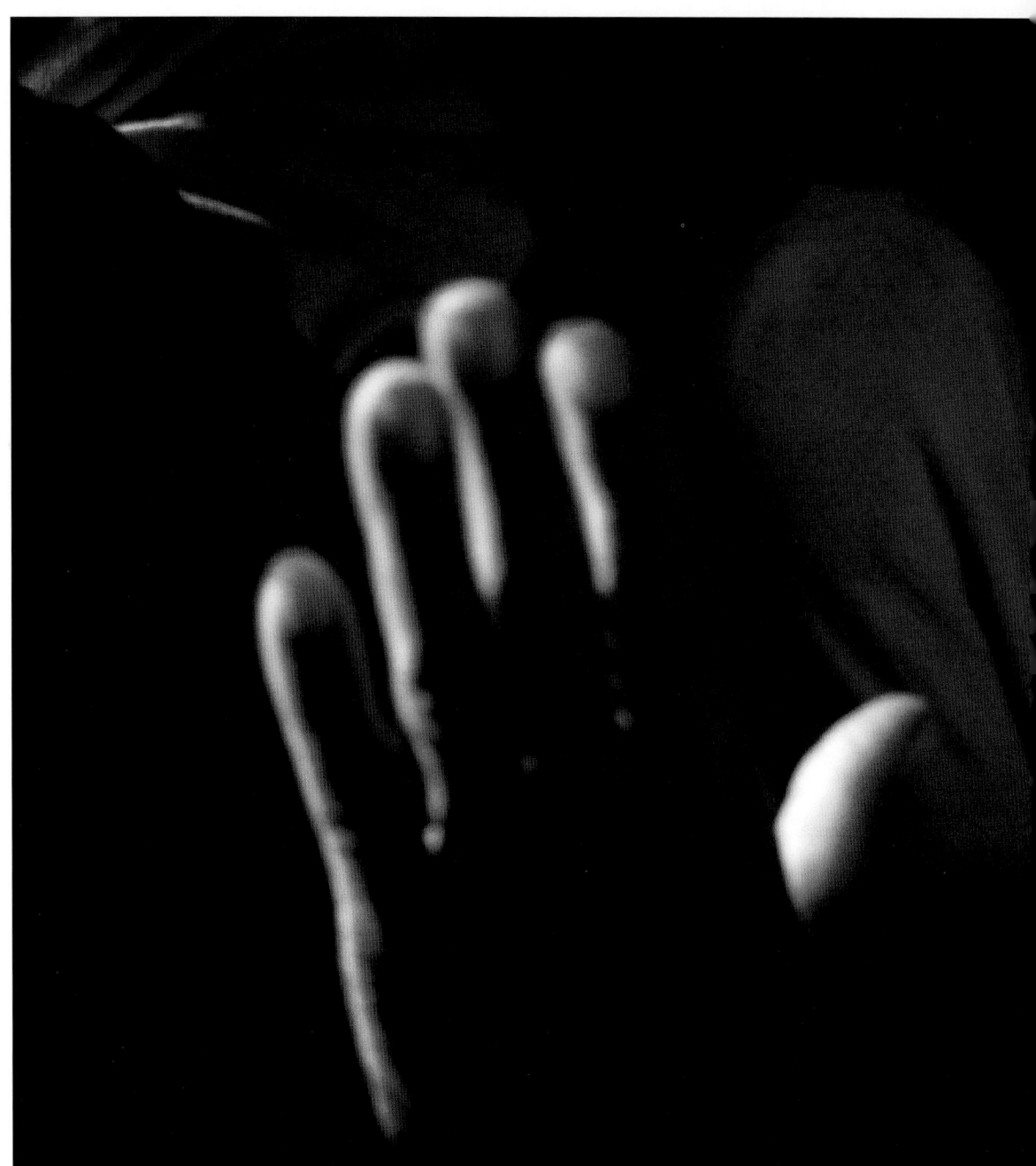

Lalibela, Ethiopia, 2017

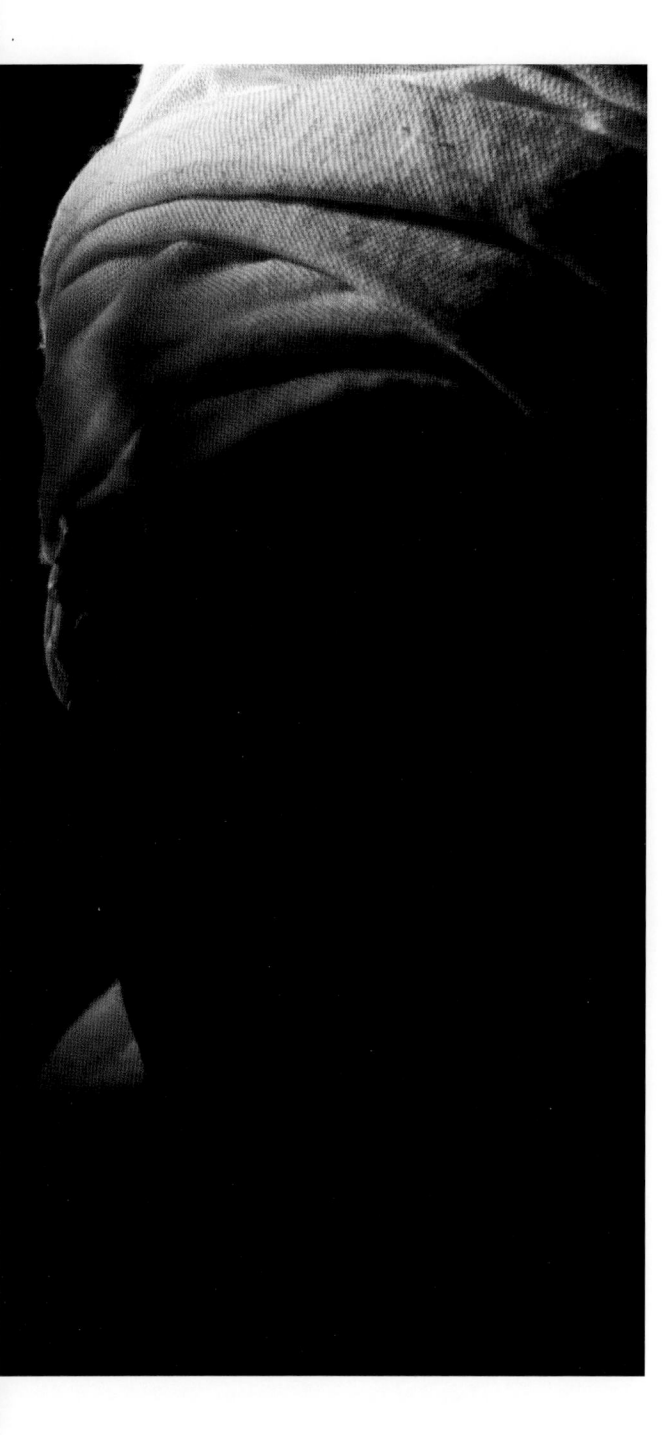

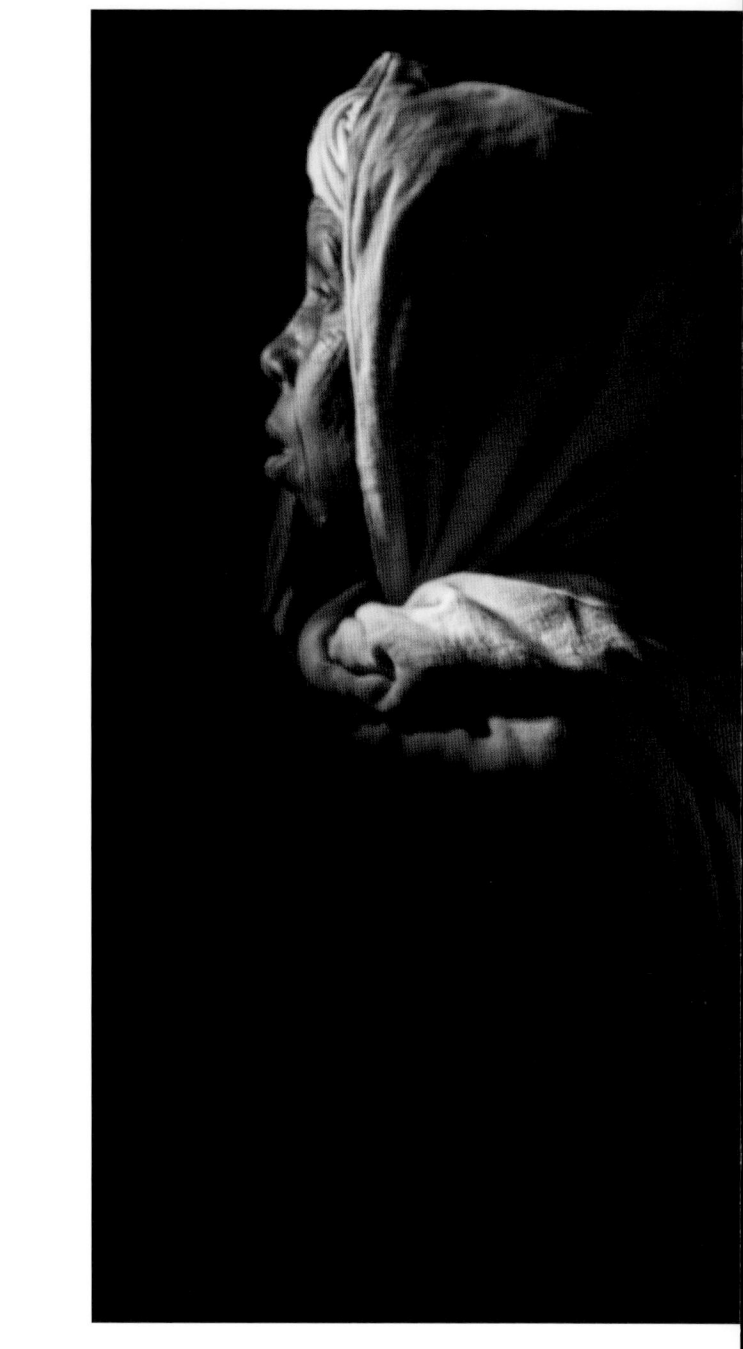

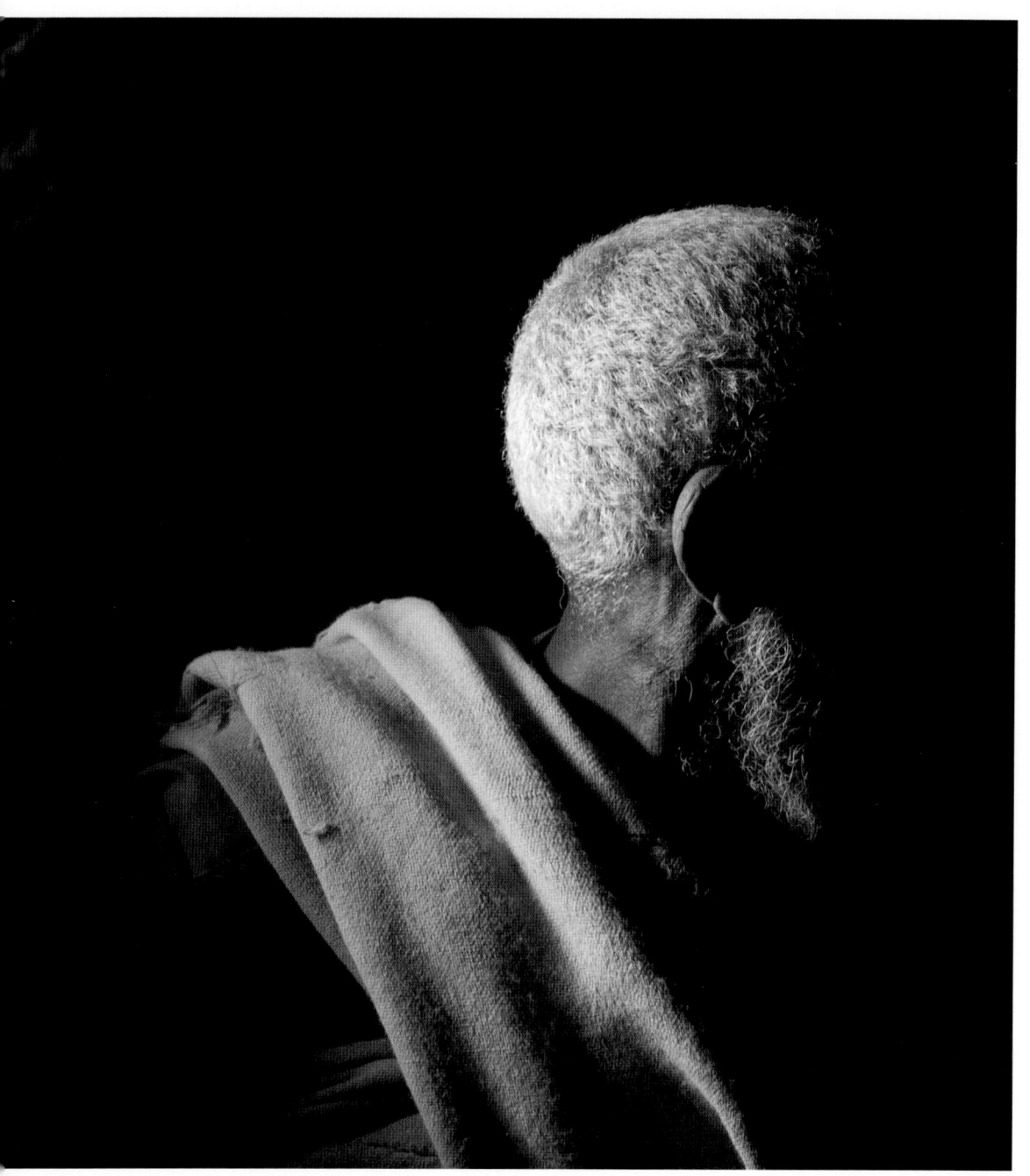

Lalibela, Ethiopia, 2017

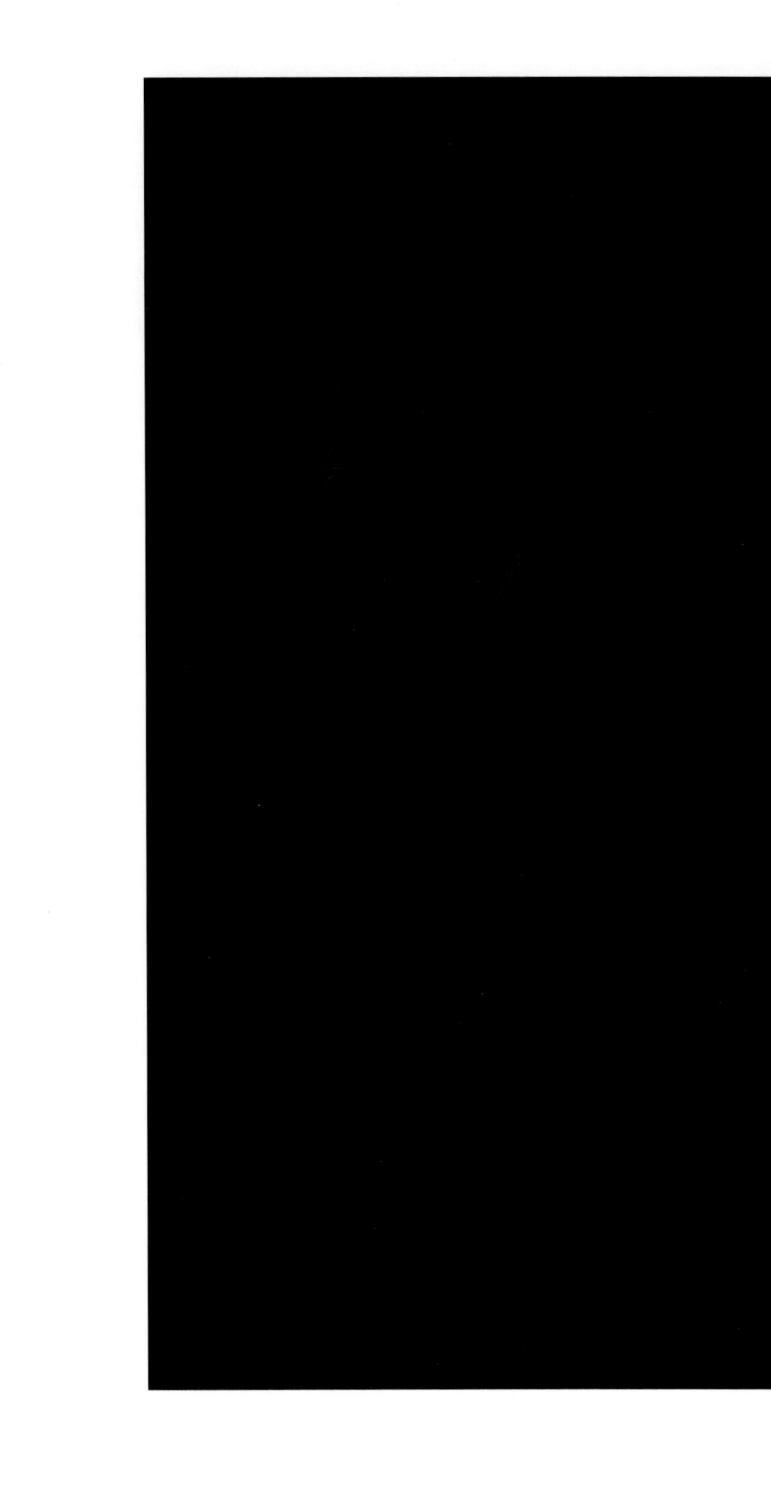

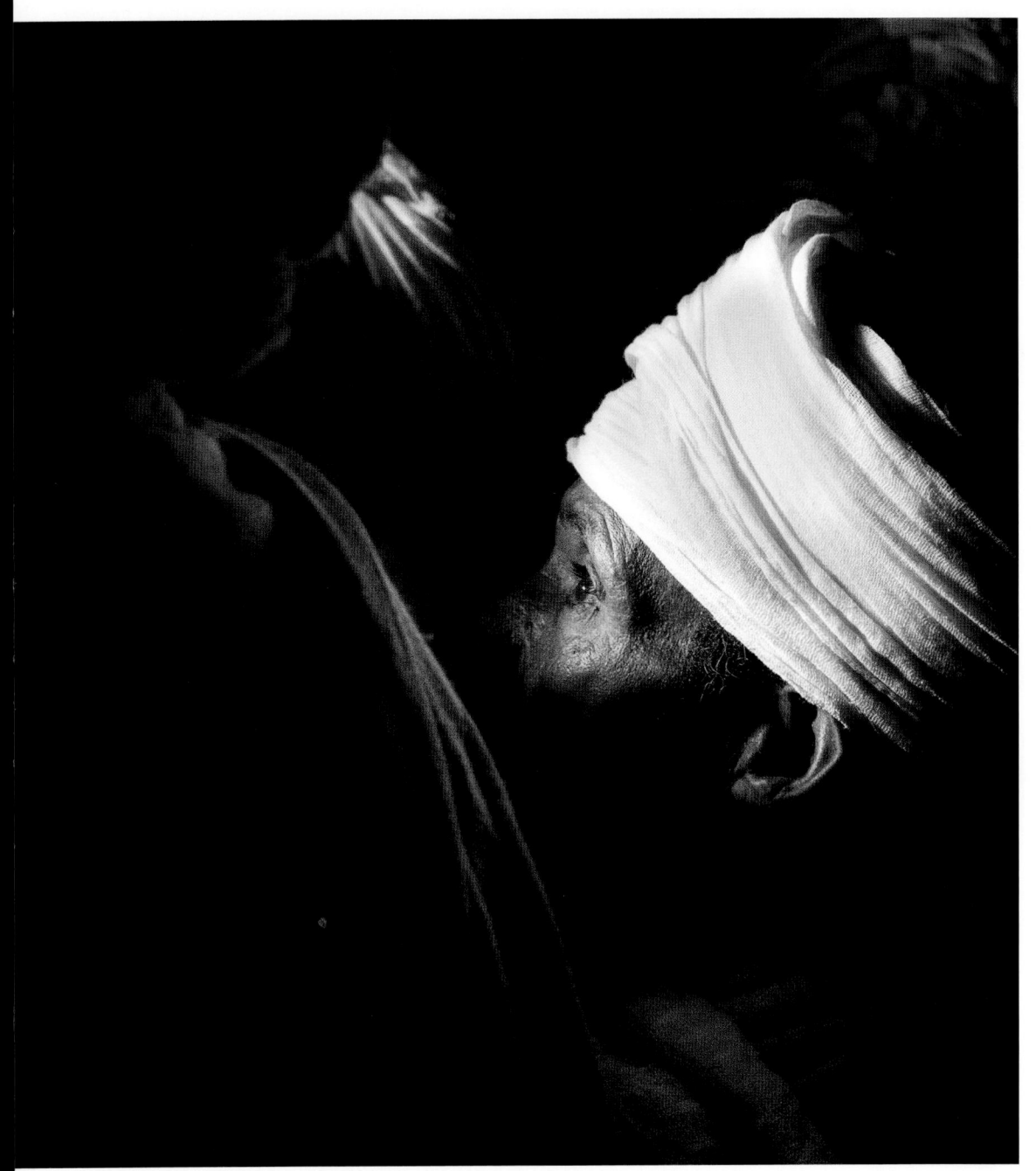

Lalibela, Ethiopia, 2017

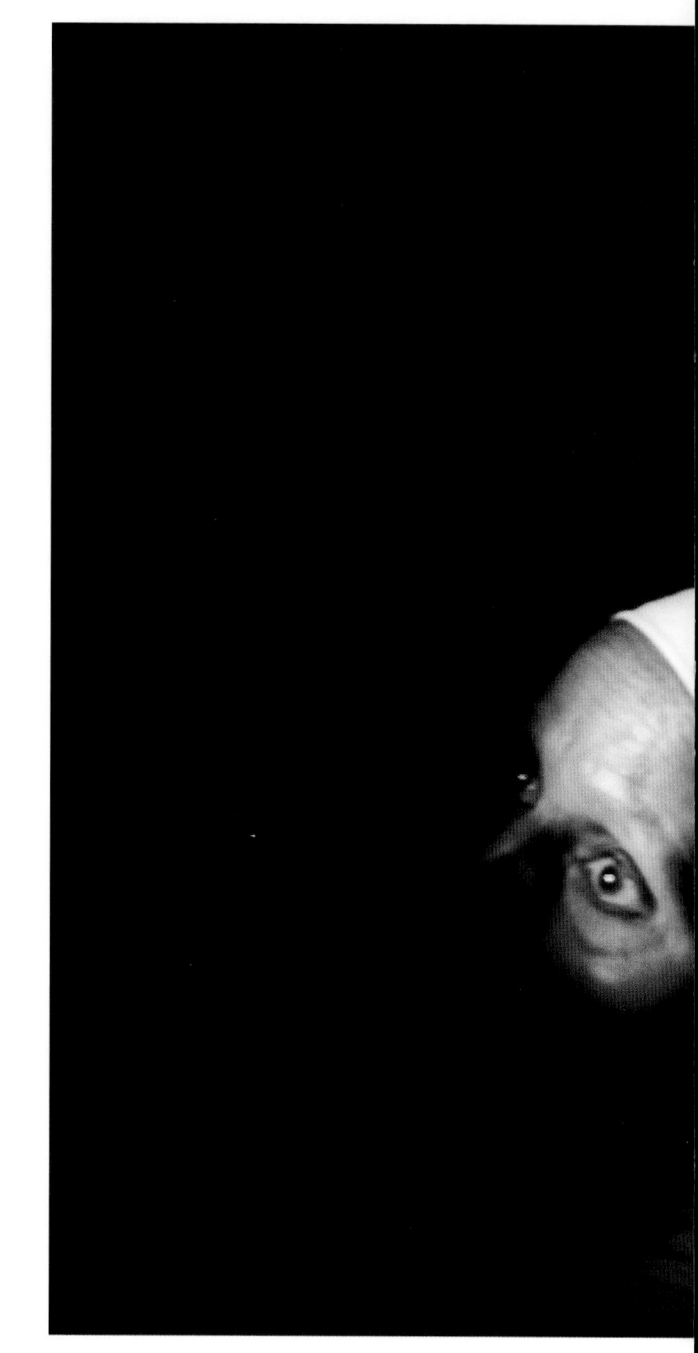

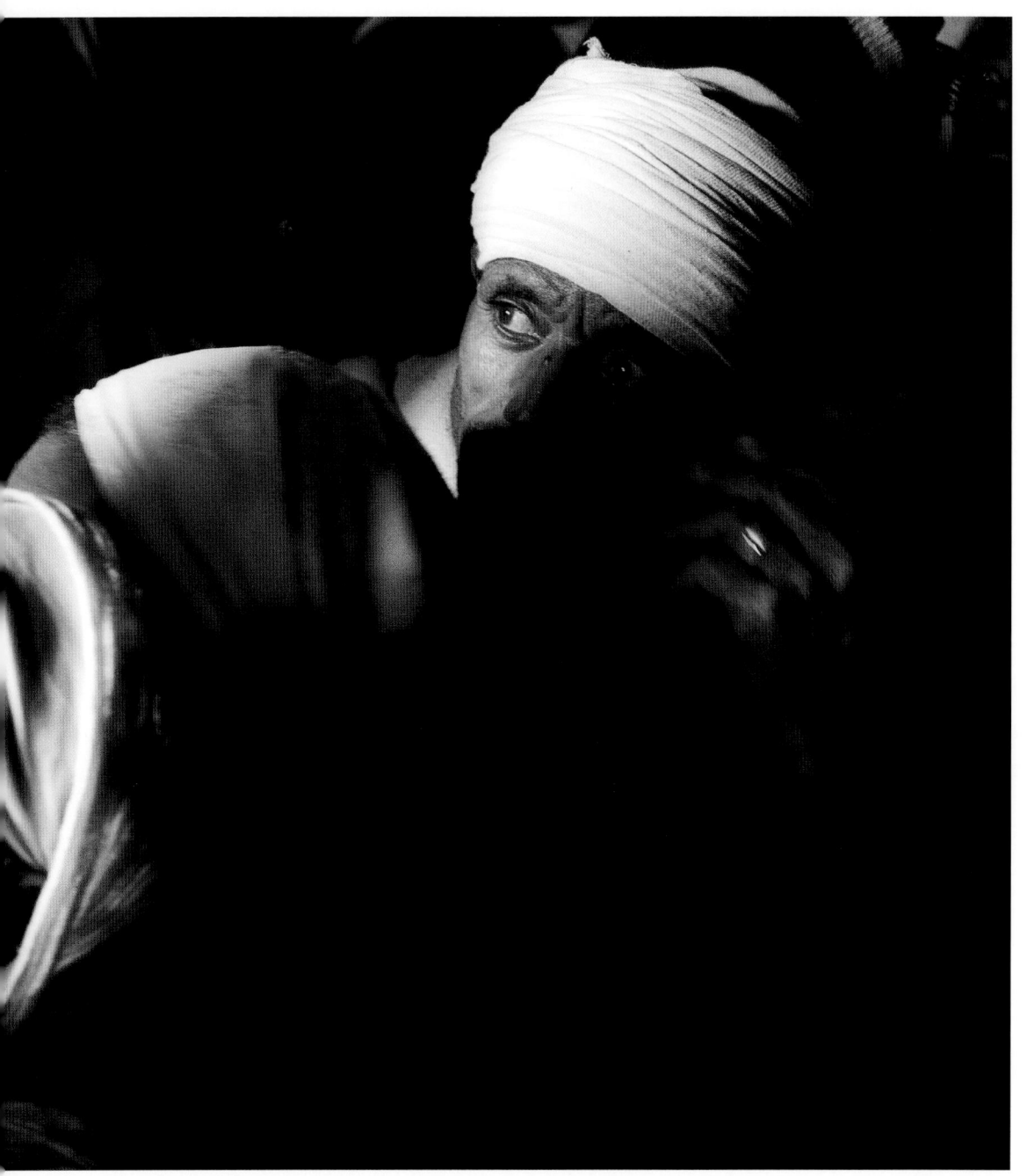

Lalibela, Ethiopia, 2017

PART TWO

Better Than Good

There's no point discussing how your subject is best expressed if you have no idea what that subject *truly* is.

04
Better Subjects

IF WE ARE TO GO BEYOND the idea of good and create a series of questions that informs our work and pushes us to make work that does what we want it to do, then we need to discuss the alternatives to "good."

The most obvious alternative to good is perfect. We often talk in terms of something being good, but when it's even better—when it can't be refined any further—it is perfect. But if the question "Is it good?" is problematic, then "Is it perfect?" is even more so. It's unanswerable. And as a goal, it's unattainable. If "Is it good?" is trying to hit a moving target, then "Is it perfect?" is trying to hit a target that doesn't exist but which has a very real and toxic effect on the creative spirit. But since the word comes up so often, I want to offer two thoughts before we move on to explore what better than good means—instead of what it doesn't.

Much as we seem to strive for it, as humans, we do not resonate with the perfect, at least not with the idea of perfect as "flawless." In fact, it is often those things with flaws to which we are most attracted. In books and movies, it is never the perfect character with whom we identify, for example. Photographically, I think one of the reasons we're seeing an increase in the use of film is that it is a less-than-perfect medium—like vinyl records, where the quality of the analog recording, while richer and more attractive to many ears, is imperfect. It is to these imperfections that we are often drawn.

The Japanese have a name that honours this notion. It is an idea called wabi sabi, and while I do not pretend to be able to communicate the finer points of it, wabi sabi is about finding beauty in the imperfect and the decaying—not *despite* those things, but because of them. The term itself and the art created from this perspective recognize that we can do better than perfect, that soul and meaning are to be found in these imperfections, that flaws have their own meaning and beauty.

The second thought is that the pursuit of this flawless perfection often results in less work getting done, and when we are paralyzed by the need to make something perfect before we release it into the world, we never finish it. This is in direct opposition to the notion that we need to be mindfully creating more and more work in order to improve our craft and make better work. So, para-doxically, the pursuit of the flawless can be the very thing that sabotages our process of learning and stops us from creating work that is better than good.

So when we talk about "better than good," we do not mean that it transcends good or that it is perfect. We mean that it is an alternative to (merely) good as a way of evaluating and talking about our images.

For example, if you understand how blurring motion can imbue a photograph with that feeling of movement, giving it both information (I understand now that the person is moving) and impact (I feel the speed of that person moving), then it can inform your choice of which shutter speed to use. The person in the photograph being blurred because of slow shutter speed does not make the photograph good or not good. What matters is your intention and vision for the image: what you hoped the photograph would do, first for you, and then for those who read the image. Remember, good is not the point. For some purposes in this example, the image in which the subject is blurred would be exactly on point, and for other purposes, that very technique would give the subject anything but its best expression.

Before we make those choices, however, we need to consider our subject, beginning with identifying what that subject really is. Traditionally, we've been taught to consider our subject as the thing we are photographing. That's not such a bad definition, so long as we're free to include ideas themselves as those things. Imagine you and two friends are photographing in a forest, all three of you pointing your lenses at the same two trees. Is your subject the trees? It could be. But it could also be the height of the trees towering above the forest floor. It could be the relationship of one tree to another, one old and dying, the other young and thriving. It could also be the small songbirds on one branch of the tree, made tiny by their context and the scale the trees give them. Or it could be the motion of the trees in the wind.

Each subject in this example is different. Though you're all photographing the same thing, the ideas being photographed are different. And because the ideas are different, each one will be best expressed differently. One photographer might choose to photograph in black and white to get the attention off the rich green colours and instead direct it to the textures. Another might use a wide lens to get more context in the frame or create a different sense of scale, while another might use a longer lens to isolate a particular juxtaposition or contrast. Each aims to include what is important to the expression of the subject the way they see it and to exclude what is not.

In my work as a teacher to photographers, I've found that often their photographs are much improved not by learning techniques or refining an ability to make a technically competent photograph, but by gaining much greater clarity on the actual subject of the image and what that photographer wants to say about it. I have found the following three questions helpful in that exploration:

- Does the photograph have a clear, single subject?

- What about this subject matter makes me care, hooks me, or pulls me in?

- What am I trying to say, or point at, about this subject?

Let's discuss each in turn.

Does the photograph have a clear, single subject?
This seems like a good first question, as there's no point discussing how your subject is best expressed if you have no idea what that subject *truly* is. If this question doesn't get you all the way there, or you need to pull back further, then try this: Don't allow yourself the luxury of your subject being a thing at all. Make it an idea.

"But I photograph landscapes; how does that work?" Make the photograph about the relationship between the land and the sea. Make it about the contrast between the rough bark of the foreground tree and the delicate wisps of cloud in the background. Make it about the play of texture and colour. Then find ways to draw that idea out—to give that relationship or contrast more impact and to reduce the impact of other competing elements or ideas.

Another way to approach this is to ask yourself what one thing this image is about.

"Well, it's about the bear."

Okay, but what about the bear? Is it about the power of the bear, the movement of the bear, the bear and his environment, the struggle for survival?

"Yes! All of those!"

No. It's not all of those. That's a list of subjects, not one subject. It's too much to ask of one still frame. No photograph can contain all of that and still have impact. The more information you try to cram in, the less impact you're likely to have.

What about this subject matter makes me care, hooks me, or pulls me in?
This is another way of looking at subject and the need to find a single hook. For those of us who ultimately do care about connecting our vision of the world with others, being able to isolate that one idea or distill it down to the one thing we most care about is a good way to find that point of connection. If you care deeply about it, there's a better than good chance that others will connect to it, too, assuming you've been faithful to yourself and your vision.

I think Russian playwright and short story writer Anton Chekhov said it beautifully: "Don't tell me the moon is shining; show me the glint of light on broken glass." The former is about facts simply stated; the latter is about interpretation. And even if your desire as a photographer is to convey information and facts, you still need to find a way to connect because no one wants to read a story without a point or a hook.

What am I trying to say, or point at, about this subject?

This is where we start to find clues about how to give our subject its best expression—by figuring out what we're trying to say about it and how that might be translated visually. It begins with basic decisions, such as the orientation of the frame. A vertical frame asks the reader to read the image up and down. There's a vertical energy created when we do that. But if your subject is much more horizontal, then there's a good chance you won't be expressing your subject well.

The same is true when you use a really dynamic aspect ratio, like a wide 16:9, to express, for example, a serene scene. It can work well, depending on the scene, but often it's a better choice to use a more serene frame, like a square, to create a better expression of that subject. Another example: a couple at a wedding is dancing, and there's movement and energy everywhere. Is the image about that energy and abandon? It could be that a slow shutter and a flash synced with the rear curtain of the shutter—often called "dragging the shutter"—gives better expression to that subject than a more literal 1/1000th of a second shutter speed that freezes it all. Sure, it's sharp as a tack. But it might also be boring. It might lose the energy that is the whole point of the image. Asking yourself what's most important, or what this image is truly about, is the first step in exploring the possibilities for how to best express it.

Because I talk in terms of a subject's best expression, please don't mistake me for saying that there is only one set of "correct" decisions out there and it is the task of the photographer to find it. I can't even imagine the pressure and creative paralysis that would happen if we approached our work this way. What I'm saying is that there are all kinds of options, and you get to choose which one works best for you, in this moment, under these circumstances, with the gear you have. There is incredible freedom in this perspective, but ultimately we have to choose. We play and risk and do what thrills us, but we have to begin with an understanding of—or a willingness to discover—what the photograph is about, and then find ways to show that.

When I teach these ideas, I am often met with dismay from photographers who say they don't always know what they want to say before they pick up their cameras, and they wonder why it's so clear and easy for others and not for them. It's not. Not always. One of the beautiful things about this craft is that the camera is not only a means of expression; it is also a means of *exploration*. So while the next part of the book is about the means of expression, I think it's probably helpful to begin talking about the camera as a tool for exploration and discovery.

PART THREE

Better Expression

It is not only what
we photograph but
how, and why, we
photograph it that
makes an image
unique, authentic,
or surprising.

05
Exploration
and Expression

THE IDEAS THAT FOLLOW are not a recipe to follow, nor are they an
inventory of effects to be pulled from our back pockets when other ideas have
run dry. They are not even a how-to manual. If anything, they are intended as
a focus on the why-to, as a list of the possibilities and the endless combinations
of devices at the photographer's disposal, all of them aspects of the final
photograph to which we respond, in which we find meaning, and which make
the image what it is. The ideas that follow offer a strong start in discovering the
ways in which, through our creativity and rigor, we can find our subjects' best
expression in the final image.

But determining the best expression of a subject is often not easy. Nor is it
always immediate. I think it's the rare photographer who consistently puts the

camera to their eye already knowing exactly what the photograph is about and how to best interpret that within the frame. If that's you, skip ahead to the next chapter while the rest of us talk about the creative process for a moment.

The camera is an astonishing tool of expression, but before that, for many of us, it is also a means of exploration. Most of us take many captures to get to the final frame that lights something up on the inside for us or accomplishes our intention or vision (however preliminary or vague that may be). Many of us begin with less of a vision and more of a curiosity, a sense of, "Hey, look at that." If you're like me, you certainly don't remotely know what the final photograph, if there is to be one at all, will look like. Some people do. I am not like them. I wrestle with my muse. I say unkind things about her under my breath while I do so. For me, it is a process, and that process begins with picking up the camera and making sketch images. Images that almost certainly won't make the final cut, but that allow me to warm up, take some risks, and try combinations of the visual devices that I'll spend the rest of the book discussing.

Sometimes we don't know what we want to say. Often, it is only by putting the camera to our faces and making those sketches, seeing not only *what* the camera sees, but *how,* that helps us arrive there. We often need to try new points of view in order to move the lines around before we press the shutter and collapse three dimensions into two. We need to move to see the light from new angles or try different exposures in order to make the image look the way that most excites us, not just the way the camera wants it to look.

This process is not just normal; it's good. It's vital that you take risks, that you consider multiple possibilities, that you get past the obvious first choices in composition and technique. If it takes you a dozen (or a couple hundred) frames to get there, there is no shame in using the camera to fully explore a scene. In fact, the only shame is in *not* doing what you need to do in order to get to the image that achieves what you finally discover you want it to. For me, that means being open to not always knowing what I want and to using questions to figure it out.

Few things are better for the creative process than good questions. Questions call us forward to new possibilities and are often only answered by trying out those possibilities. What, for example, would this scene look like if I moved around until it was backlit? What would it look like if I reduced my exposure and allowed the people to become silhouettes? What would it feel like if I used a wider lens and got in tight? While doing all these things, in the back of the mind I'm asking, "What's this image really about for me, and am I getting closer to that or farther away?"

If it sounds like there are a lot of things going on in the brain all at once, there often are. But with time, these things begin to feel intuitive, and you begin to trust your gut more. I'm not suggesting you overthink your way into paralysis, just that you understand that there are a tremendous number of possibilities. The more willing you are to explore them and let them guide you to more clearly understanding your true subject and get you closer to expressing that subject in a way that feels right to you, the closer you'll be to making the kinds of photographs that are not just good, but yours.

The chapters that follow are not only about questions; they are also invitations to having a more open and receptive creative process, a way of making photographs that allows for one decision to lead to another, rather than bowing to the pressure to get it right all at once. Not every question will be relevant to every scene or purpose. And not everything that makes a meaningful photograph is represented here, though I've tried to be thorough. What is most

Few things are better for the creative process than good questions.

important is remembering that it is in the combinations of these questions and the willingness to risk answering them in unexpected ways that will bring the greatest rewards.

There's a well-worn trope among the photographically dissatisfied that mourns the idea that "everything has been photographed," forgetting that it is not only what we photograph but how, and why, we photograph it that makes an image unique, authentic, or surprising. Yes, it's all been photographed. What now? We transcend cliché and find our way out of the ruts that were once exciting creative grooves by exploring these ideas in ways new to us, and in combinations we've not yet played with. This is too important to most of us to take so seriously that we forget to play.

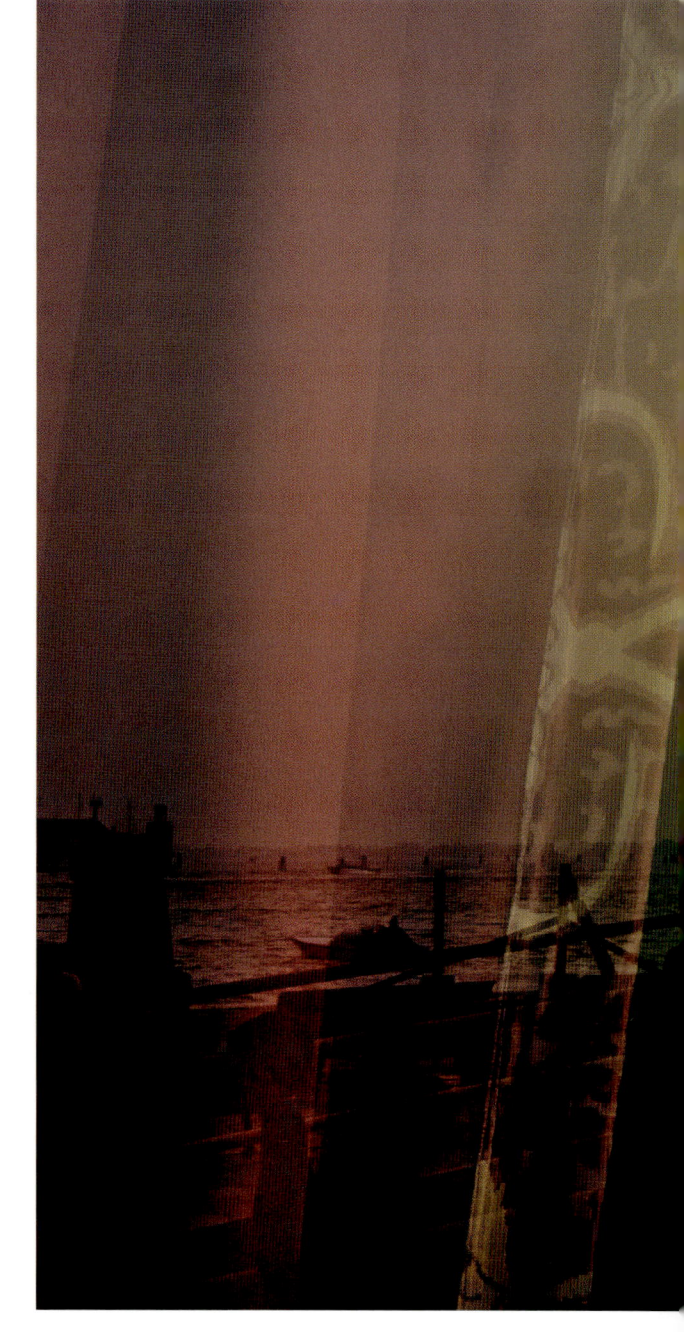

Venice, Italy, 2017

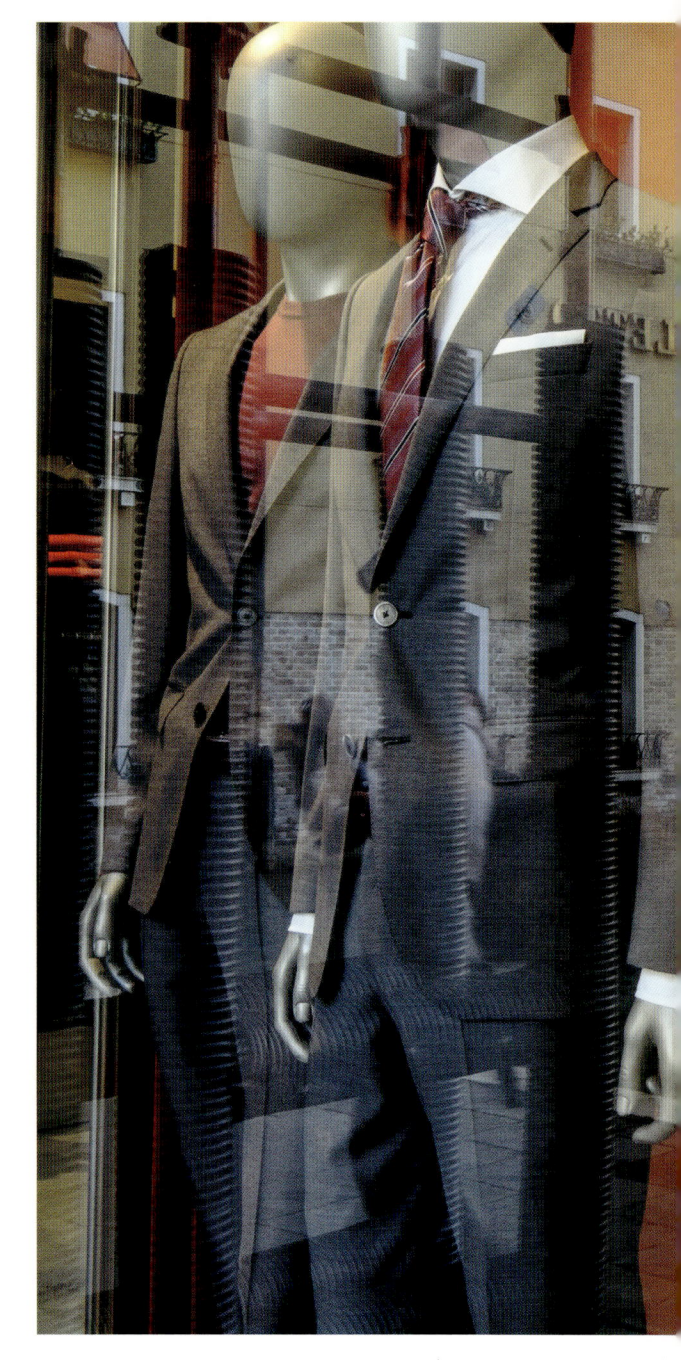

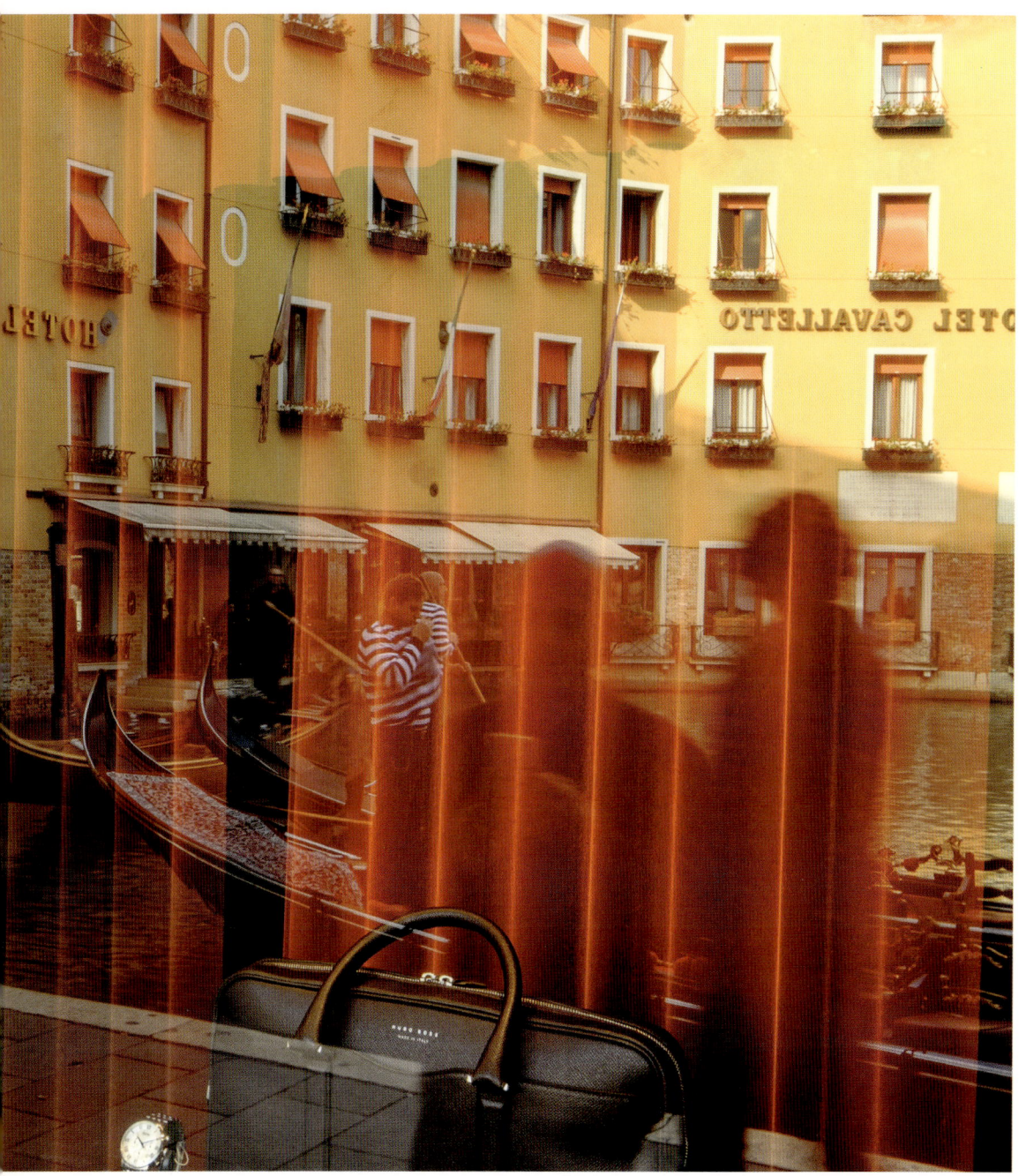

Venice, Italy, 2017

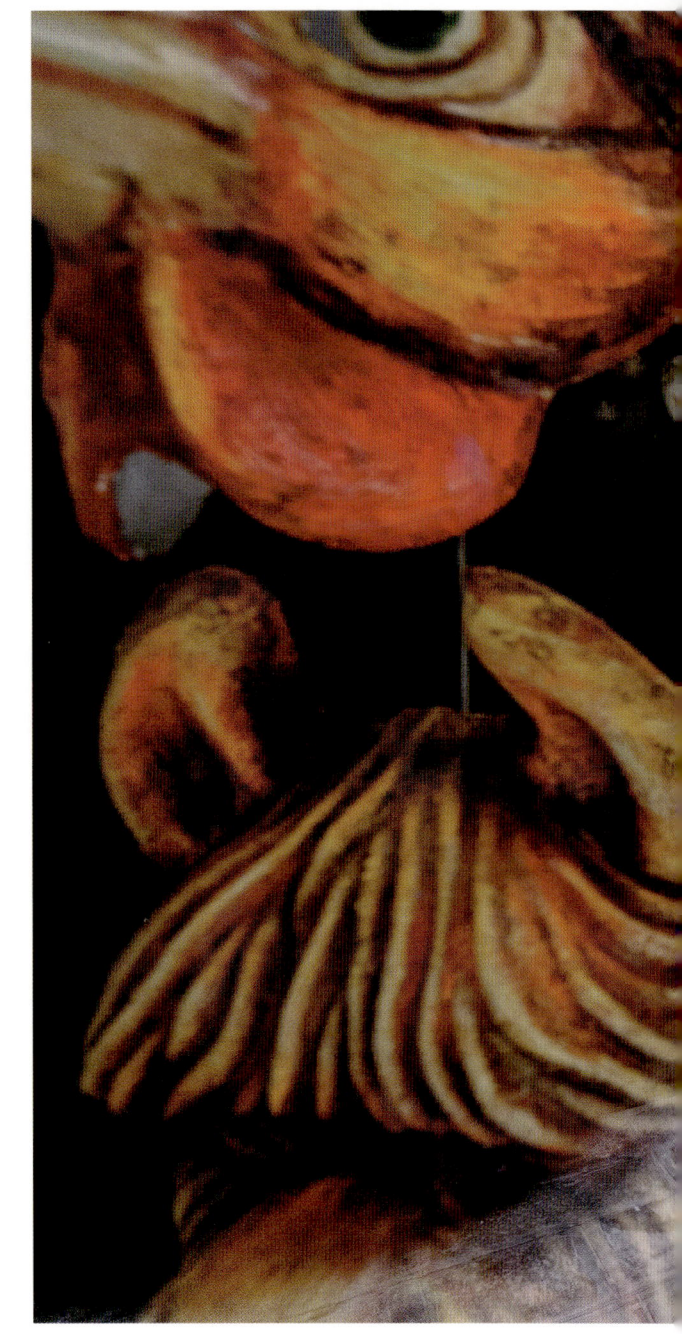

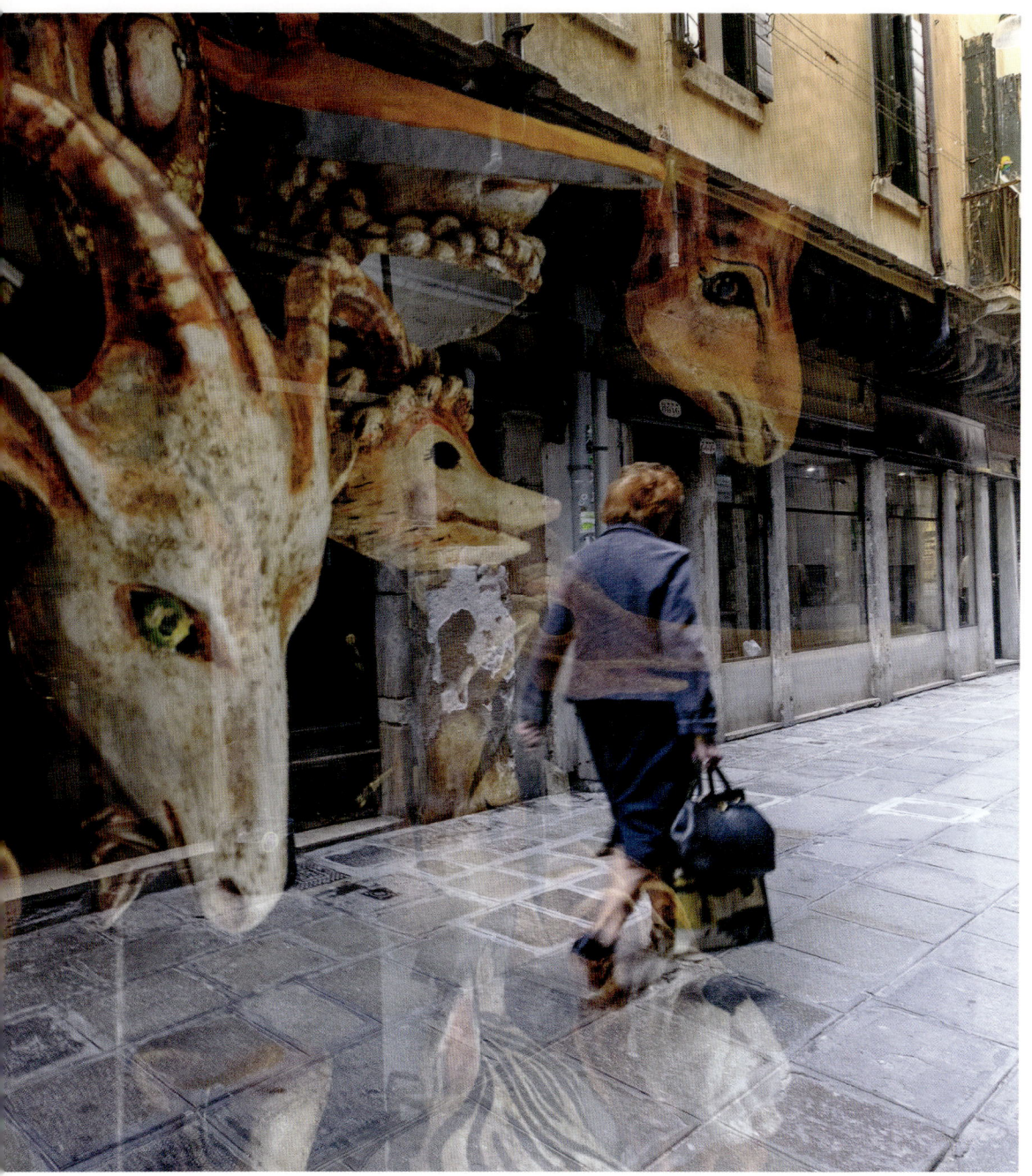

Venice, Italy, 2017

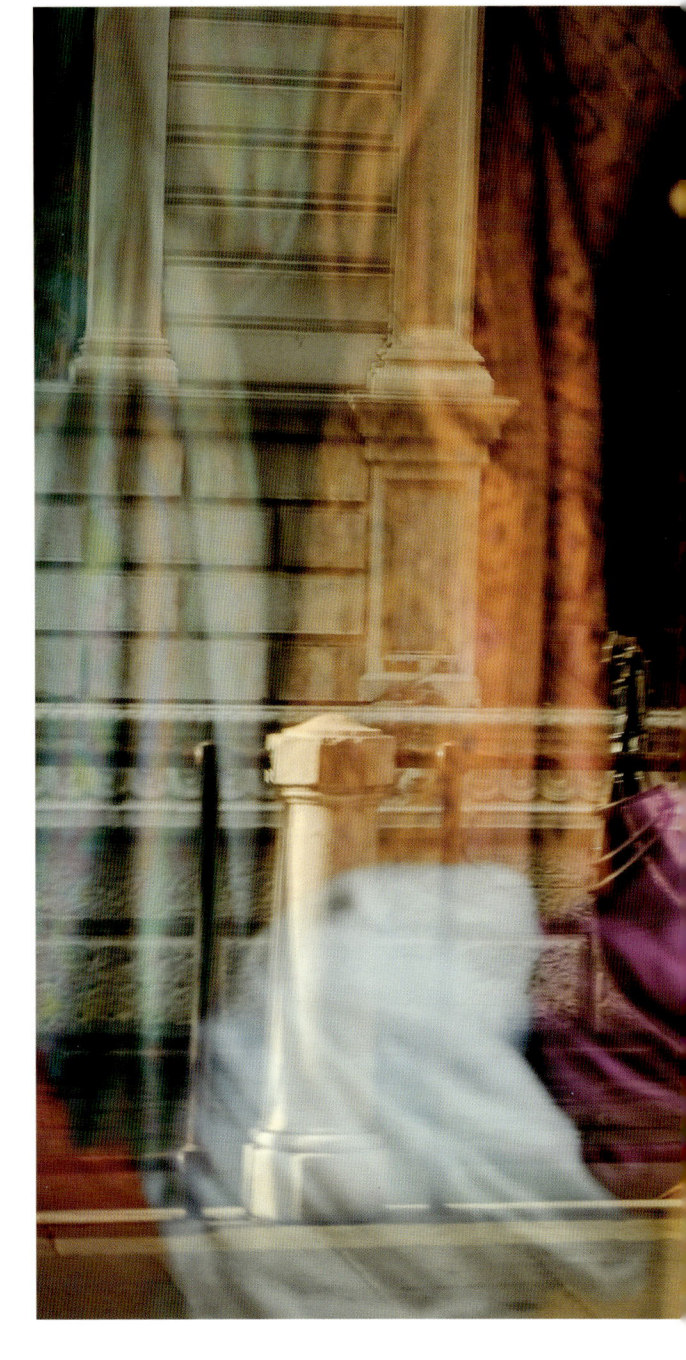

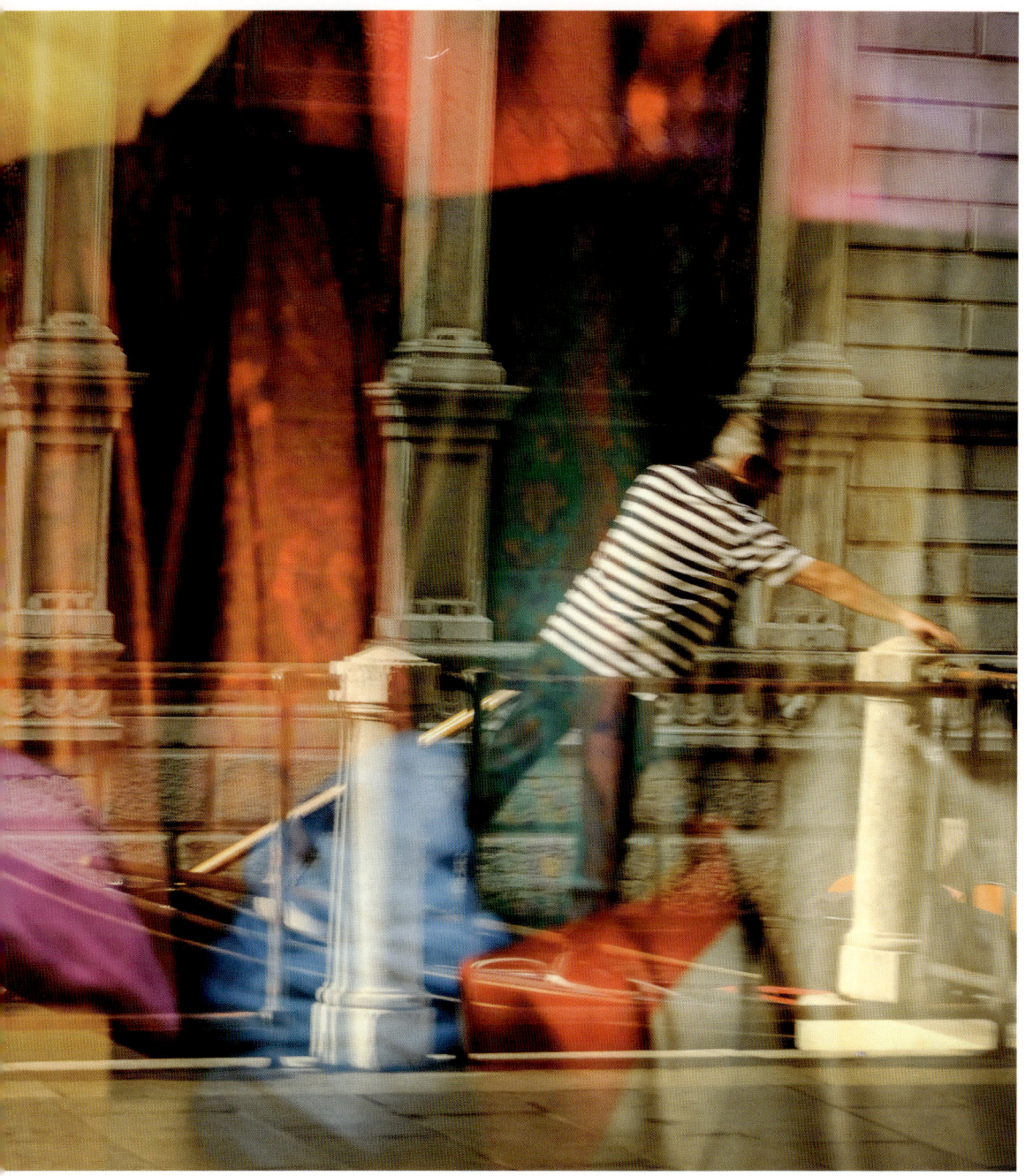

Venice, Italy, 2017

It is tempting to think in terms of good light and bad light, but that is a distinction I urge you not to make.

06
What Is the
Light Doing?

WE HAVE ONLY A FEW RAW MATERIALS in photography: light, space, and time. What we do with these using the box in our hands determines what our photograph will look like. Being able to see them and understand them, especially knowing how the camera sees them, is the lifelong pursuit of the photographer. For my purposes as a teacher, I have often reduced my approach to a scene to three questions that serve as reminders of these raw materials: What is the light doing, what are the lines doing, and when is the moment? This book further unpacks these questions, not only by asking, for example, about the light itself, but what choices we can make with that light.

When we first learn to use a camera, we most often approach it more as a capture device—a tool for making correct, literal exposures—rather than a creative tool full of possibilities. We rarely begin our journey of craft being told that the camera sees the world differently than we do, and that in those differences—the constraints of shutter speeds and apertures, film and sensor sensitivity, and optics—lie worlds of possibilities.

So while the first question I often ask is "What is the light doing?" my next one is usually "What can I do with the light?" And each of these questions contains galaxies of other questions, all of them giving me devices with which to both explore and express my subject.

As photographers, light gives us assets. It creates effects, though we often take those for granted without a camera in our hands. Light gives us shadows and reflections. The quality of the light determines the quality of the shadows: Are they long and bold, or soft and feathered? In which direction do they run? What do they hide or reveal? It is very tempting to think in terms of good light and bad light, but that is a distinction I urge you not to make. Light is neither good nor bad, but rather gives certain assets we can either use or not. It is either helpful to your specific intent for an image (if you have one) or it is not. But it's a creatively hobbled mind that doesn't see the light for what it is and ask, "What can I do with this?"

For several years, I favoured soft light. I knew what to do with it and how to work it. Seeing harder light and bold shadows, I would retreat behind the too-convenient belief that "the light was bad" rather than making something with what I had. There's nothing wrong with favouring a certain kind of light, but that's not the same thing as being too lazy or too scared to take the creative or technical risks that allow you to discover the possibilities that other light offers.

What's your preference in light? Could it be that your belief in the so-called magic hour is blinding you to the other 23 hours, all with their own magic, all of them giving you something you could use? Could your belief that some light is fundamentally not good or useful create expectations for you that are stopping you from seeing it as it truly is and for what it can contribute to your image?

Perhaps it's not about the hard or soft quality of the light for you. Maybe it's about the direction of the light—the way you've always preferred to have the sun coming over your shoulder, evenly front-lighting your subject, and you've forgotten that a subject all about texture or dimension might be better expressed using sidelight. Nothing gives better expression to texture or dimension than sidelight.

If your subject isn't about texture but instead is all about gesture (a man leading his camel train across the desert, for example), then backlight is a great choice. All you have to do is get to a position where you can shoot into the sun, placing it between you and the man and his camels. In this case, the details don't matter because it's all about shape.

This is where the question expands from being about what the light is doing to what you do with the light. This is the dance. So you underexpose the image relative to what the camera wants, knowing that the camera is going to nudge you toward seeing detail in the man and his camels, and knowing you don't want those details. No one is ever going to ask who that man is or which particular camels he's walking. If the subject of the photograph is about the shape of the camels and the colour of the setting sun, then it will not likely find better expression, at least where light is concerned, than with a backlit silhouette.

Remember, my hope here is not to teach you all about light; that's a book in itself. My hope is to connect the dots between what you already know about light and the camera's way of dealing with it to help make you increasingly aware of the many possibilities of using that light to interpret the subject. Another way of exploring this might be, "How can I use the light to best convey the point of the image I want to make?" Would moving around to see the light from all angles give you fresh eyes on this? Would waiting an hour give you new shadows or more intense colours? Would overriding the camera meter and underexposing it to make those shadows darker or those colours more saturated help make your image stronger when it's about mystery or about the play of those colours?

I do not use a lot of strobes in my photography, but for those who do, there are further questions and possibilities because you can change the position of those lights, adjust their power and direction, modify their colours, and more. But it's easy to get carried away with those effects—to use an effect for its own sake— and in so doing, to forget that the photograph is probably not *about* the effect. I'm not saying you shouldn't experiment and play with your strobes in an effort to develop your intention and vision for an image; I'm saying you shouldn't let lighting techniques override everything else. Clever lighting itself is not the point of the image. Remember to identify your *actual subject*. What is the photograph really about? Now find ways to make it powerfully and creatively about that. If others talk more about the effects and devices you used to make the image than they do about what you had hoped the picture would actually achieve, then you've made a photograph in which the subject is the effect itself, and not many of us will be moved by that.

Considering questions like these can help bring us new ideas and directions:

- What is the light doing? What does it give me in this moment?

- What decisions can I make with my exposure to best use this light? Would my subject be better expressed by being under- or overexposed?

- What direction is the light coming from, and can I change that by moving the position of the camera?

- Can I modify the light by bouncing it, diffusing it, or supplementing it?

- Would waiting for the light to change be more effective than using what I've got right now?

Sometimes the light isn't the point. Sometimes other choices will give your subject the strongest expression, such as a moment so powerful that the photograph could be made in any light at all. But that's the case with all the elements and decisions that go into making a photograph. Remember that this is about possibilities, not prescriptions. If the answer to my initial question of, "What is the light doing?" is "It really doesn't matter," then move on. But light is one of the few raw materials we have, so you still need to ask the question, then make an exposure that considers your subject and what you want to say about it.

We assign
tremendous
emotional weight
to colour, so it
is an important
consideration.

07
What Does Colour Contribute?

BECAUSE COLOUR IS ENTIRELY A FUNCTION OF LIGHT, this is as good a place as any to discuss it, though these chapters should not be considered necessarily sequential. As these are all questions related to the making of images, you could ask them at any point. In fact, these questions can also be asked in an *evaluative* way when you're making edits and selecting one image over another or in post-production when, for example, you're trying to decide if adjustments to the colour are needed and why your eye keeps drifting off to that one element in the frame that captures so much of your attention but is not the point of the image.

Colour is really seductive. Our brains are hardwired to pay attention to colours and assign them meaning. Colour has tremendous *visual mass*, a term related to how much an element pulls at our eyes, though in reality it's about how much meaning and attention our *brain* gives one element over another. In the case of colour, we are drawn to brighter colours over more muted hues, and to colours that provide the most contrast with the rest of the scene—especially reds and yellows, the colours of choice for emergency vehicles, caution signs, and the big Buy Now buttons on websites that grab our attention. That's good when you want it, but not helpful when what you want, for example, is harmony in the image or for the eye to rest elsewhere in the frame.

Paying attention to the colours within the frame and asking whether they support or fight against your intention is important. It's counterproductive to have colour pulling at your viewer's attention when you're trying to guide that attention elsewhere. We also assign tremendous emotional weight to colour, so when it comes to the kind of mood you want the image to have, colour is an important consideration. Chapter 22 is devoted to the question of mood and whether it matches the subject you're trying to express so I won't steal that thunder, but it's important to remember the connection. If the image's mood isn't what you want it to be on an emotional level, ask yourself if the colour fits.

Since the big idea of this book is to provide a series of questions to get you thinking about matching your choices about elements and devices with the subject of the photograph, the obvious next question, at least for me, is "Does the colour contribute at all?" Colour is not always easy to work with. In the real world, we have very little control over the colours in our scene, which makes having a unified colour palette in a single image—let alone a series of photographs—often hard or impossible to achieve. One solution is to change the colours in post-production, and since our work in post-production is often as much a part of the creative process as the initial image capture, it's worth a nod. Software tools now make it easy to make your greens a little more blue or a little more yellow, to desaturate the reds, or even to replace colours entirely. How much you choose to adjust in post-production is very much a matter of taste, but if you choose to do that kind of colour work, the question about the colour's contribution to the best expression of the subject is even more relevant.

Even if you don't opt for that kind of colour work in post-production, the question remains; it's one of the reasons I do so much of my work in black and white. I want my images to have a harmony about them, and most of the situations in which I photograph make finding colour harmony a challenge. But my decision to remove colour is based on other criteria as well. If the image just isn't about colour (or the colour isn't the point), a more powerful image is often made when that colour is removed. If, for example, the image is about the relationship between two people—the moment at which they kiss, perhaps—then I want the photograph to be about that moment, about the tenderness, the intimacy. If there's a bright-red element in the background that constantly pulls attention past the lovers and their moment, then I am allowing that moment to be robbed of its impact if I don't remove the colour.

Photographing in black and white, or choosing to render colour work in black and white later in post-production, allows other elements to play more powerfully. With colour gone, the eyes can give more attention to texture, gesture, lines, moments, or story. When those things are more important in the image, colour might be an unnecessary distraction. I often remove colour because removing it unifies my work and allows photographs that are neither about colour nor the mood it provides to be more powerfully about something else.

More often than not, it's the interplay between my chosen subject, my own tastes, and the real-world constraints in which I photograph that determines whether my photographs end up in full colour or in monochrome. But always, in every case, the question that guides these choices is "Does the colour

contribute—not just to the image, but to the *strongest expression* of my subject—
and can I use it to strengthen what I want to say about the subject?" If it doesn't
contribute, or worse, if it competes for my attention, then I remove it in one
way or another. I might move my perspective to exclude that red element, use
a different lens, or wait for a better moment. And when those possibilities fail,
I exclude it in post-production (usually by converting the image to black and
white), but with the knowledge that hue, saturation, and luminance can all be
adjusted so that the colour contributes rather than competes.

Questions to explore about the possibilities that colour gives us include:

- What colours are present in this scene, and do they work together?

- Are there colours that compete with the more important elements in the
  scene, and can I exclude them?

- Do the colours in the photograph help establish the mood?

- Is colour important to this subject, and could black and white be a
  stronger choice?

- In post-production, could subtle changes to hue, saturation, or luminance
  create a stronger, more unified colour palette?

What you do with the answers to these questions will always be a matter of
taste and your vision for the photograph itself, but colour is too important to the
way we experience a photograph, and too powerful a tool in the way we make
that photograph, not to be intentional about exploring and using it.

Our brains are hardwired to pay attention to colours and assign them meaning.

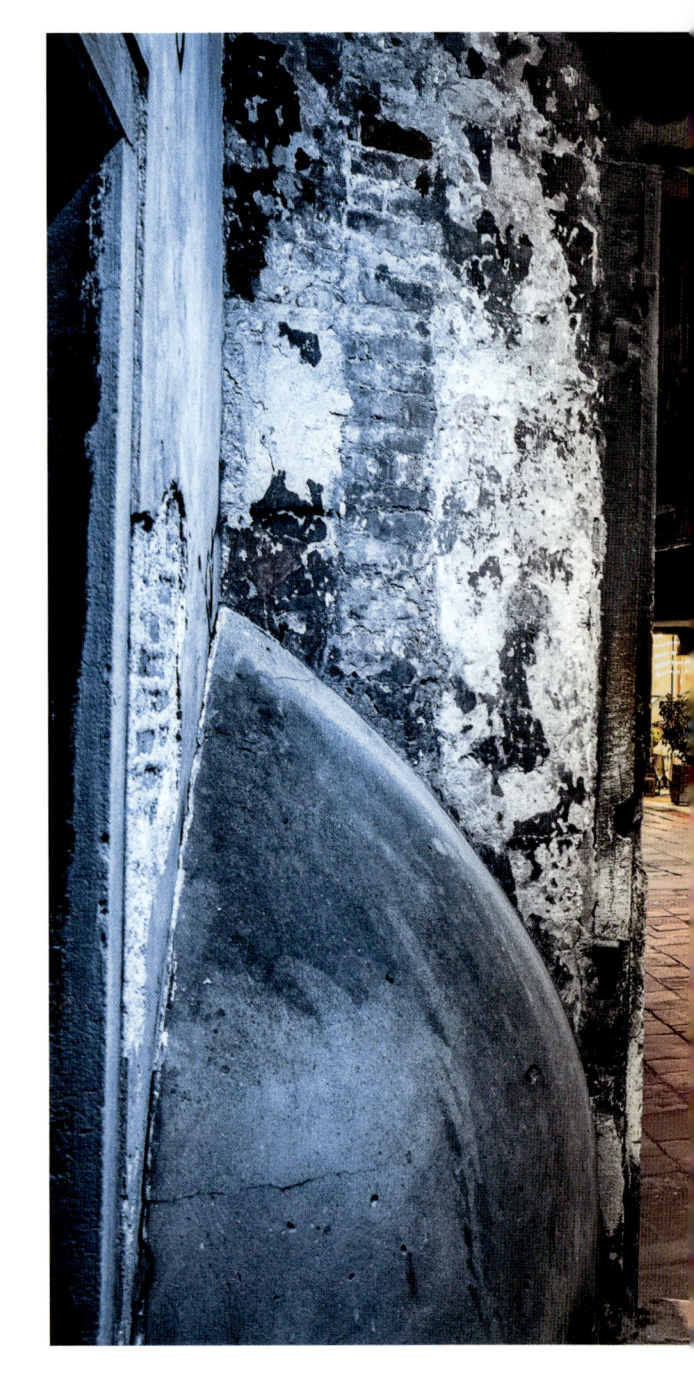

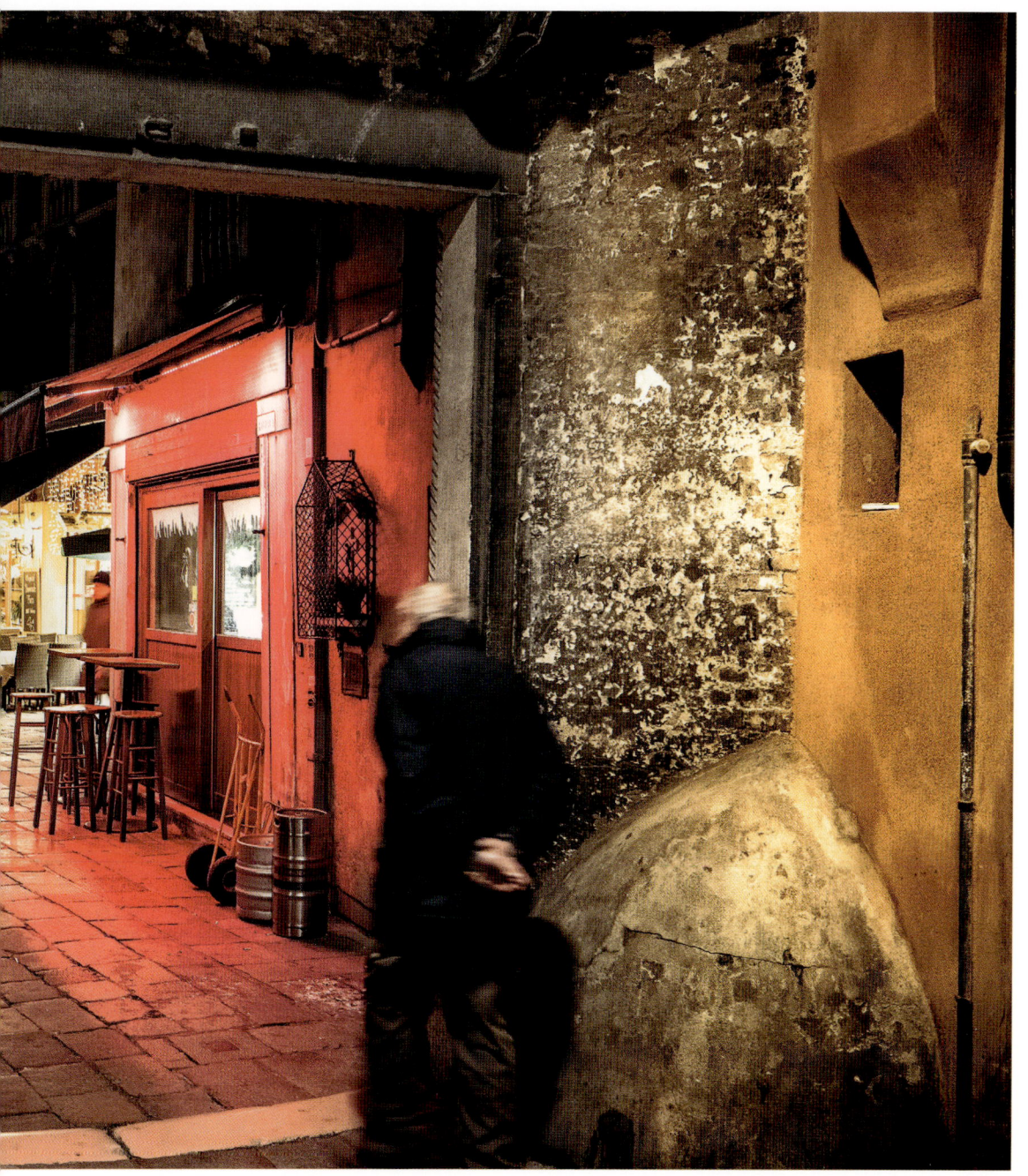

Venice, Italy, 2018

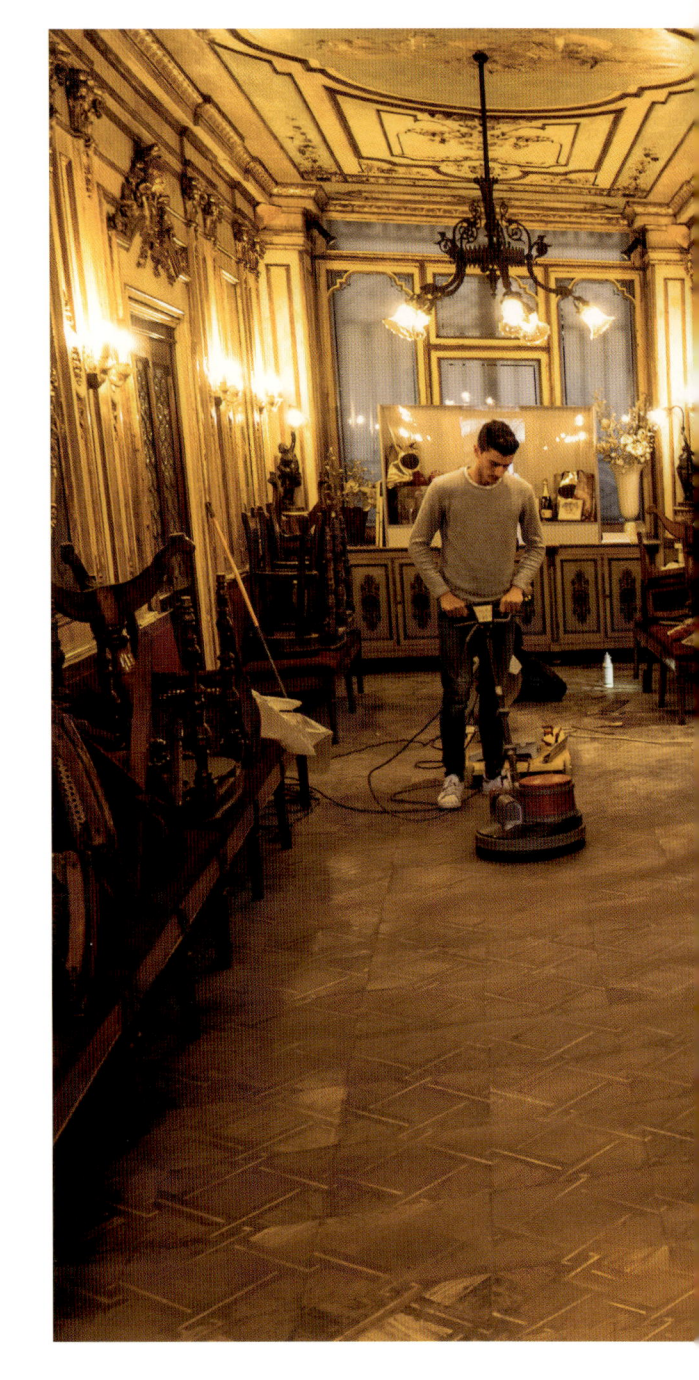

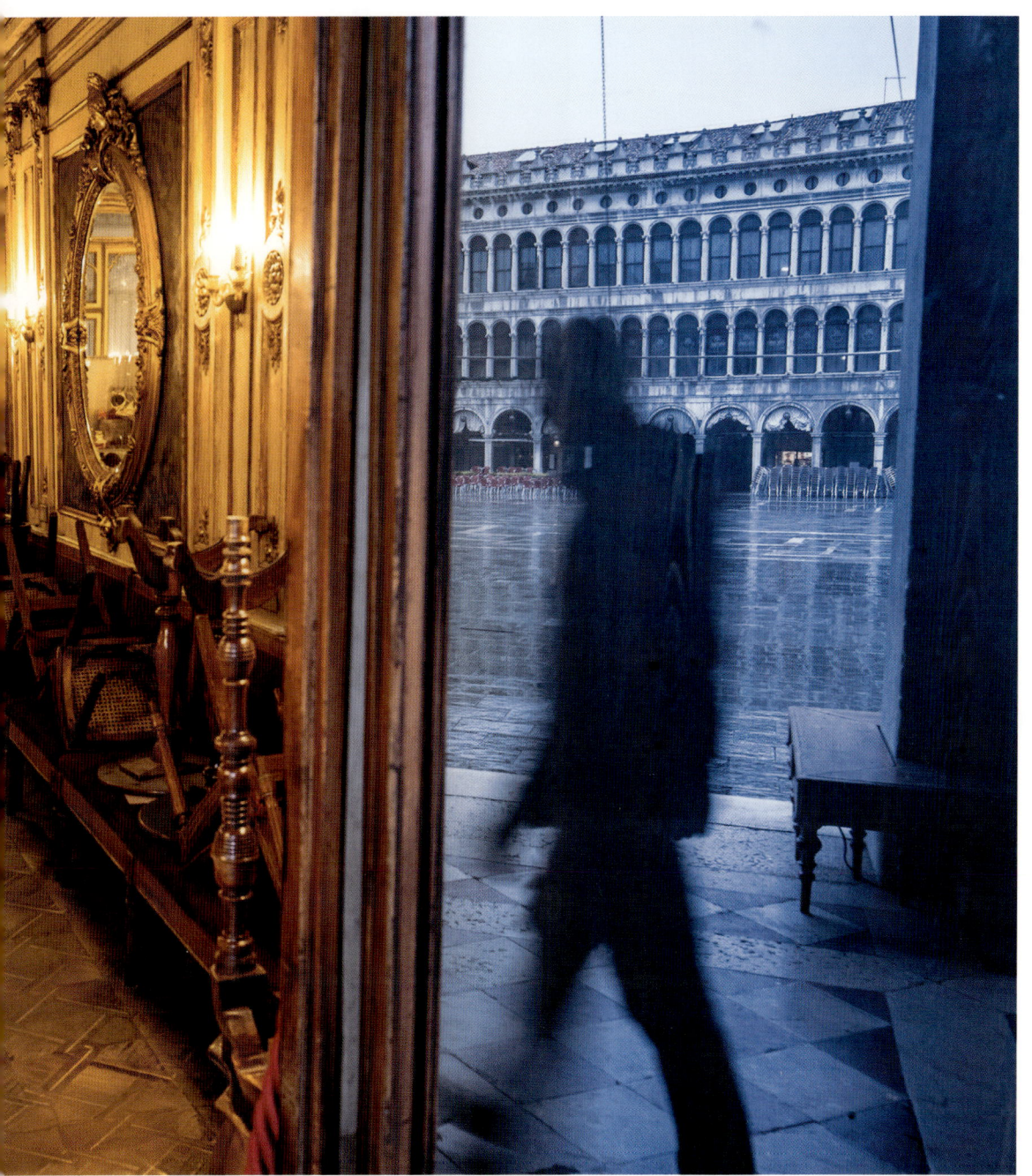

Venice, Italy, 2018

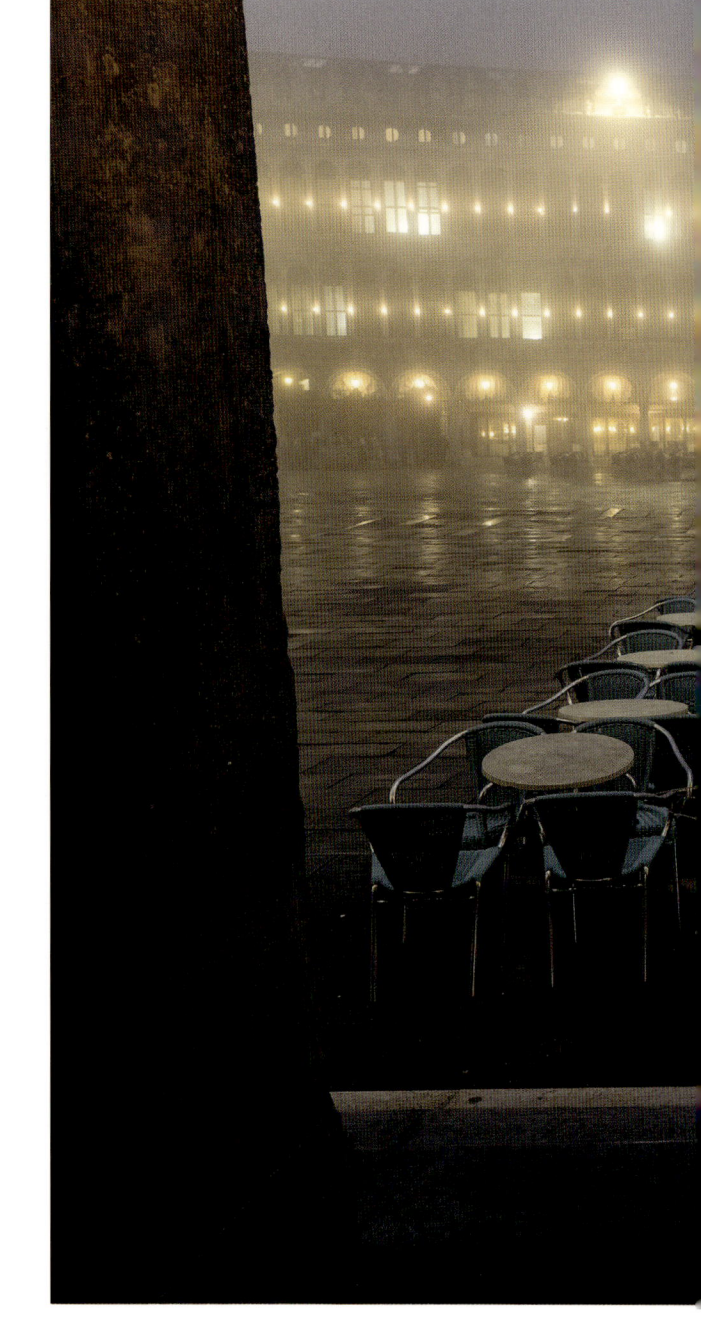

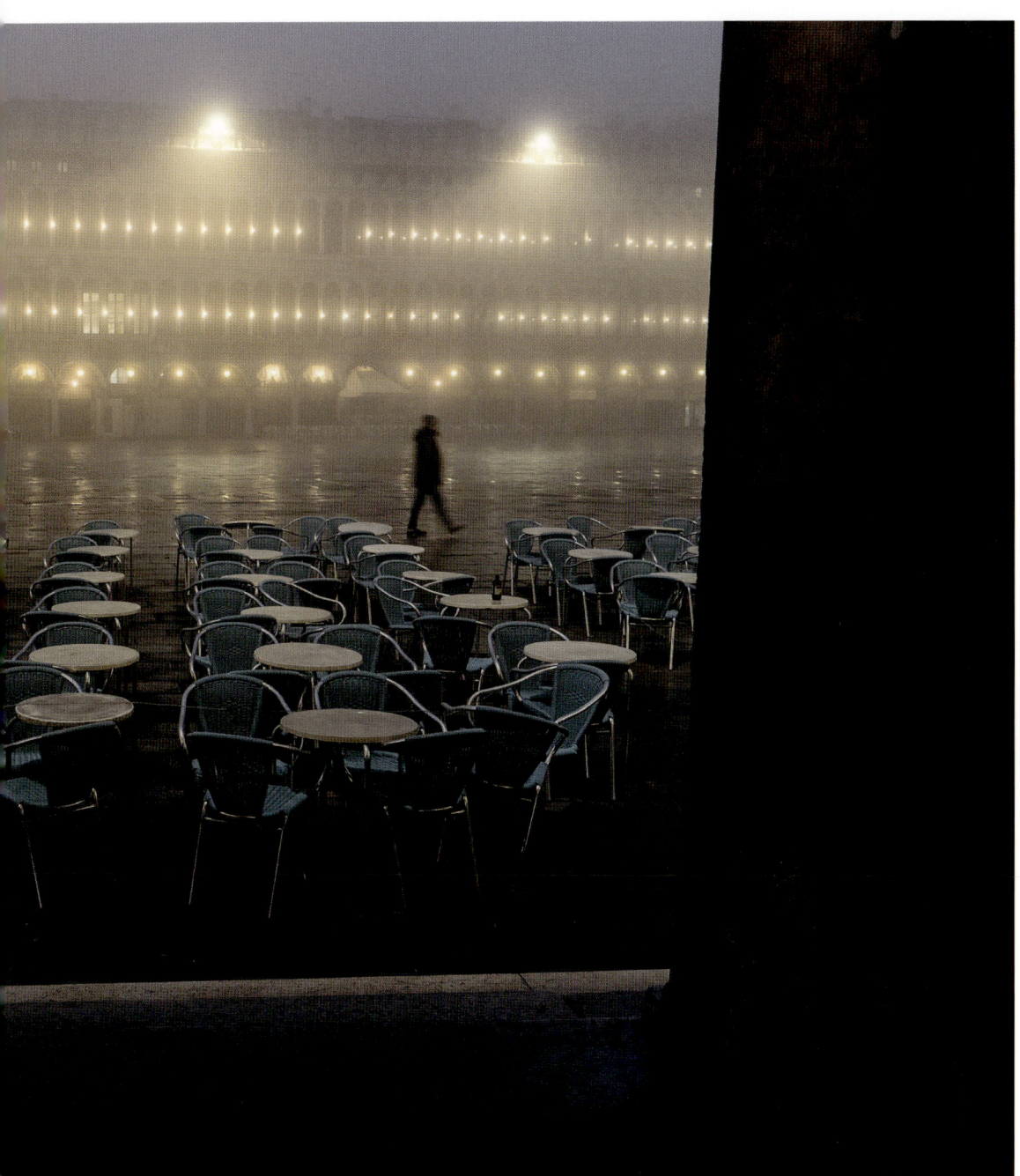

Venice, Italy, 2018

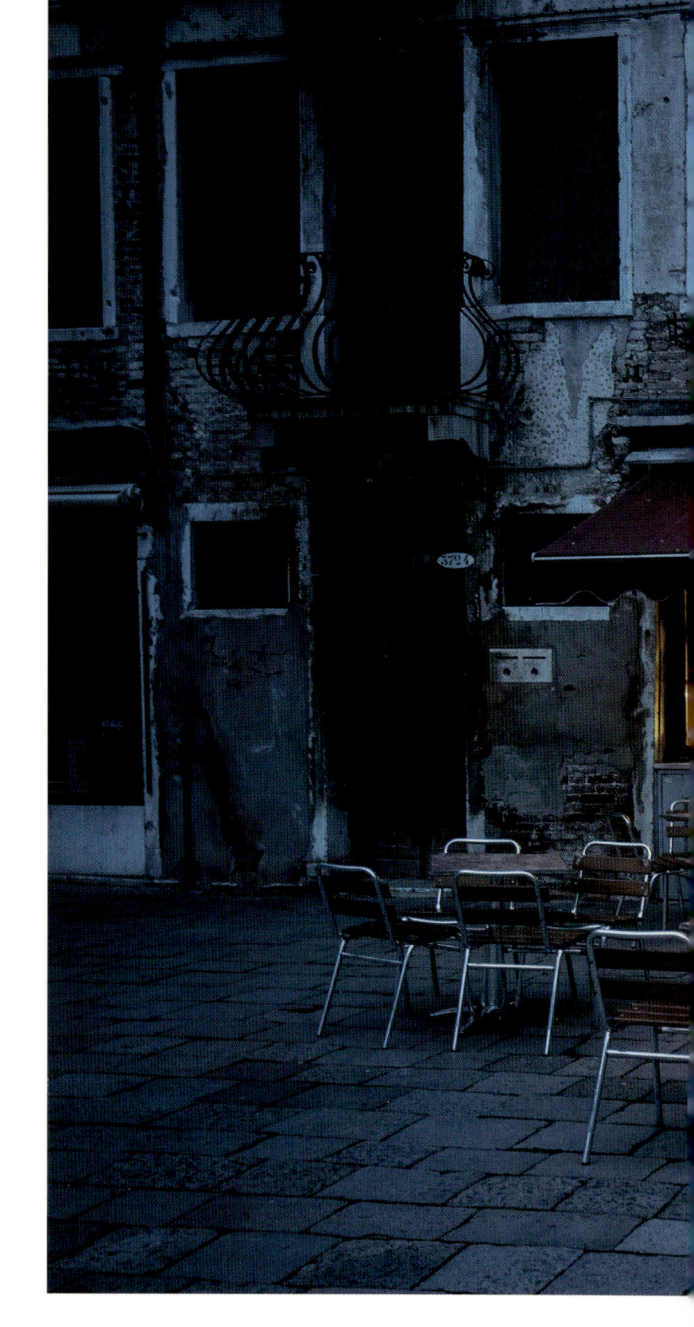

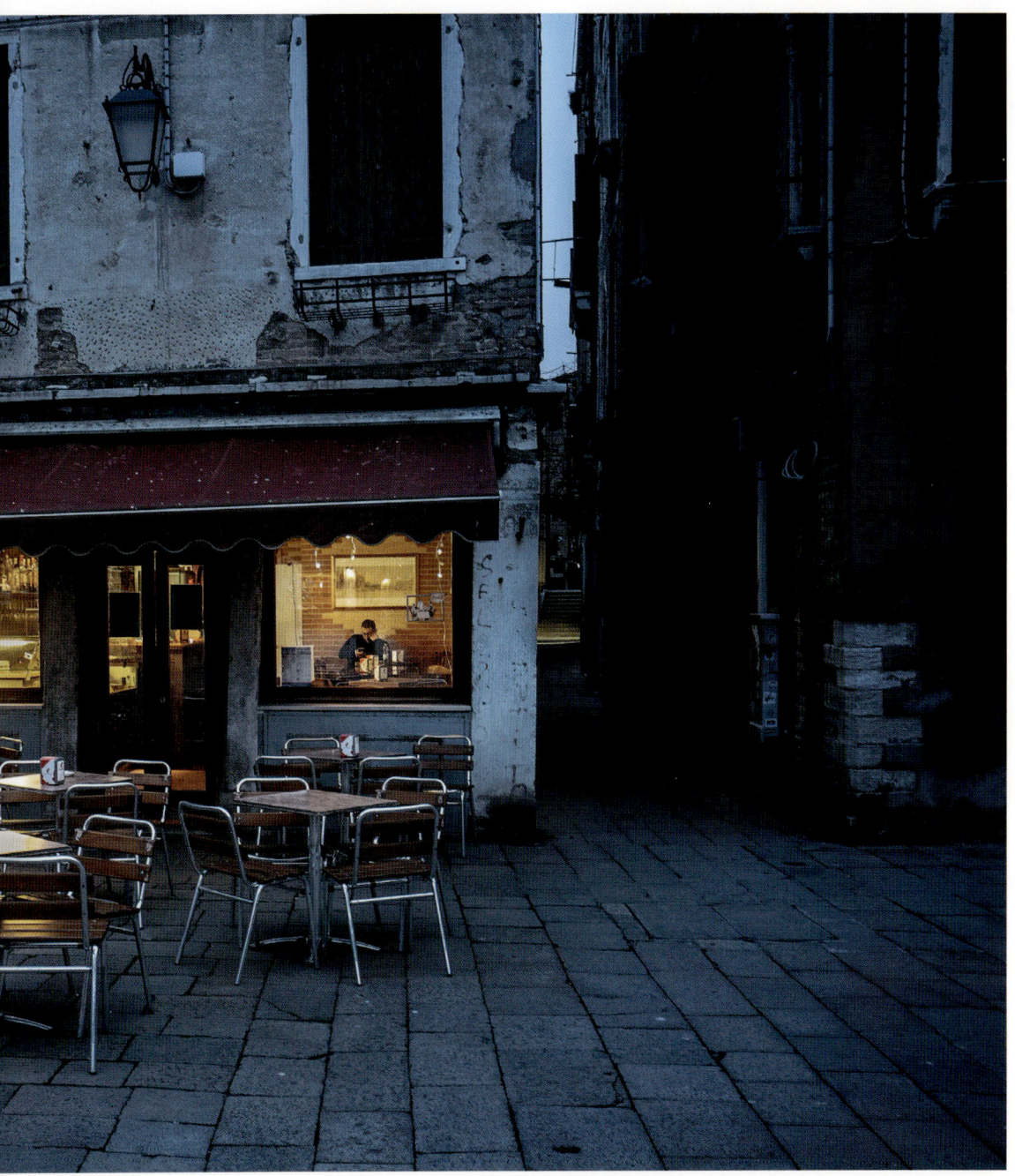

Venice, Italy, 2018

The final image is an *interpretation* in line, shape, tone, and colour of what we saw.

08
What Role Do the Lines and Shapes Play?

THE CAMERA HAS A WAY OF TRICKING US into believing it sees the world the way we do, immersed as we are in three dimensions and the sensuality of real life. It tricks us into thinking we photograph trees and buildings, people, and flowers—whatever it is you point your lens at. But the final image is an *interpretation* in line, shape, tone, and colour of what we saw. It is a graphic thing, and like all graphics, the materials with which we make them are simple: point, line, and shape.

I say this because we too often forget this. We are seduced by the depth of the real world and everything that's going on in front of the lens; it is only later, when we return to the final image, that we see the lines do not line up, the shapes do not successfully represent the person whose spirit we wanted to capture, or the energy of the scene we wanted never to forget. As it is with all of photography, the trick is to be conscious—truly aware—of what the lines are doing. Questions can help us with that perception:

- Where are the lines leading my eye? Is there a vanishing point? To where does that point take me?

- Do those lines have energy to them? Are they static horizontals or energetic diagonals?

- Do the lines intersect in ways that might later surprise me? The power lines running through my subject's head, for example?

- Do the lines connect with the frame in ways that help or hinder the visual journey around the photograph?

- Do the lines form shapes?

- Do the lines and shapes please me? Are they interesting? Sensual? Strong? Delicate?

Beyond questions that help bring our awareness to the graphic possibilities for the image itself, perhaps the most important question becomes this: How can you use or change these lines and shapes to help write the photographic poem or story you want to tell? What choices can you make to have that silhouette of a cowboy look the most like a cowboy possible? A silhouette is just a long line, filled with black, that describes a thing. But it is in our choice of moment or our position relative to the man himself that gives that silhouette its best chance at being the best line possible, one that—for anyone who wasn't there—can mostly clearly describe that it's a cowboy, sitting on a hill, shoulders slumped and tired. Or is it just a dark blob on the horizon?

The trick is to be conscious—truly aware—of what the lines are doing.

It's the same subject in one frame as it is in the other, but one finds a stronger expression in the final image because of the photographer's conscious effort to make those lines describe exactly what was intended.

Remember that these questions are not only about the making of more intentional photographs, but about recognizing the possibilities before the camera even comes to your face, and later in choosing that one final frame from the many you took to get there. When you ask what the lines and shapes are doing, you give yourself a chance to see the scene as close to what it is, especially in terms of how the camera sees, as possible. You begin to see the circles formed by certain elements, you see repeating triangles, you become aware of the geometry of the scene and how certain elements form large rectangles and divide the frame. And in that awareness, the lines and shapes offer you a chance to move them around and make more pleasing relationships or give the picture more energy as you change it from static to dynamic. Or perhaps you notice the ways in which one line intersects with the top of the frame and forms one of those little triangles in the corners that trap the eye, so you nudge the camera down to give the image a chance to be stronger, free from that distraction.

It has always seemed a shame to me that photography has been treated as though it were primarily a technical pursuit. That perspective has forced us to learn how to use a camera often at the expense of learning how to *see*. It takes years for many photographers to notice how the camera, particularly in collaboration with lenses and our own perspective, sees and represents lines. In the next chapter, I'll explore the latter. Here, I think it fitting to point out that this chapter's overall question is not just about lines and shapes, but about how the camera sees them; specifically, how our optics see them.

If you're asking what the lines are doing or what possibilities they present in the making of your photograph, then an obvious next question might be: What lens are you using? Knowing how lenses behave is like knowing how different brushes put paint on the canvas. I'm not a painter, so let's not take this metaphor too far, but different brushes will put colour on the canvas in different ways. So, too, with lenses and their treatment of lines.

Long lenses create a visually compressed effect on lines, pushing lines together, isolating them, and often robbing them of their energy by making them shorter. Wider lenses do the opposite, pushing elements apart, exaggerating lines and any energy they might have, especially when we use them closer to those elements in the scene. This is neither good nor bad, unless you want your photograph to have strong energy and your choice of lens robs the image of what could have been a more dynamic representation of the lines. Or, conversely, if you want a more serene scene and perhaps your choice of lens combined with your point of view makes that serenity impossible because you created a picture that doesn't let the eye rest for all the energy you've given the lines.

One of the exercises I give my students to bring a greater awareness to the lines and shapes in an image might help here. You'll need two things: a marker (I like red) and a handful of images. Print out a dozen of your own photographs or tear some from a magazine. Use that marker to trace on the paper the primary lines of the image. Doing this with an actual marker helps make you aware of the lines and shapes in an image, and it eventually gives way to doing it with your mind's eye. It helps make you more conscious later, when you've got a camera in hand, of the direction and energy of lines, where they intersect, what shapes they form, and how they relate to each other and to the frame. Only once you're aware of them can you begin to make choices about what to *do* with them in order to make the image say or feel what you intend.

It is the combination of both lens choice and physical position that has the most potential creative power over the lines in the final picture.

09
What's Your
Point of View?

IN THE LAST CHAPTER'S DISCUSSION of line and shape, I mentioned that our perspective with the camera (our position or point of view) plays a part in how the lines and shapes find their final relationships in the photograph itself. It is one thing to accept this on a fundamental level, but it's another thing entirely to embrace it as an extraordinary creative tool in the making of our photographs.

When painters paint their pictures, they are unbound by anything but the limits of their imagination and skill. They put the barn where they choose in order to balance it against the mountain in the background, and they strategically place the tree where it will balance out the whole canvas. You and I have fewer choices, but setting aside the obvious conversation (and subsequent rabbit holes and arguments) about the possibilities we have with software, that doesn't mean we're powerless. Limited as we are by the constraints of the real world, the photographer still has an astonishing ability to move the elements within a scene, in relationship not only to each other but to the frame itself. We leverage that ability with our choice of lens and by moving our feet. It is the latter that's relevant now.

Have you heard the expression "zoom with your feet"? It's a well-worn platitude that, like so many platitudes, is used to sound pithy and wise but gets applied far more broadly than initially intended. I'm quite sure it was initially meant to suggest that we not be lazy and use a zoom lens when we could just as easily, and perhaps with stronger effect, get physically closer to the subject. It's solid advice. But when we misunderstand it to mean that zooming and using our feet are the same thing, we are not recognizing that what a particular focal length does to lines and shapes in an image is different from what moving our feet does to those same lines and shapes. In fact, it is the combination of both lens choice and physical position that has the most potential creative power over the lines in the final picture.

Your lens cannot change your perspective. Only your point of view (often abbreviated POV) or position relative to the scene can do this. The lenses only help to exaggerate this position. Together they are very powerful. And this power is lost the moment a photographer arrives on a scene, plunks down a tripod, and uses only a few half-hearted twists of the zoom lens to refine the composition. He or she completely misses the ability to change it all by walking around, crawling on the belly, standing on a rock, and in doing so to change the relationships of all the elements one to another and to the frame.

Imagine you're standing on the edge of a lake, which forms your midground. In front of you is a large rock, your potential foreground. And in the background, at the far side of the lake, is a mountain. You could walk to the rock, choose whatever focal length allows you to get it all in, and make the image. But you'd miss a hundred potential photographs, maybe thousands of possibilities, by not noticing how a longer lens (perhaps a focal length of 200mm) has the effect of pulling the rock and the mountain together, making the similarity between them even more apparent. Or how a wider focal length, perhaps 24mm, makes everything much smaller. But wait, don't put the camera down just yet. Keep that 24mm lens on and walk closer to the big rock. Notice how it gets larger relative to the mountain in the background; it gains more mass in the frame. The photograph is now more about the foreground rock than the background mountain. Move even closer and the rock obfuscates the mountain entirely—a 10,000-foot peak hidden behind a 3-foot rock.

Now move back a little and to the left. The rock moves to the right of the frame, and the mountain moves, relatively, to the left. Lie on your belly and now the rock breaks the horizon, just like the mountain does. Nothing but you has moved, but in the photograph, everything has changed. Most of us know this. But it's important to truly understand the impact of these choices, not just on the aesthetics of the photograph (what it looks like) but on the message (what are you trying to say?). How does what you are saying or implying in the photograph change when you intentionally create distance between elements or bring them together? How does your point of view on the scene determine what is included and excluded, and what do those choices say about your intended subject? In the case of photographing people or making portraits, would a change in POV make your photograph feel less condescending (by looking down at them) or give your subject greater power (by looking up at them)? Would photographing lions from a lower perspective, say at eye level, make the image more empathetic to the plight of its prey?

Nothing but you has moved, but in the photograph, everything has changed.

If you know (or are willing to discover) what your photograph is about, then being aware of the impact of your own perspective, especially in combination with your lens choice, gives you much greater control and creativity in making the final image. Asking yourself these questions can be tremendously helpful:

- Does my current point of view allow me to include or exclude what I need?

- Would a different POV do that better?

- Can I make the relationships between the included elements and the frame itself stronger by moving?

- Can I change the balance in the photograph by moving the elements around with a change in POV?

- What possibilities are there if I changed my POV and my focal length, particularly in manipulating the relationship between foreground and background?

- Is there a different perspective that might give better expression to my subject by changing the feeling or messaging?

- Would a change in perspective, perhaps from extremely high or low, say something different about a familiar subject, or make it more interesting?

One final note: please don't read this as a criticism of tripods! Tripods help slow us down, which is often a good thing. They also allow effects that we couldn't achieve by holding the camera in our hands. But if you must use one, do so only after you've fully explored the scene, gotten past the obvious first compositions, and have a greater sense of the desired relationship between the elements. And if a tripod isn't suitable for the kind of work you do, as is the case with so much of my own work, then take advantage of that freedom and find answers to the question, "What's my point of view?" by moving around until you've discovered the strongest possibilities.

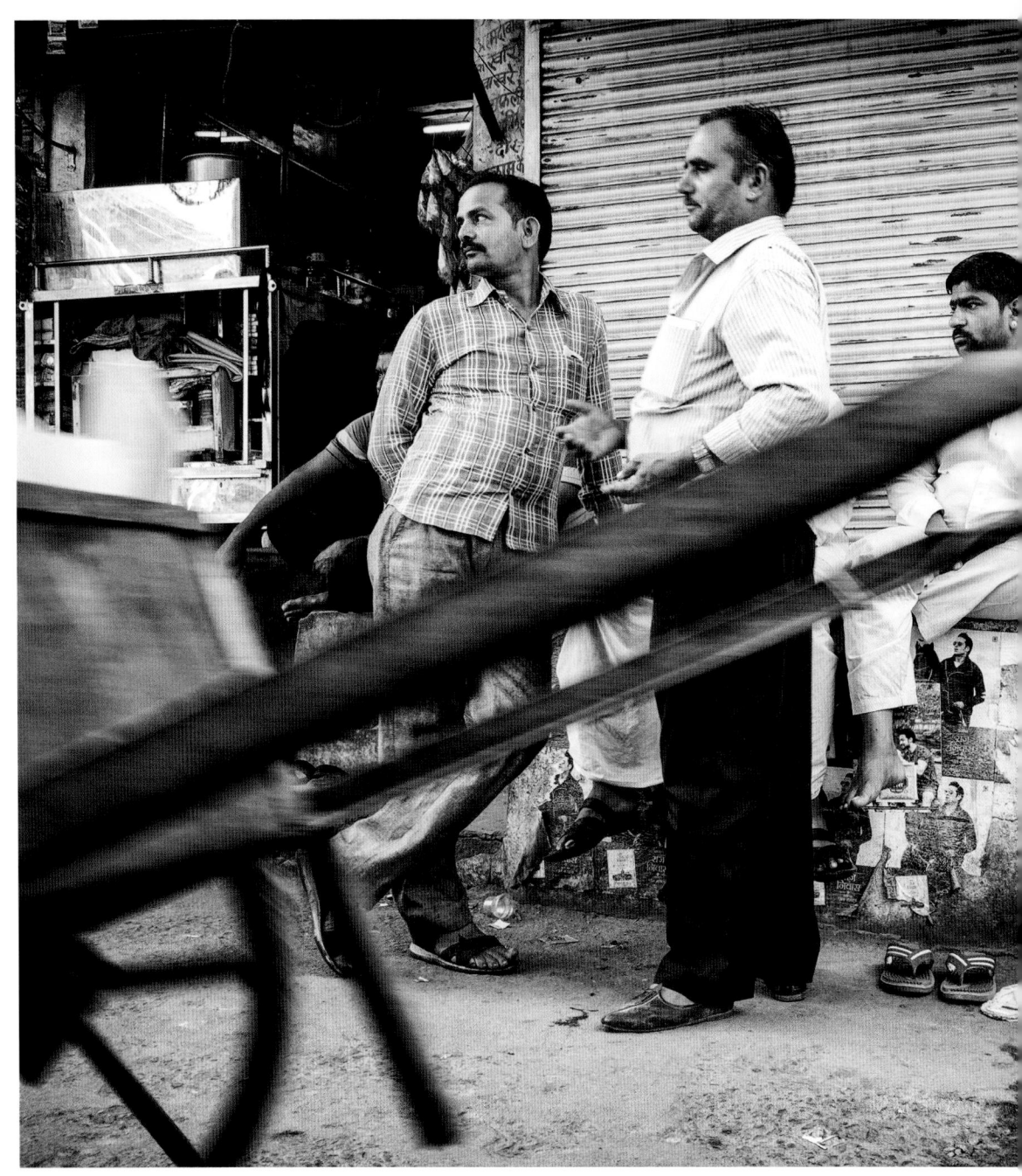

Jodhpur, India, 2017

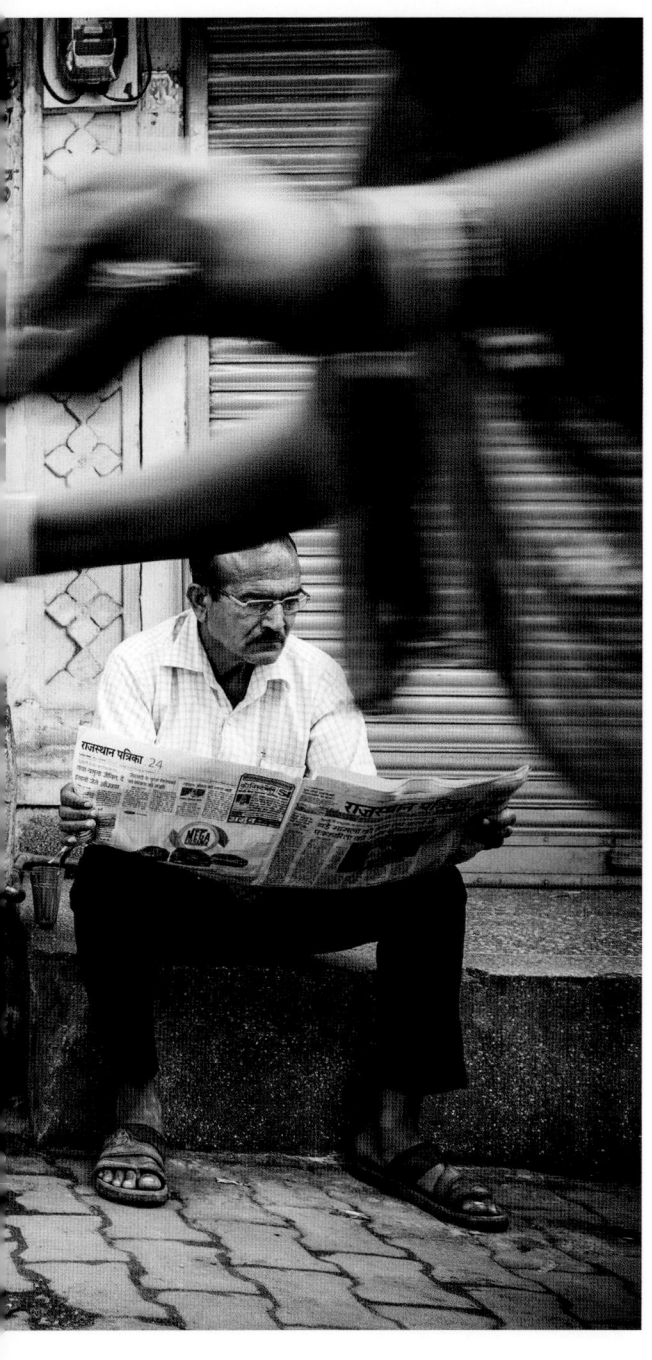

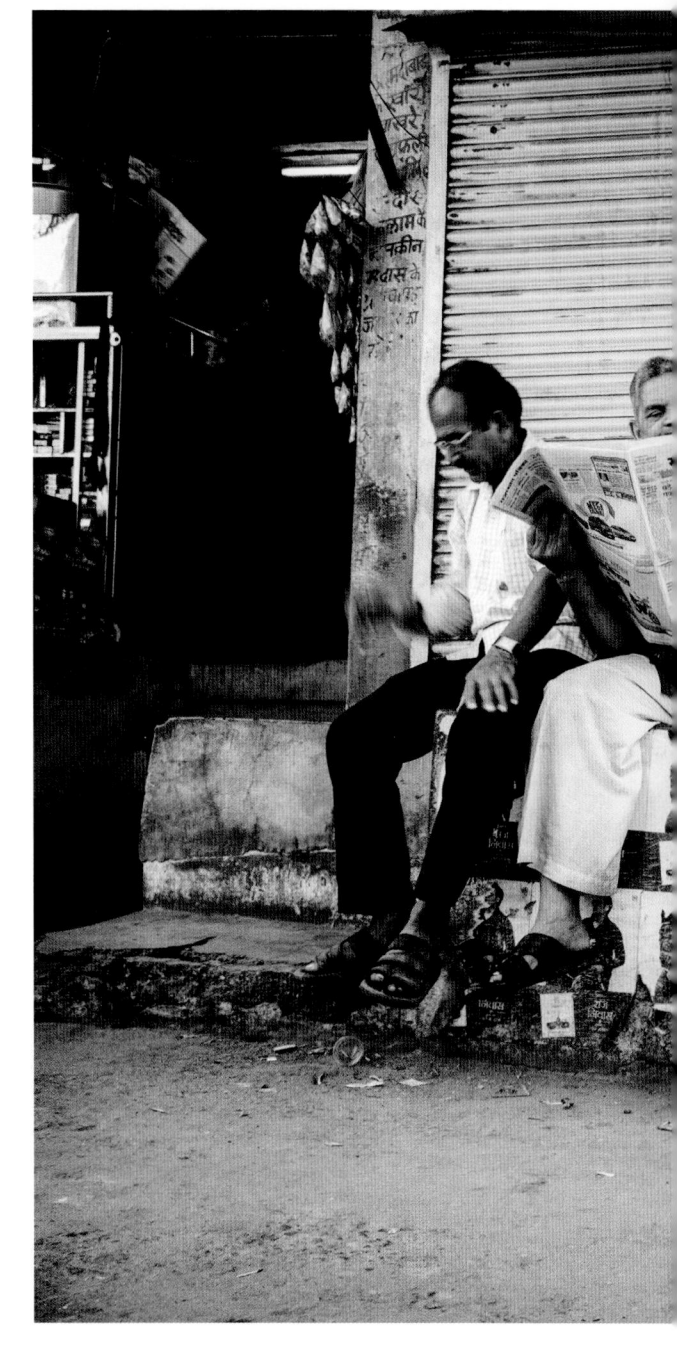

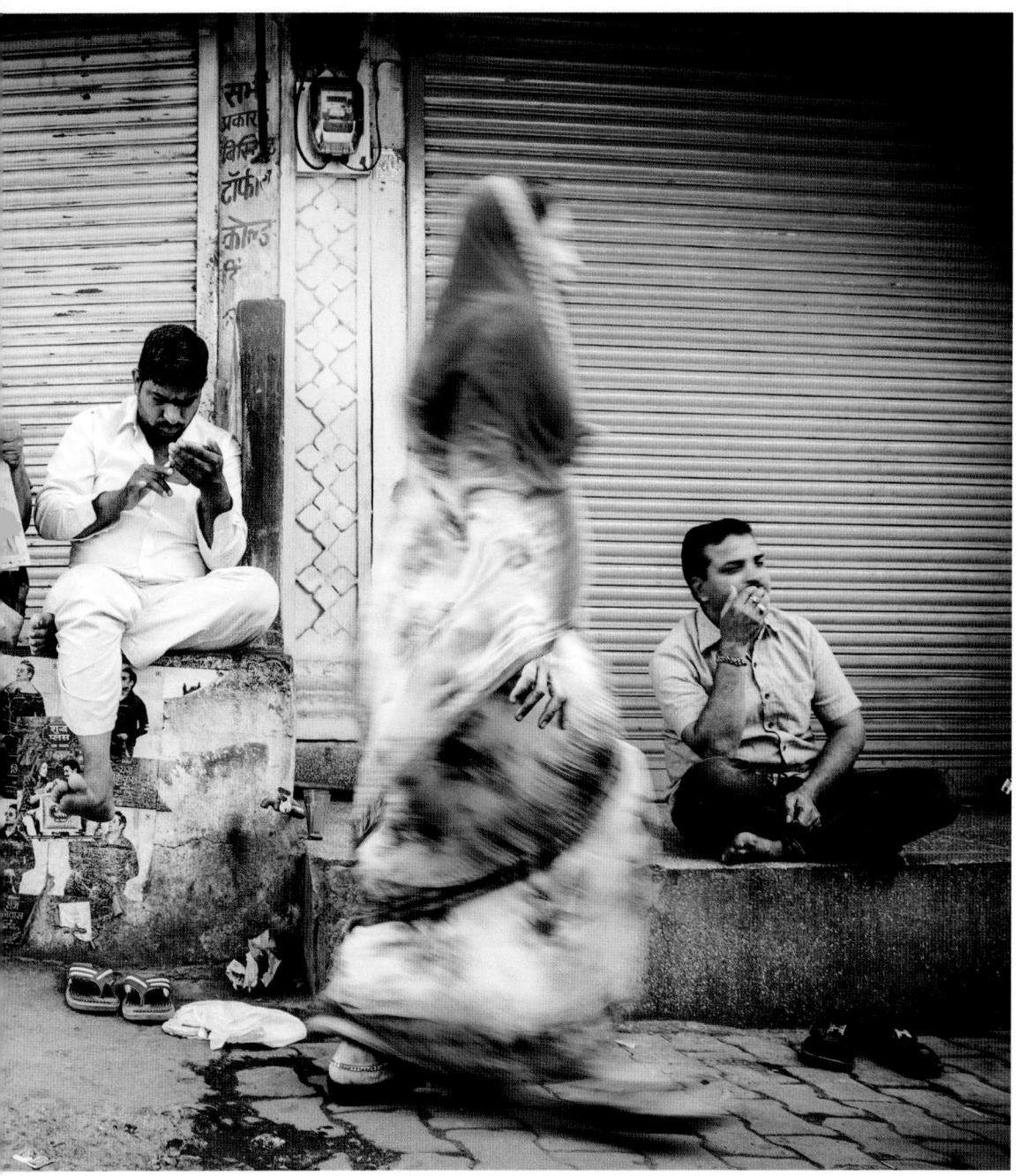

Jodhpur, India, 2017

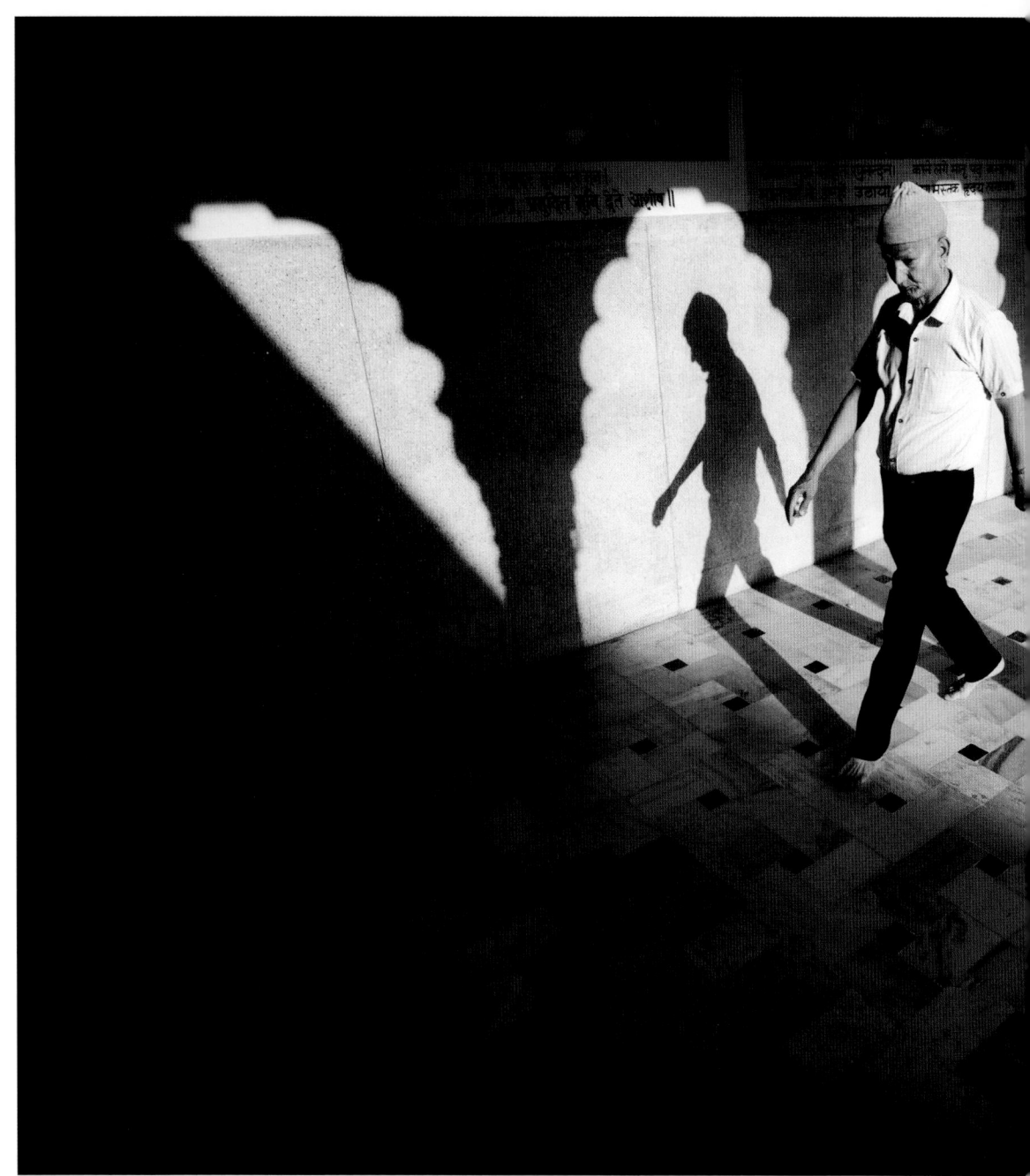

Jodhpur, India, 2017

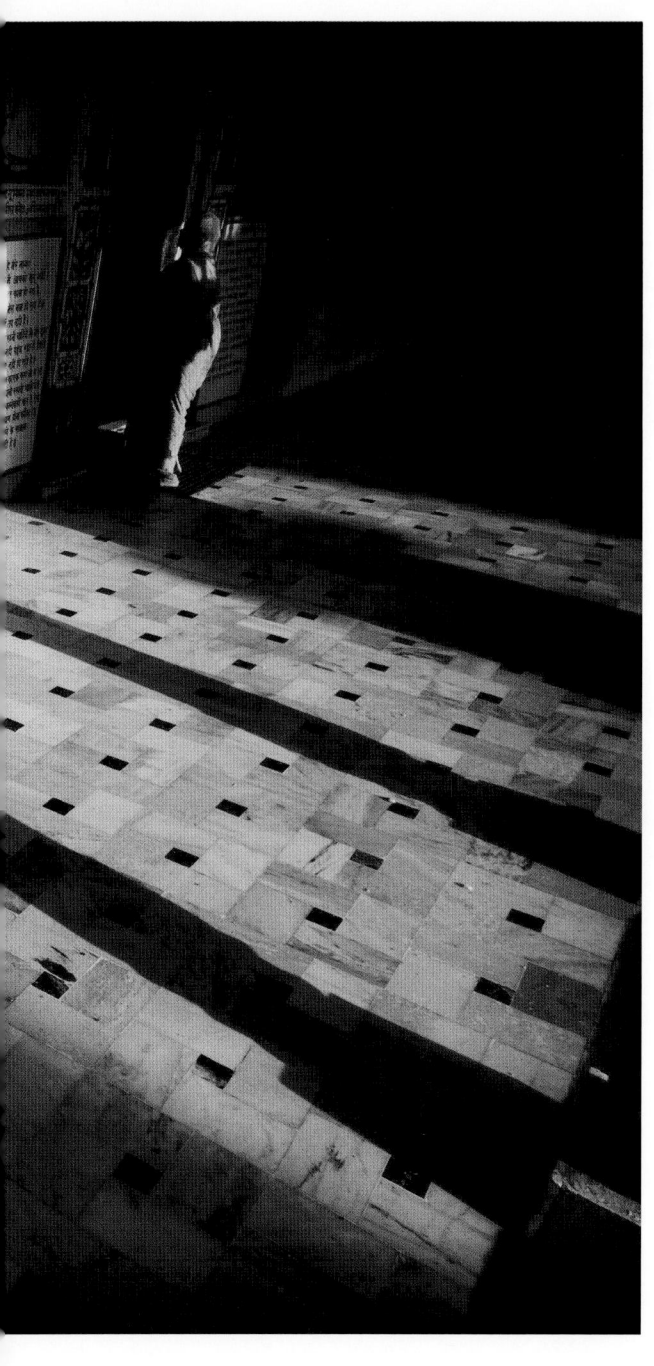

Timing can be everything, which is not surprising for a craft so dependent on time.

10
What Is the Quality of the Moment?

NOT EVERY PHOTOGRAPH BENEFITS from quality of moment the same way. In some images, the role of moment is blindingly obvious: a kiss, a gesture, or just a glance at a wedding; a bear catching a salmon; a man leaping over a puddle. All of these depend not only on time, but on timing. But it is no less powerful a tool in the hands of the landscape photographer who relies on seasonality, light, and weather, though that photographer may prefer to think of "moments" that span minutes, hours, or weeks, rather than the fragments of seconds that most street, travel, sports, or even portrait photographers usually consider so important.

Timing can be everything, which is not surprising for a craft so dependent on time. In order to make an exposure, we must consider not only which moment, but the duration of that moment. This means we have some choices to make,

and these choices are not always simple. Often, they are a balance of making a
good exposure in the sense of getting the right amount of light onto the sensor
or film, along with what those choices imply for the look of the image. A narrow
or wide aperture will have consequences for what is in and out of focus. A fast
or slow shutter speed will have consequences for how the passing, or slowing,
of time is captured in the image. And with these choices, we say certain things
about our subjects.

Where time is concerned, a subject that is about motion, and is particularly
about the feeling or experience of motion, will want to be treated differently
from a subject that depends on precision of timing. A cheetah on the Serengeti
might be best photographed with a slower shutter speed while panning the
camera, giving that sense of motion and speed. The same technique used with a
bear catching a salmon in Alaska might not be so well served. But to know that,
you have to have a sense of the quality of the moment and what possibilities
it presents. That bear standing still on a rock and looking for salmon might
be very well served with a stable camera and a 1/8 of a second shutter speed
that allows the waterfalls around him to blur and gain a sense of motion that
contrasts with his own stillness, bringing attention not only to the motion of
the waterfall but to the patience of the hunting bear. Unless the bear moves, in
which case it's just a blurry mess.

The feeling of the moment is not the only thing that will or won't be well
expressed by our choices; so too will the meaning of that moment. If you
photograph a child throwing a baseball and you're a little late on the shutter, you
may end up with a photograph with no visual clues that a ball has been thrown.
In this case, the potential quality of the moment has been missed and won't at
all communicate the true intended subject of the image, which is the throwing
of the ball, the action, the implied story of the baseball game.

What does this moment need to look like to best express the idea or subject?

Reverse engineering this, you could ask yourself: What does this moment need to look like to best express the idea or subject? Is it important that the bear catch the fish, or is it more powerful for the shutter to release just a fraction of a second before that moment, creating a photograph in which the fish is perpetually suspended in front of the waiting mouth of the bear, creating tension and encouraging us to forever ask ourselves whether the bear gets a meal or the fish goes free?

Our ability to play with both time and timing gives us incredible creative options that we can use as powerful emotional and storytelling tools. Here are some of the questions I consider as I'm photographing:

- Does time, or timing, play a role in this image?

- Could my choices about when to press the shutter and how long to keep it open give me options that better express my intended subject?

- If there's movement, can I better express that movement with a longer shutter and/or camera motion?

- Would waiting a little longer bring me a stronger moment than the one I have now?

- Would coming back to this scene bring me a different quality of moment, perhaps a change of light, weather, or story?

- What about this moment is essential? Or to put it another way, which smaller moment in the context of the larger flow of moments is the apex of the action, the one that best represents it all?

These same questions can be asked later when editing, helping you choose the one frame that best tells the story or conveys the mood. But for all the things we can change with software after the fact, there are few fixes for a missed moment, for time treated without intention or anticipation. It's hard. It's frustrating when we miss it, but it's that challenge, and the beauty of it when it pays off, that makes this craft the beautiful, time-dependent thing it is, so bound to our memories and emotions.

This consideration of moments, perhaps more than anything else in our journey toward mastering this craft, is the hardest to gain. These questions are helpful, but sometimes we don't have the time to reflect on them, much less do anything about them, before that moment is gone and the chance is missed. That only makes it more important that we learn to anticipate these moments and when they arise, recognize more quickly what our options are. Intuitive photographers usually only become so because they've been doing this kind of work for a long time. Intentionally asking these kinds of questions, and often, gives us all a better chance of getting there sooner.

The power of a photograph to tell a story comes from its power to get the human imagination started.

11
Where Is
the Story?

HAVING WRITTEN ABOUT STORY in several of my previous books, I don't want to repeat myself, but story is important enough that it bears at least a nod in its direction. Story can give much of the meaning to certain photographs, so it's important those stories are told well by way of the conscious decisions we make to tell, or imply, them.

It's also important to recognize that story is not the *only* way to convey meaning in photographs. I've had many students over the years come to me almost in tears because they just couldn't figure out how to make their macro photographs of flowers tell a story. Landscape photographers have said the same to me. So have photographers who prefer to work in more abstract ways.

Story is only *one* way to create impact in images, just like it's only one way to create impact or relay information in written form. Go to a bookstore and you'll see many books, many of which will do exceedingly well what they were written to do. And many of them will *not* be novels or short stories. They will be books of poetry, and they will be nonfiction books about topics too numerous to list. Imagine how frustrated many of these writers would be if they were told they had to say what they wanted to say only in story. That's like telling cookbook authors that they can only use haiku.

Story is about change. In a photograph, it's usually about implied change because it's hard to show change actually happening in just one image. So it's change about to happen. Change that might happen. Change that has happened. With a series of images, I can make this story much clearer. And with enough images, they become a movie, a medium much more adept at the nuance of story. But can one single frame have strong story elements in it?

Story is also about conflict. In fact, it's the conflict that brings about change in a story, often by forcing it. So how do we show this in a photograph? My theory is that one of the best ways to do this is through contrast or juxtaposition, which we'll explore in the next chapter. So, aside from this, how do we incorporate story?

I'm simplifying here, but all great stories have a combination of character, action, setting, timing, and theme. Who. What. Where. When. Why. And if you can tie them together or suggest relationships, our imaginations take over and tell the rest of the story. The power of a photograph to tell a story comes from its power to get the human imagination started.

If you believe there's a story to be told or suggested in your image, these
questions can guide you to possibilities for implying that story more powerfully:

- Is the setting clear? If it matters at all, can I tell where and when the story
  takes place? What visual clues might help those who experience this
  photograph discern that? For example, does the writing on the wall help
  establish that this story takes place in India?

- Are the characters clear? If it's important that I know something specific
  about that character, what visual clues suggest that? What gives it away?

- Is the relationship between the characters clear? What can I tell from
  their gestures that helps establish this relationship? For example, are they
  close? Is one larger than the other? Does it tie into a larger, universally
  understood relationship, like predator versus prey, or adult versus child?

- Does the relationship between these characters imply change? For example, does the dark and threatening sky over a small town imply danger?
  Remember, nature can be a character, too. When you look at an image
  and think, "Tornado is coming!" then you can bet there's change about to
  happen—and that's story.

Don't overthink this. And don't let it get you worrying that your images don't
tell stories. They won't always, and they don't have to. But when story matters,
you'll be able to make a stronger photograph by asking if any of the above
applies, and understanding that the more clearly you can incorporate these
elements, the more impact they will have in the final image.

If this kind of approach interests you, then you should also consider the role of
contrast and juxtaposition, tools that hook our interest but that are not unique
to stories, so they're best discussed as their own devices. Because no matter
what kind of image you're making, without contrast, you've got almost nothing.

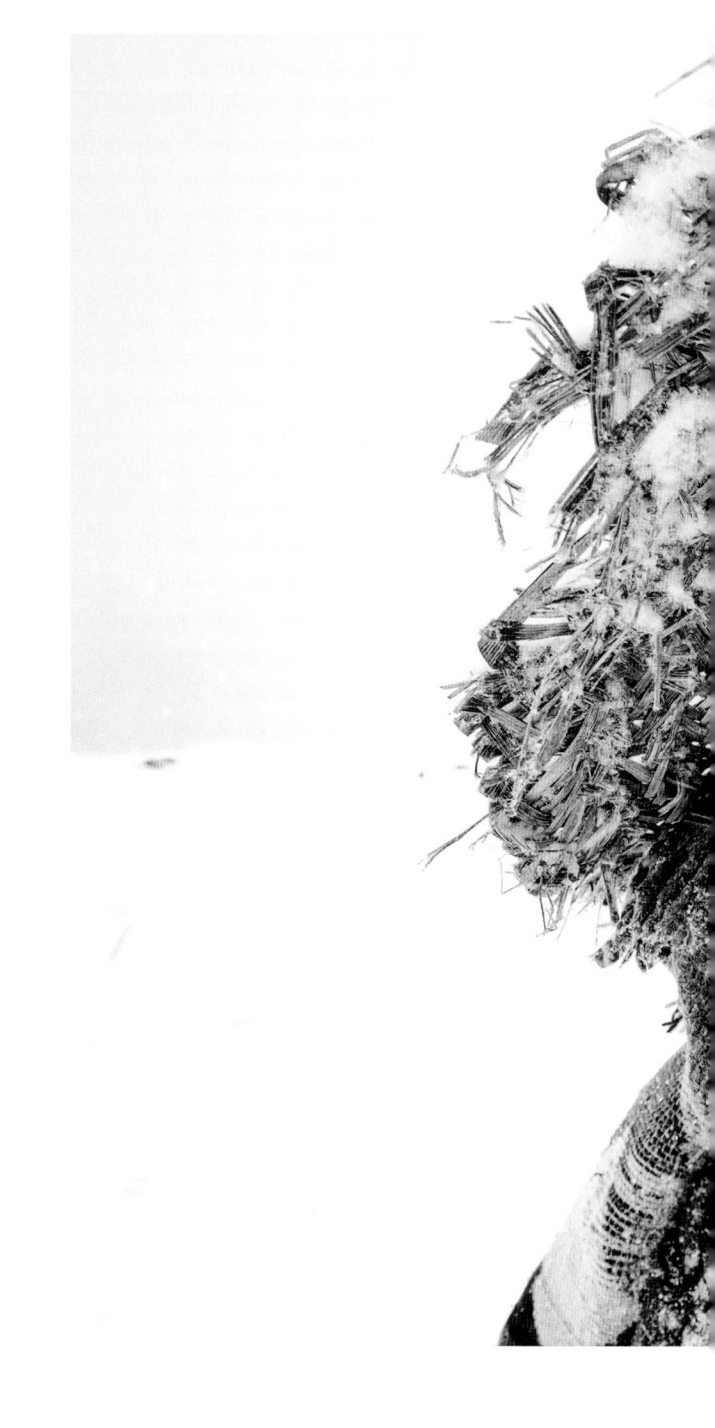

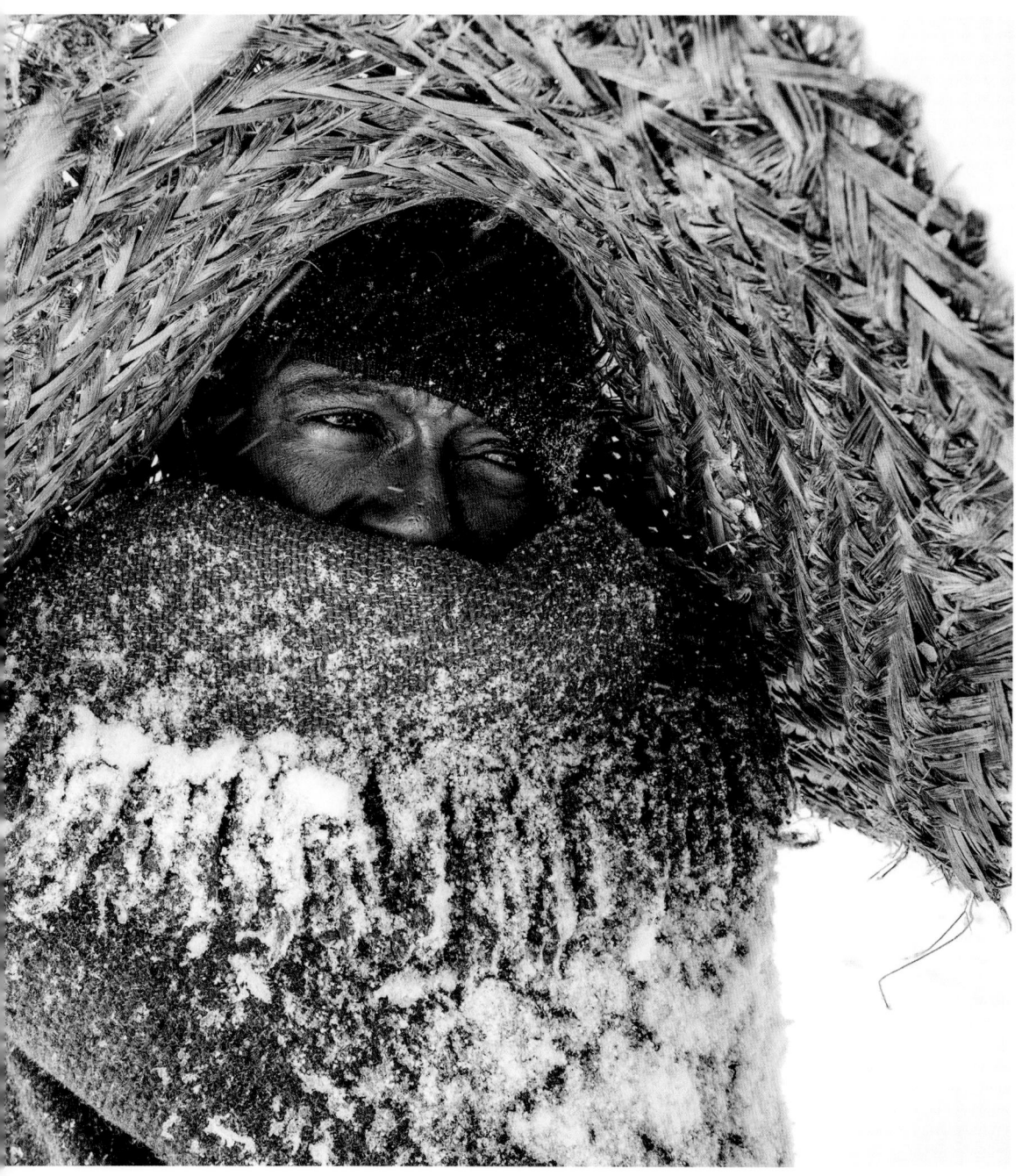

Mokhotlong, Lesotho, 2017

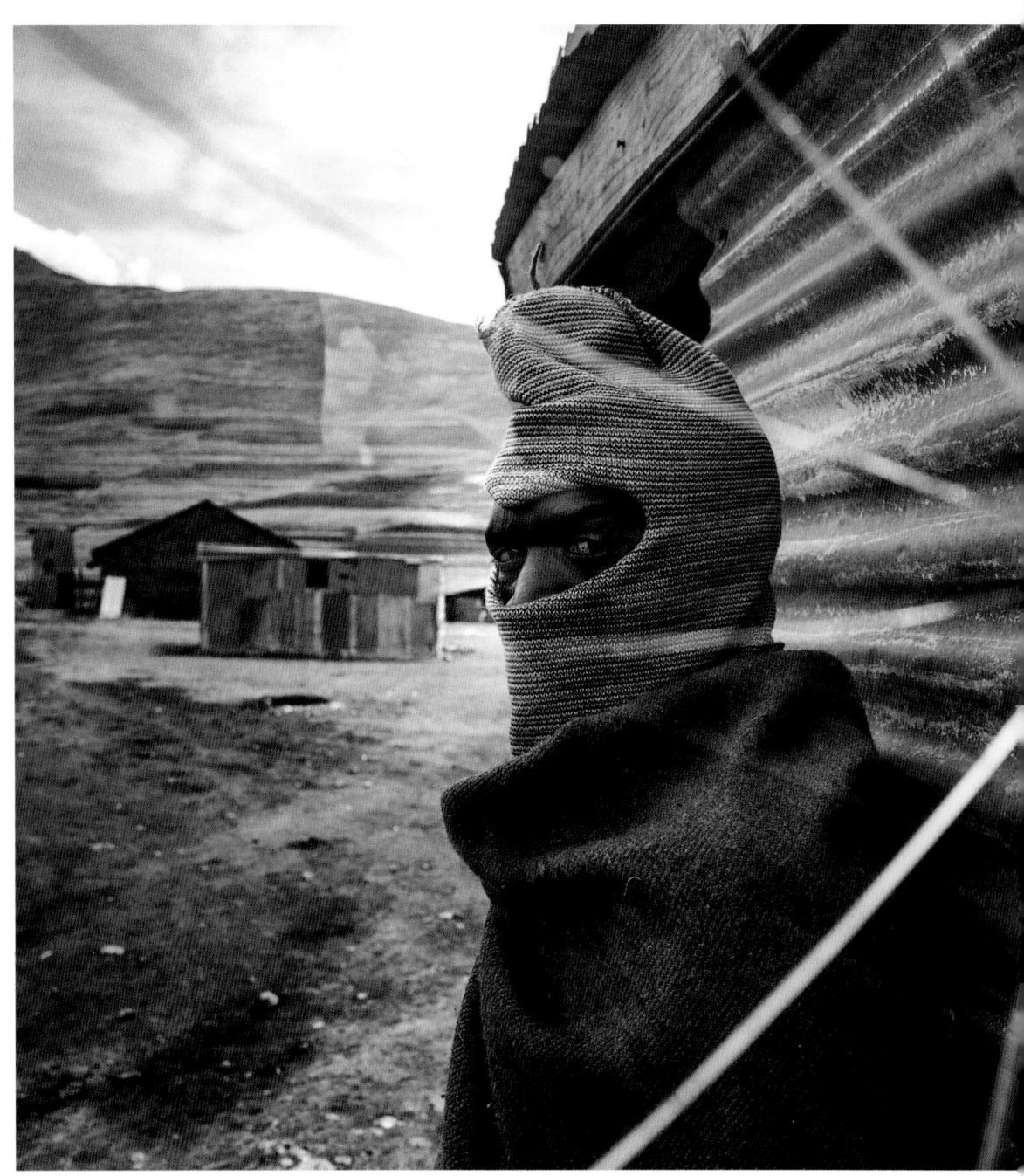

Mokhotlong, Lesotho, 2017

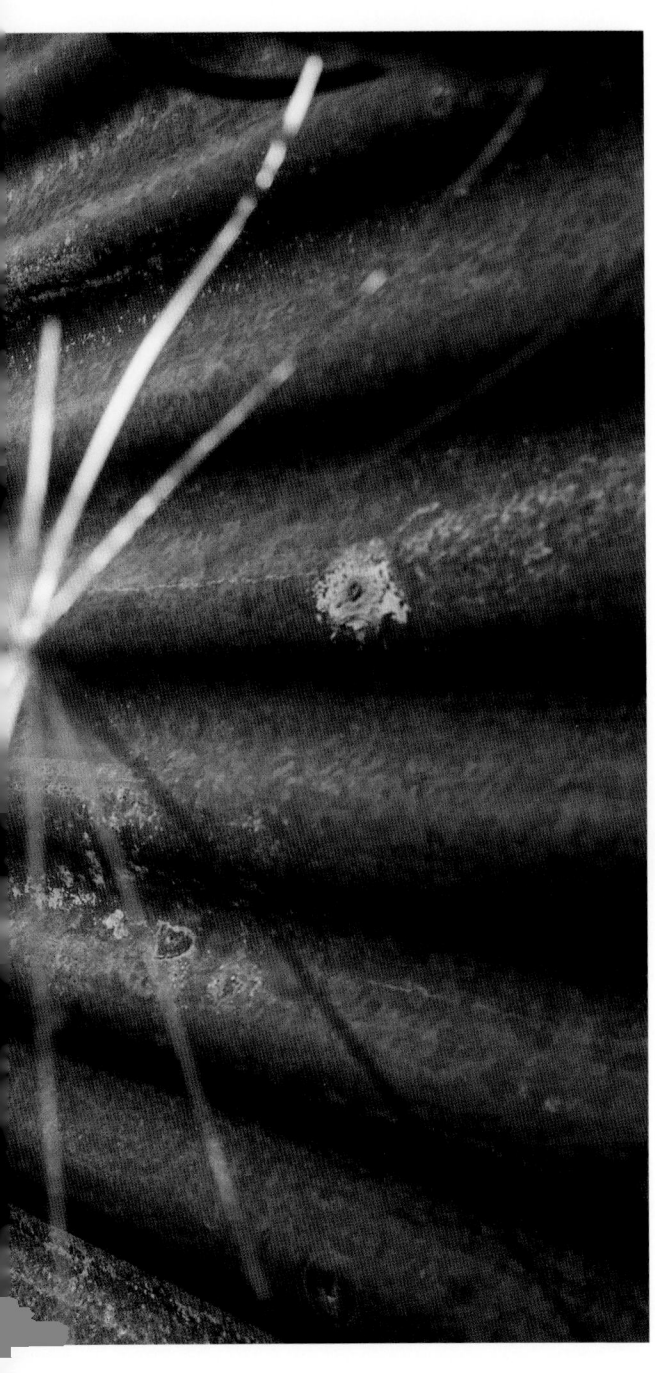

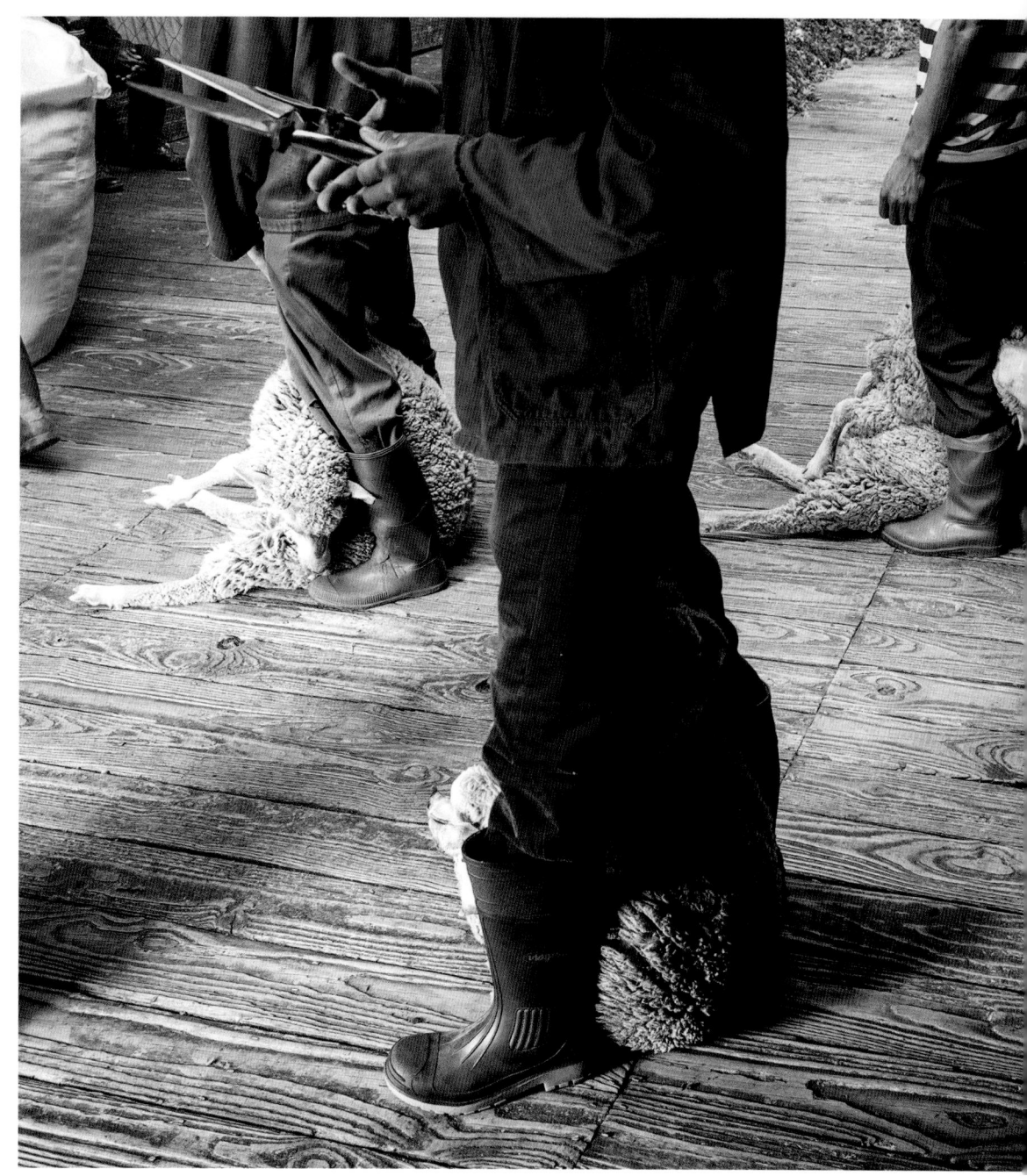

Mokhotlong, Lesotho, 2017

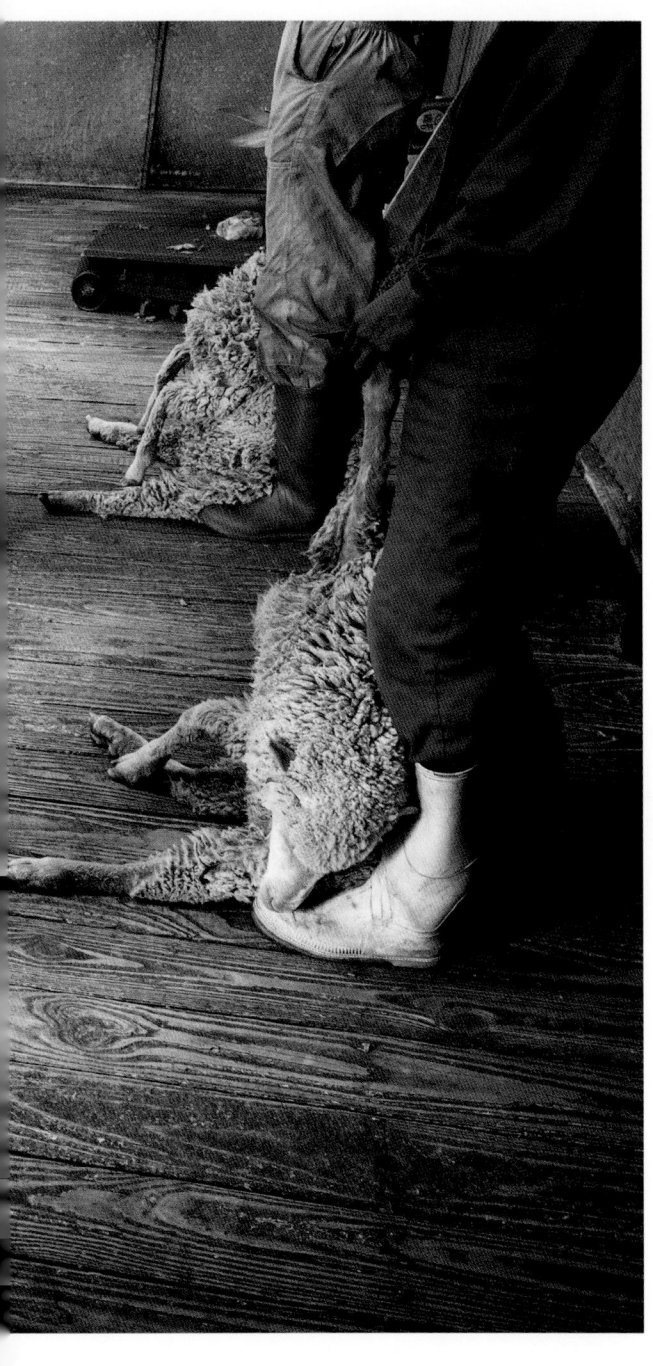

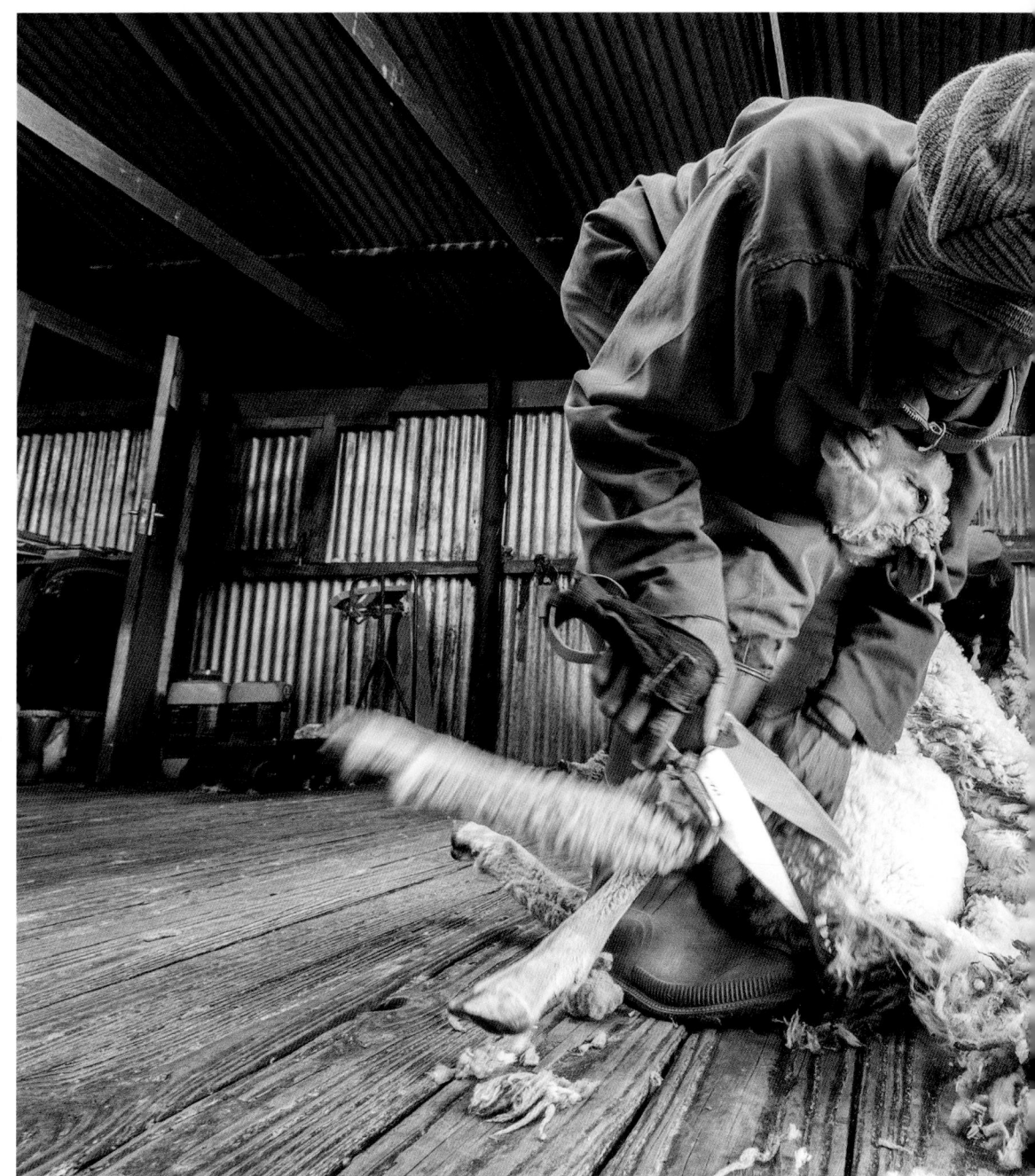

Mokhotlong, Lesotho, 2017

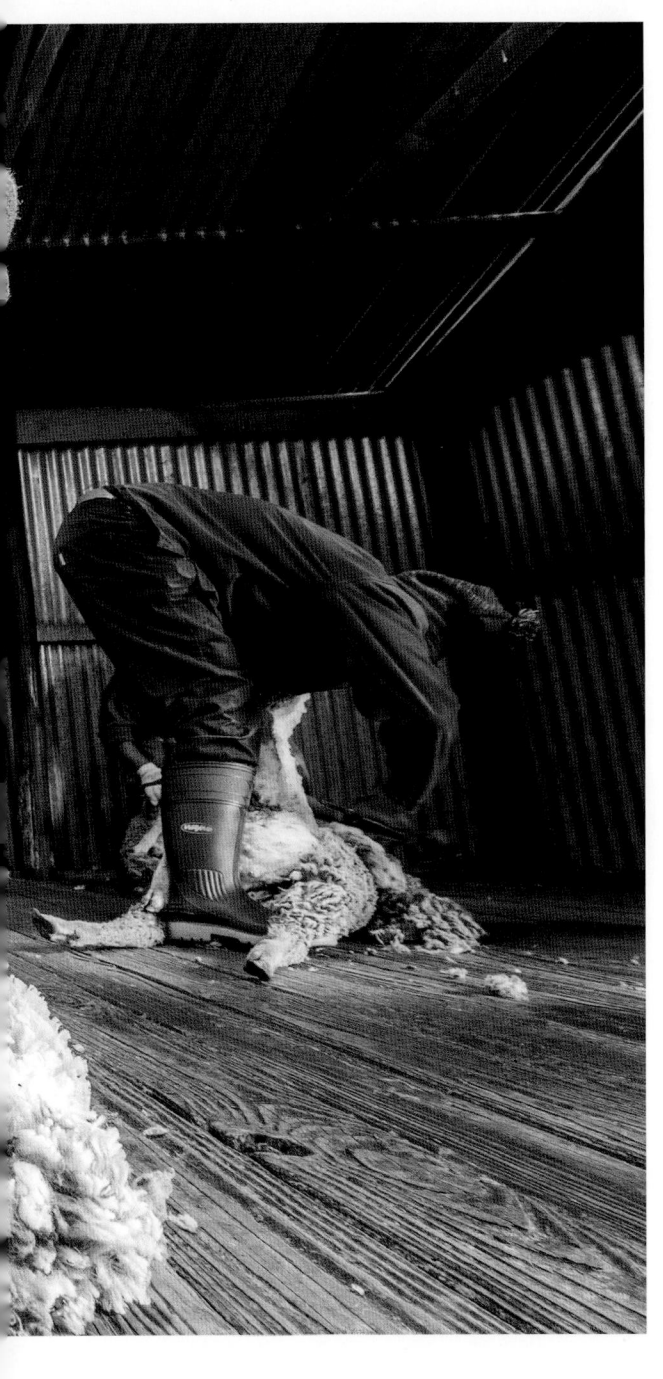

If you want your viewer to pay attention to something, an increase in any kind of contrast will pull their eye to that area.

12
Where Is the Contrast?

CONTRAST IS ABOUT DIFFERENCE. The way tones or colours differ from one another—that's contrast. But so, too, is the way lines or shapes differ. You can even have contrasting *ideas*. When you place a newborn baby in the hands of a grandfather, you create contrast. When you place a small human in a vast building, that is contrast. It's actually several contrasts, including a contrast of human versus architectural, and small versus large. The degree of success that contrast achieves in drawing our eye and making us pay attention to a photograph comes from the amount of difference between the elements. Yellow contrasted with orange might be a little too subtle to make you look twice, but yellow with blue is a contrast with strong visual mass, so we pay attention to it. If you want to draw attention to an image, or to elements within an image, creating strong contrasts is a good start.

Many of the images I've seen as I've worked with younger photographers leave me wondering exactly what they want me to be looking at. The subject is unclear. A sea of faces in a crowd, everyone wearing the same clothes, the same expression, and looking the same way, won't likely elicit a response from me. Where do you want me to look? What's interesting here? But give one of those faces a different expression, or give one person different clothes, and by those contrasts you've given me something to consider. Now I know what you're showing me.

Contrast done well can also help carry the meaning in an image. It can help establish or comment on an idea. Photographers exploring the fine art nude genre have used this to good effect for decades. When you put a light-skinned nude woman among large black rocks or towering cacti, you are pointing out certain qualities of the female form by showing us what it is not. The woman's skin seems lighter by being surrounded by the dark rocks. It seems softer, her form more sensual, her curves more organic, and in contrast to the cacti, she seems more vulnerable.

Because contrast focuses our attention on difference, it can be used to raise questions and point to incongruences that we find amusing, or heartbreaking. Elliott Erwitt, whom I have long held up as one of my favourite photographers of this century, is a master of using juxtaposition to create something like a visual pun or gag. Naked painters at their easels painting a fully dressed model, for example. An art gallery in which a single woman admires a painting of a fully dressed woman, while a dozen men stand ogling a painting of a naked woman. A small dog dwarfed by the legs of a dog so large we can see nothing but those legs.

It is human nature to be drawn to the differences among things. Look for them. Call them out.

Documentary photographers have long used contrast to point out injustice. Images of the living among the dead, the powerless and vulnerable among the powerful, the beautiful in a setting of atrocity, or vice versa.

The larger question then is "How can contrasts and juxtapositions be used to strengthen the aspects of the subject you want to highlight?" Here are some further questions that can help you unpack that:

- What makes my subject stand out, and how can I make it stand out more? Could a change in my perspective make the subject larger relative to the smaller elements, or vice versa?

- Could a change in my optics allow me to better isolate that contrast, eliminating not just clutter but competing visual ideas? Would a wider lens moved closer to my foreground create more contrast by making that foreground larger relative to the background, for example? Would a longer lens with a narrower angle of view give me a more direct view of a contrast already present but less discernible?

- Would more or less depth of field help show the contrasts more clearly, or hide other contrasting elements that I don't want to be as prominent and might otherwise be distracting?

- Does my treatment of time, using shutter speed, create possibilities for showing more contrast, especially if the subject is moving and I want to contrast it more powerfully with those elements that are stationary?

- Where moment is important, would waiting longer or being more intentional about my choice of moment give me a stronger contrast? Particularly important where people or wildlife is concerned, this also applies to landscape work, when waiting a little could give you not only greater contrast in light and colour, but in weather.

It is human nature to be drawn to the differences among things. Look for them. Call them out. If there are contrasts in the scene, we can make our images more powerful, and give them more emotional pull or visual interest, by working to highlight or exaggerate those contrasts, and doing whatever it takes to minimize competing elements.

This same consideration can be applied in post-production, which is why darkroom techniques have always included dodging and burning, the practice of making some areas lighter and some darker. Areas of high contrast have high visual mass. If you want your viewer to pay attention to something, an increase in any kind of contrast—tonal contrast of light to dark, colour contrasts between one hue and another, even contrasts in focus or sharpness—will pull their eye to that area. The reverse is also true: lowering the contrast in less important areas allows their eye to return to what matters in the image.

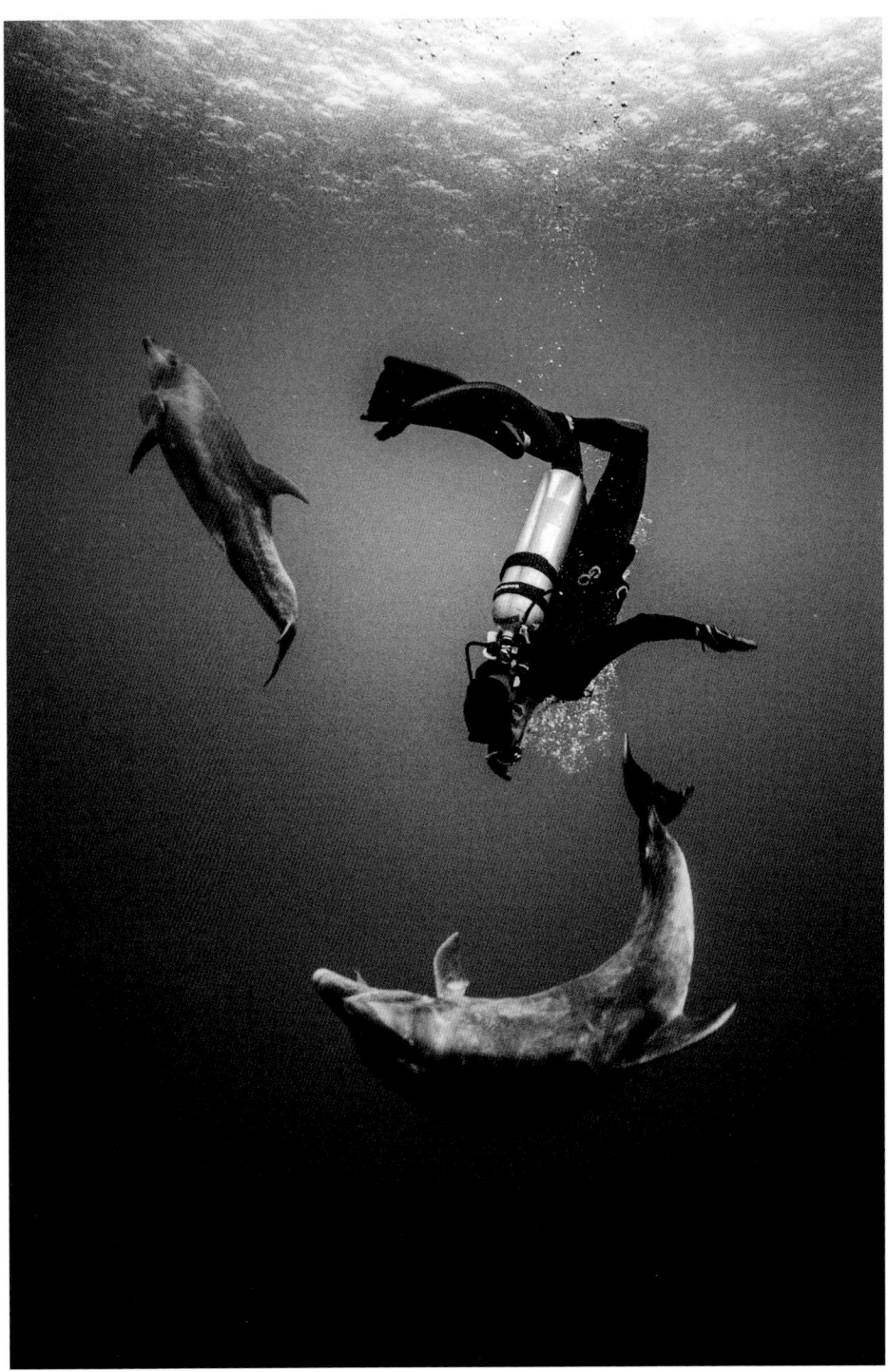

Revillagigedo Archipelago, Mexico, 2017

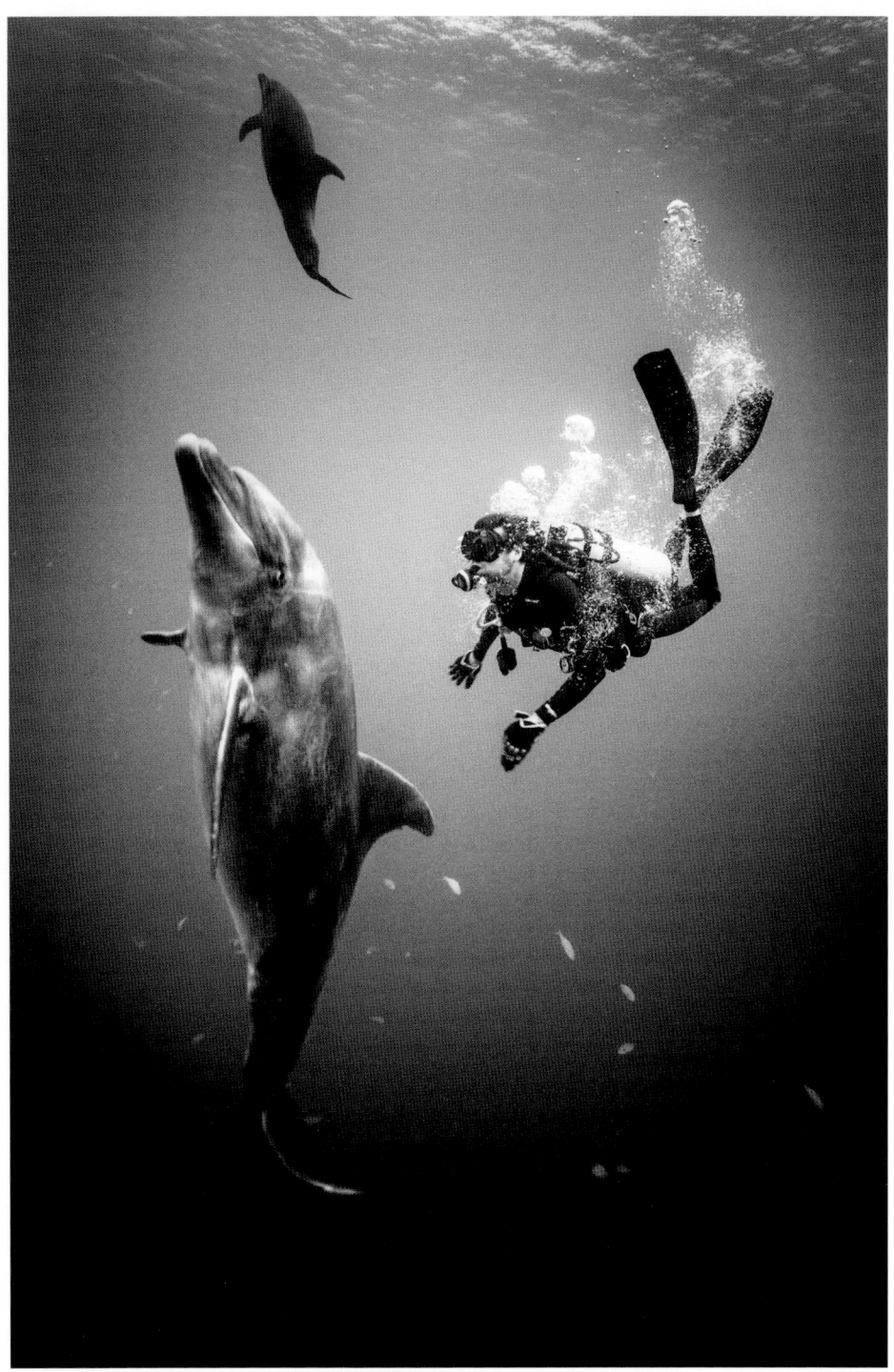

Revillagigedo Archipelago, Mexico, 2017

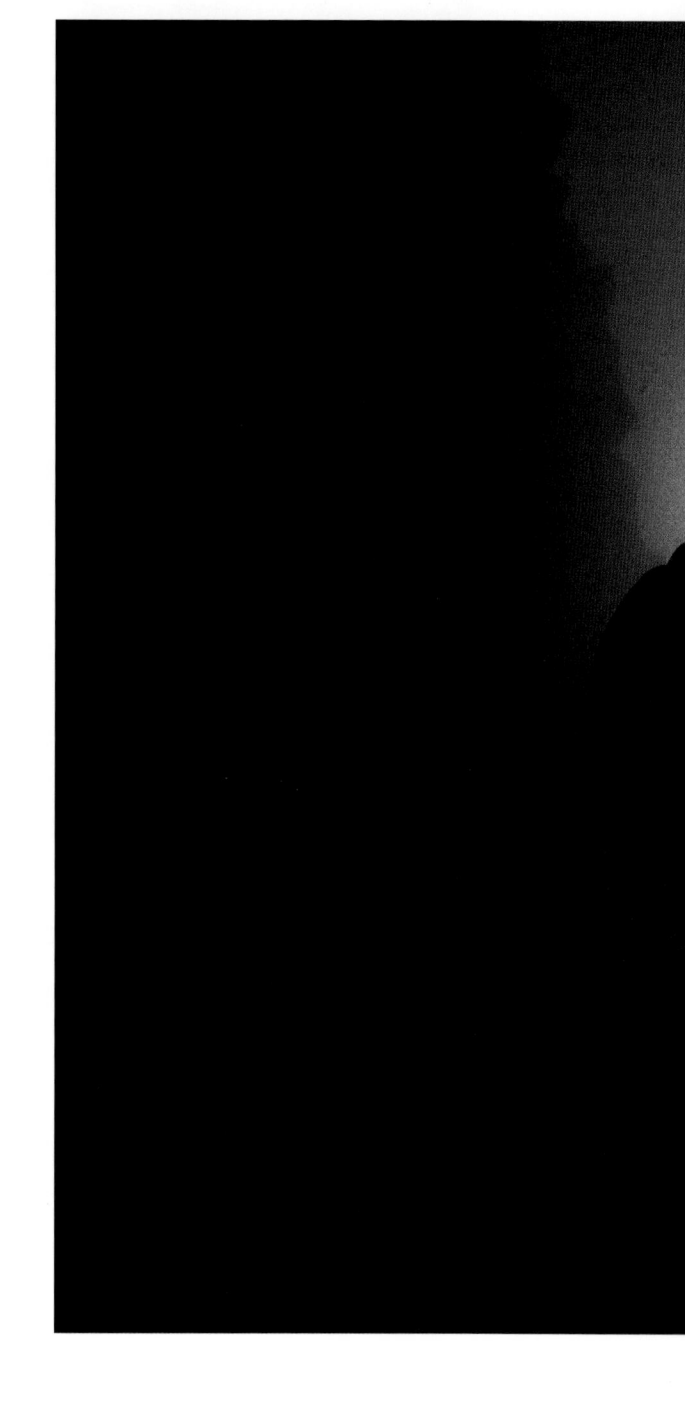

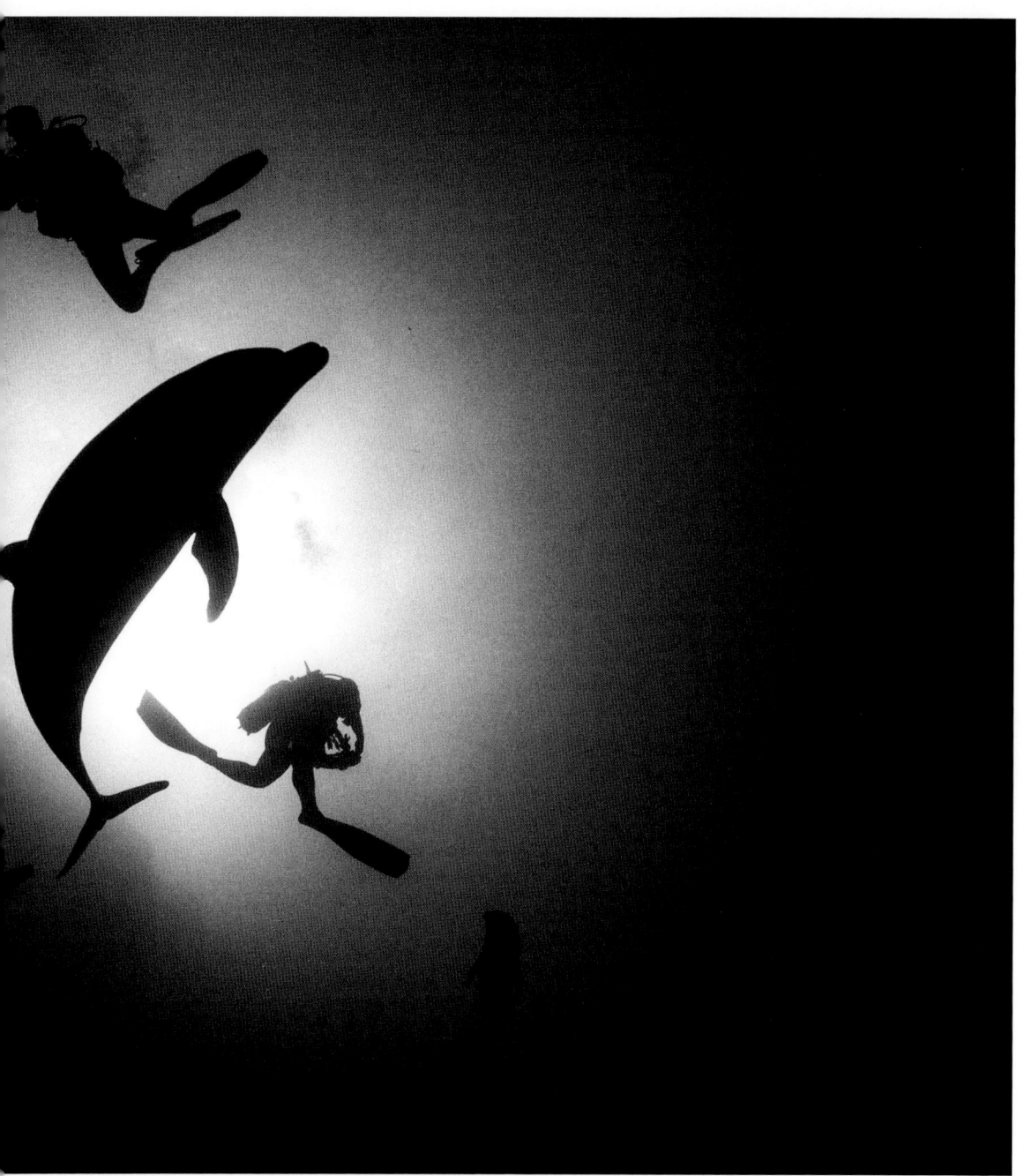

Revillagigedo Archipelago, Mexico, 2017

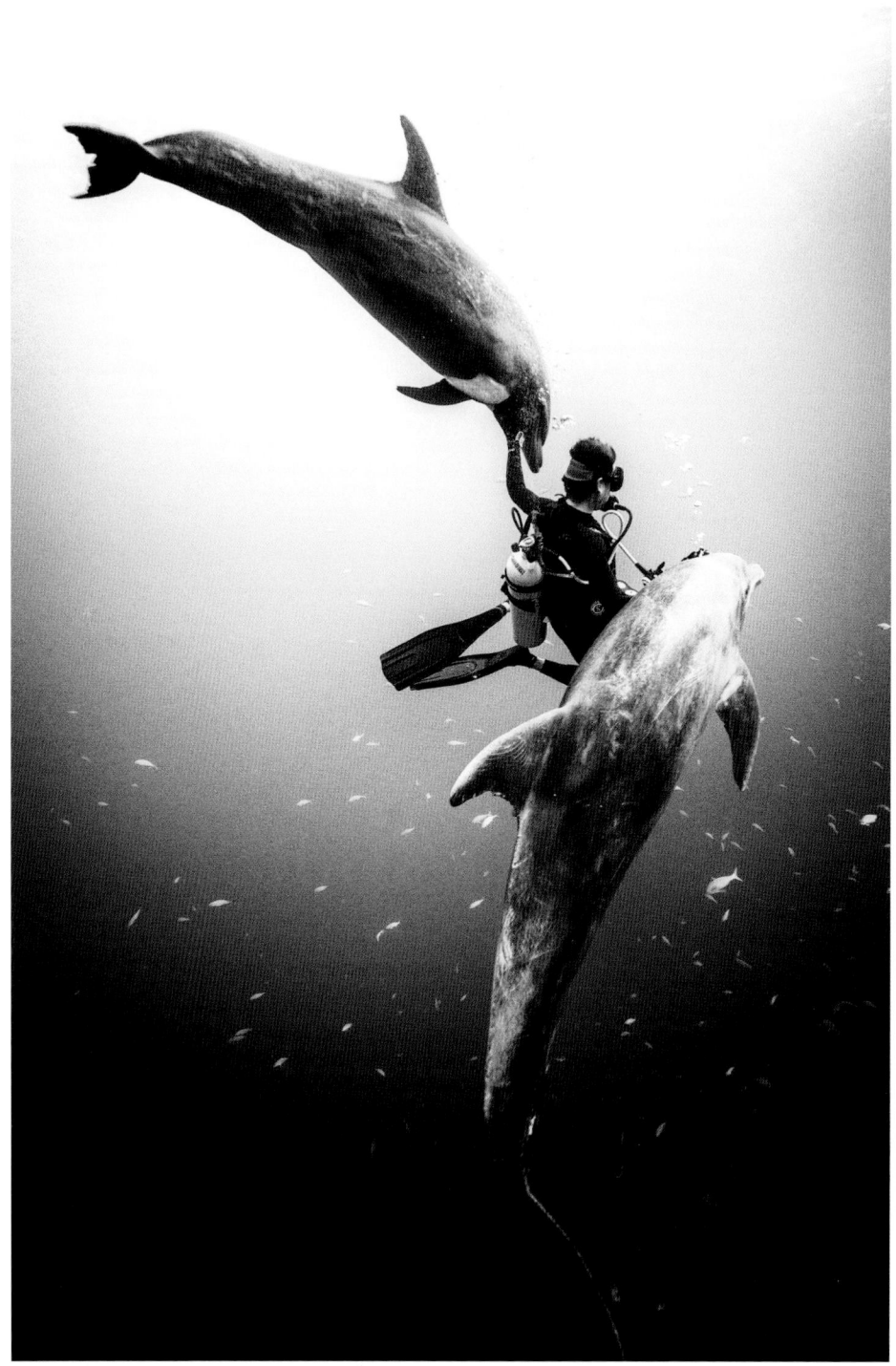

Revillagigedo Archipelago, Mexico, 2017

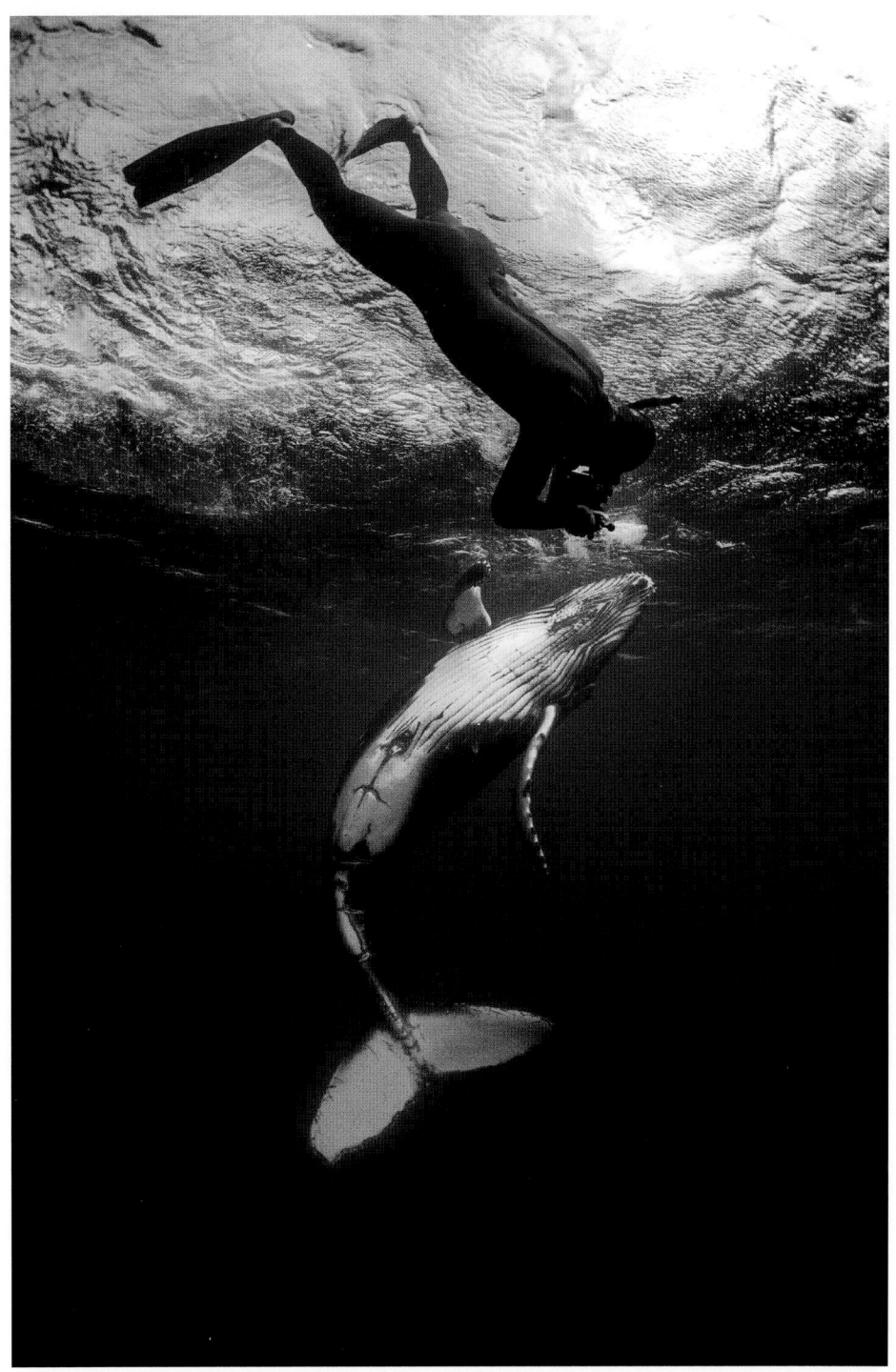

Vava'u, Tonga, 2018

This is not a math problem for which there is a formula to apply. It's experiential. We feel it.

13
What About Balance and Tension?

ASK A PHOTOGRAPHER ABOUT BALANCE AND TENSION in a photograph and they'll look at you like you just asked them about the mathematics of hyperfocal distance. Actually, that's unfair; I know a number of photographers who could speak at length about the latter. I know fewer who can speak about the former. But ask a painter or sculptor the same question, and they'll have thoughts on the matter.

Balance and tension have a great deal to do with the *feel* of an image. But for all their importance, I have yet to read a good definition of balance or tension, which I think is okay here, as I'm less interested in defining the terms than I am in talking about them and posing questions and ideas that will help you use

them more effectively. I think you can work with balance and tension as tools
and understand their effect on how we read an image without being able to
perfectly define the concepts themselves.

It all begins with terms we borrow from the physical world: pull and weight. I've
mentioned the idea of visual mass a few times already, and understanding this
concept is really important for wrapping your head around both balance and
tension. Here's how I see it: every element in a photograph pulls the eye—some
more, some less. Much of it has to do with contrast. So the large, bright, sharply
focused yellow ball is likely to draw your attention much more than the muted,
out-of-focus background because there's massive contrast between the two,
and we're interested in that. That ball, in this context, has visual mass. So far,
so good?

But in this hypothetical image, imagine the large yellow ball is not the only
element in the frame. Perhaps there's a smaller red ball. Now you have two
elements in the same photograph that are pulling at the eye. Do they pull the eye
the same amount? Probably not. The large yellow ball probably has more visual
mass than the red one. Why "probably"? Because the frame itself matters as
well. If the rest of the image is filled with blue (the sky, for example), then that
yellow ball has a lot of contrast, and therefore, visual mass. And because it's
larger, it probably has more mass than the red ball. But what if the background
of the image is yellow? That would create much lower contrast for the yellow
ball, and the red ball would jump out, and your whole experience of the image
would change.

Why does this matter? Because if all the elements in the frame pull the eye
with unequal force, then how we arrange those elements determines whether
the image is balanced, and how, and it helps us understand tension. And both

balance and tension determine where we look and how we feel about an image. This is not a math problem for which there is a formula to apply. It's experiential. We feel it. Here are some questions to help you explore this:

- More visual mass on one side of the frame than the other will throw the photograph out of balance. Can I put something else in the other half of the frame to provide a counterbalance?

- Can I remove something from the heavier side of the frame to lighten it up? What about giving the image a little more negative space?

- How can I use the so-called rule of thirds here? It suggests we place the most important element a third of the way (or two-thirds) into the image, either horizontally or vertically. The rule is silly, but there's an important principle that it encourages: dynamic balance. All other things being equal, if the element with the most amount of mass is on a third, then the less important elements that fill the other two-thirds of the frame offer counterbalance to the heavier third of the frame. The photograph stays balanced but not in a static way. Understand this as a principle but be suspicious of it as a rule.

- Placing all the visual mass in the middle of the frame will be balanced—but potentially boring if the subject is intended to be energetic or dynamic. Is my subject best expressed with words like "serene," "symmetrical," or "calm"? If so, this static balance might be just what you need.

- Some elements in the frame not only pull the eye to them but pull in a particular direction. Imagine a man in the image looking toward the left of the frame. The viewer's eye will not only go to the man but along the direction of his gaze. Now imagine two people in the frame, each looking in opposite directions. Now the viewer's eye is pulled in different directions, toward both the left and right edges of the frame. This creates tension. So ask yourself: Am I aware of the tension in this image? Does it work for me? Would waiting for a moment when these two people both look in the same direction reduce that tension? If I want more tension, would waiting for a change in their gaze create that?

You don't need to understand or be able to articulate all of this, at least not at first, but you do need to understand that the eye gets pulled, and how it gets pulled creates a feeling of balance or tension. The big questions are these:

- Is that balance or tension helping to express my subject?

- How does it feel to me?

- Does that feeling complement or contradict what I want to say about the subject?

As balance and tension are better experienced than explained, it might be helpful to ask these questions as you study photographs, either your own or those of others. Ask yourself if the image feels balanced to you and how that balance is achieved. Is it heavier on one side of the frame than the other? Ask yourself if the photograph creates tension and, if so, how that was accomplished and whether you think it serves the subject or not. The longer you consider and experiment with visual mass, balance, and tension, the more you'll be able to control them as you make your photographs.

The eye gets pulled, and how it gets pulled creates a feeling of balance or tension.

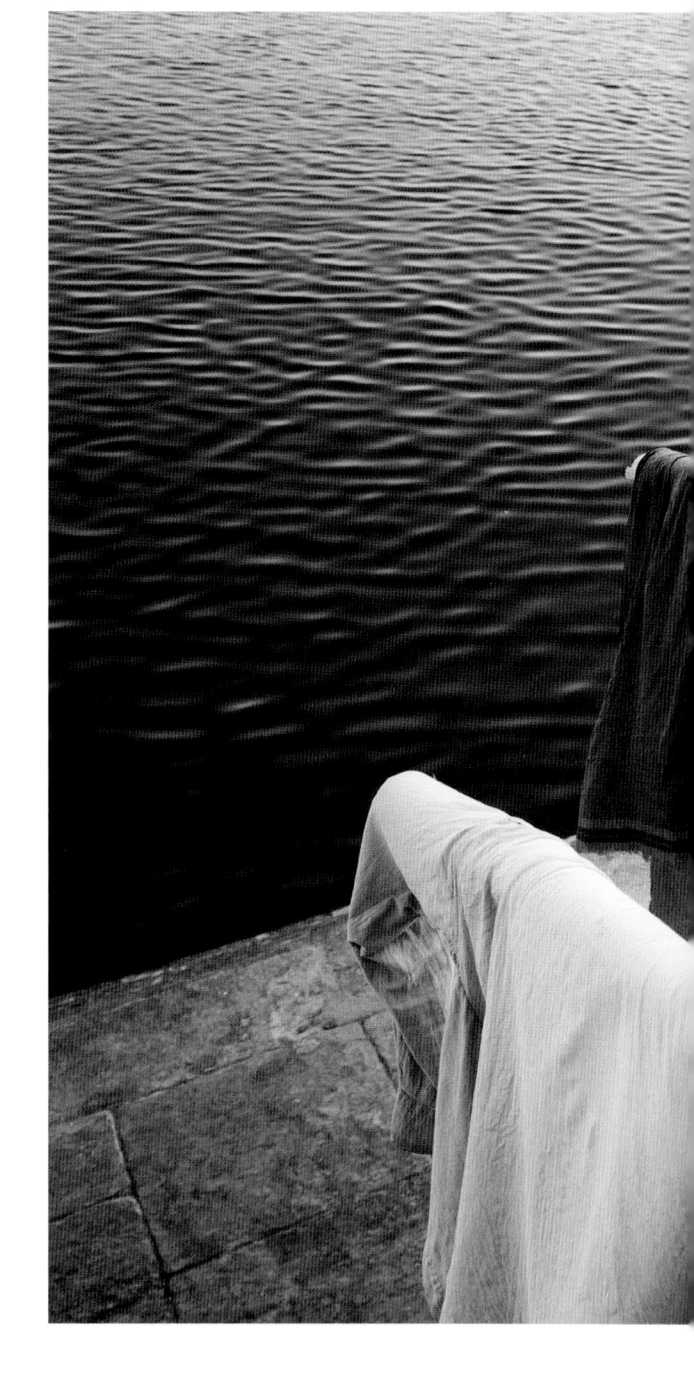

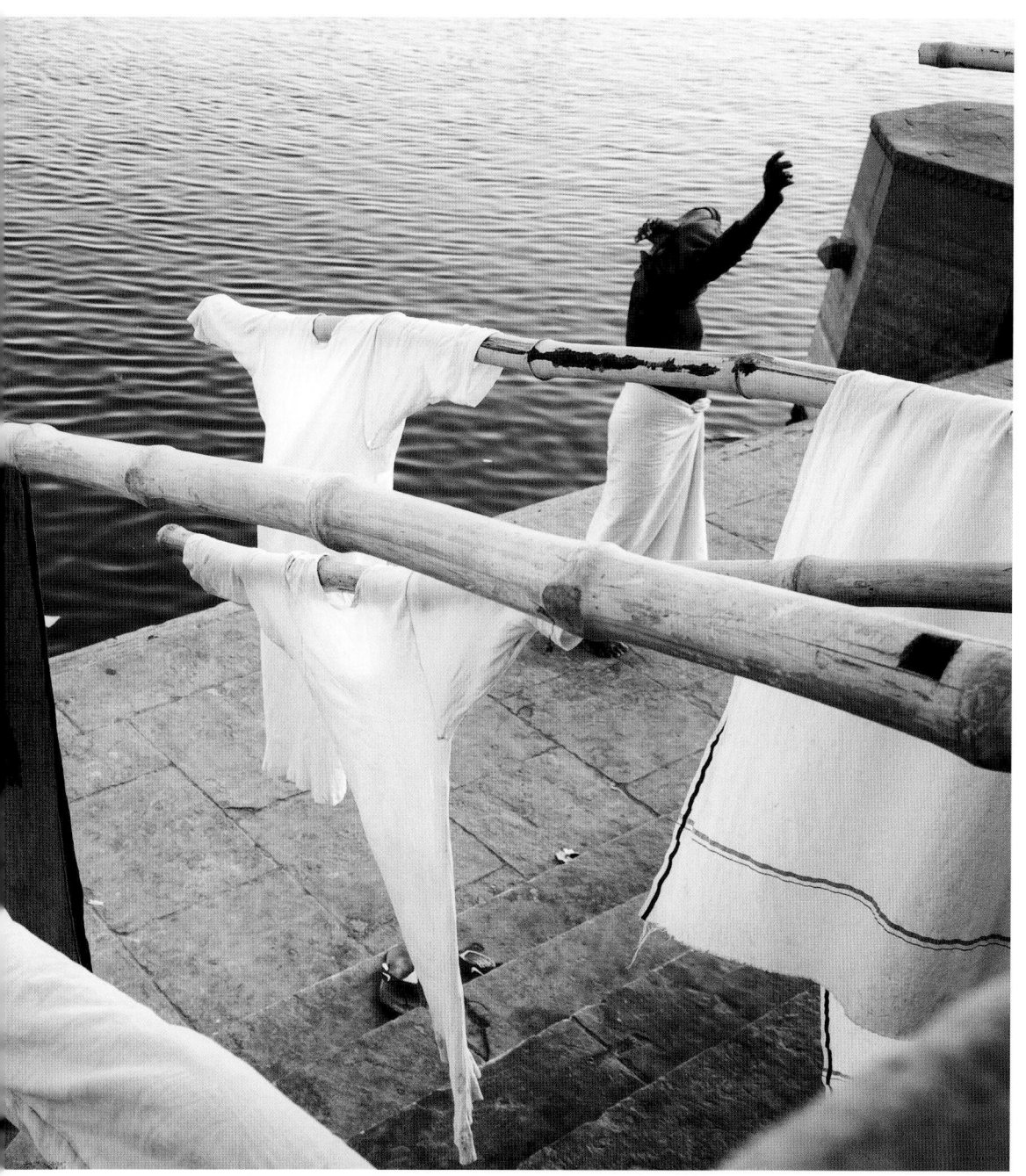

Varanasi, India, 2018

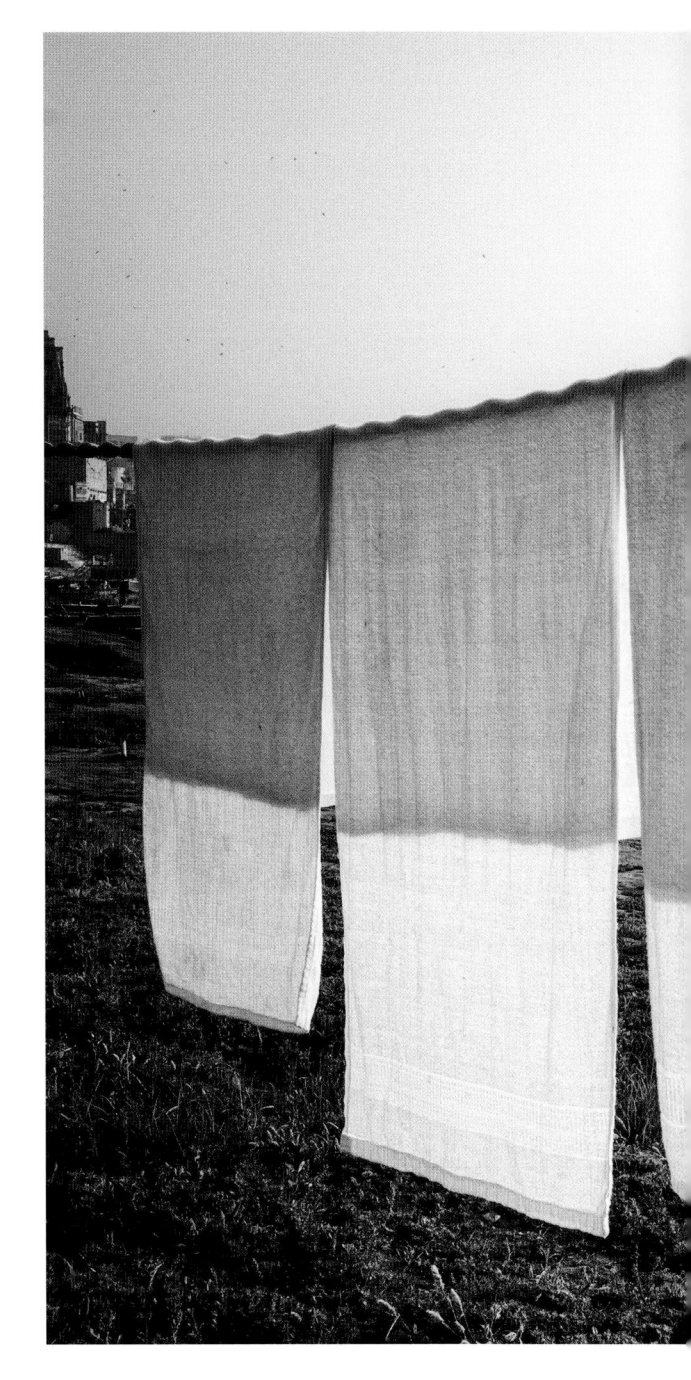

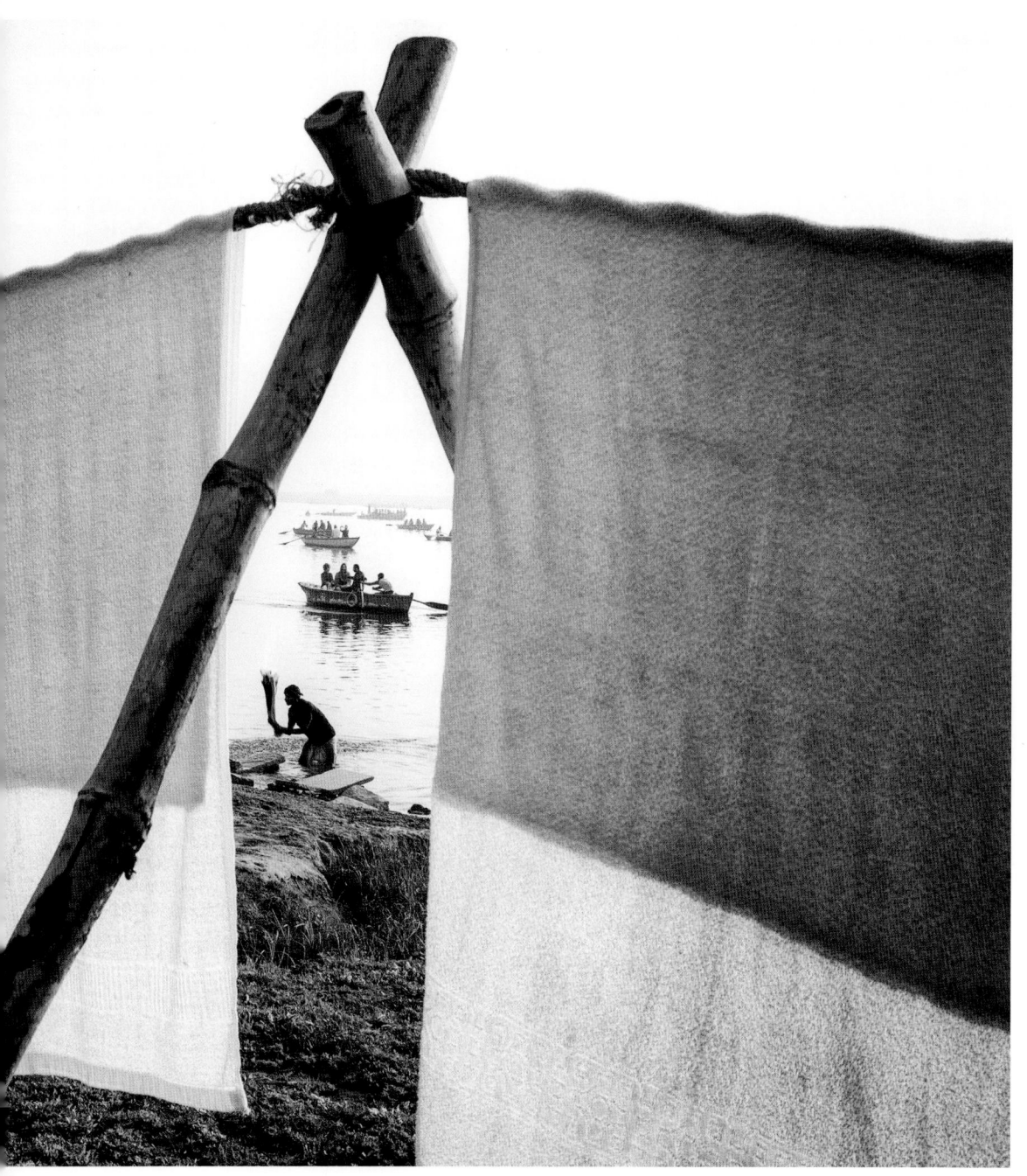

Varanasi, India, 2018

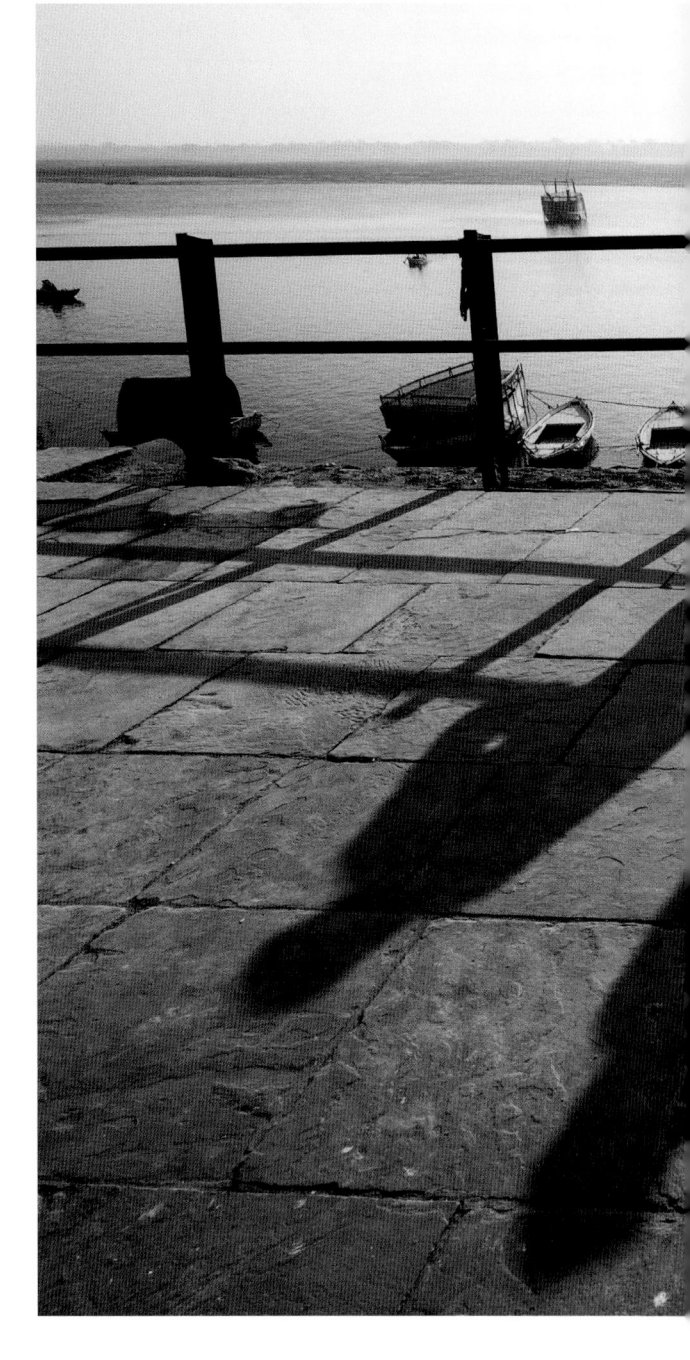

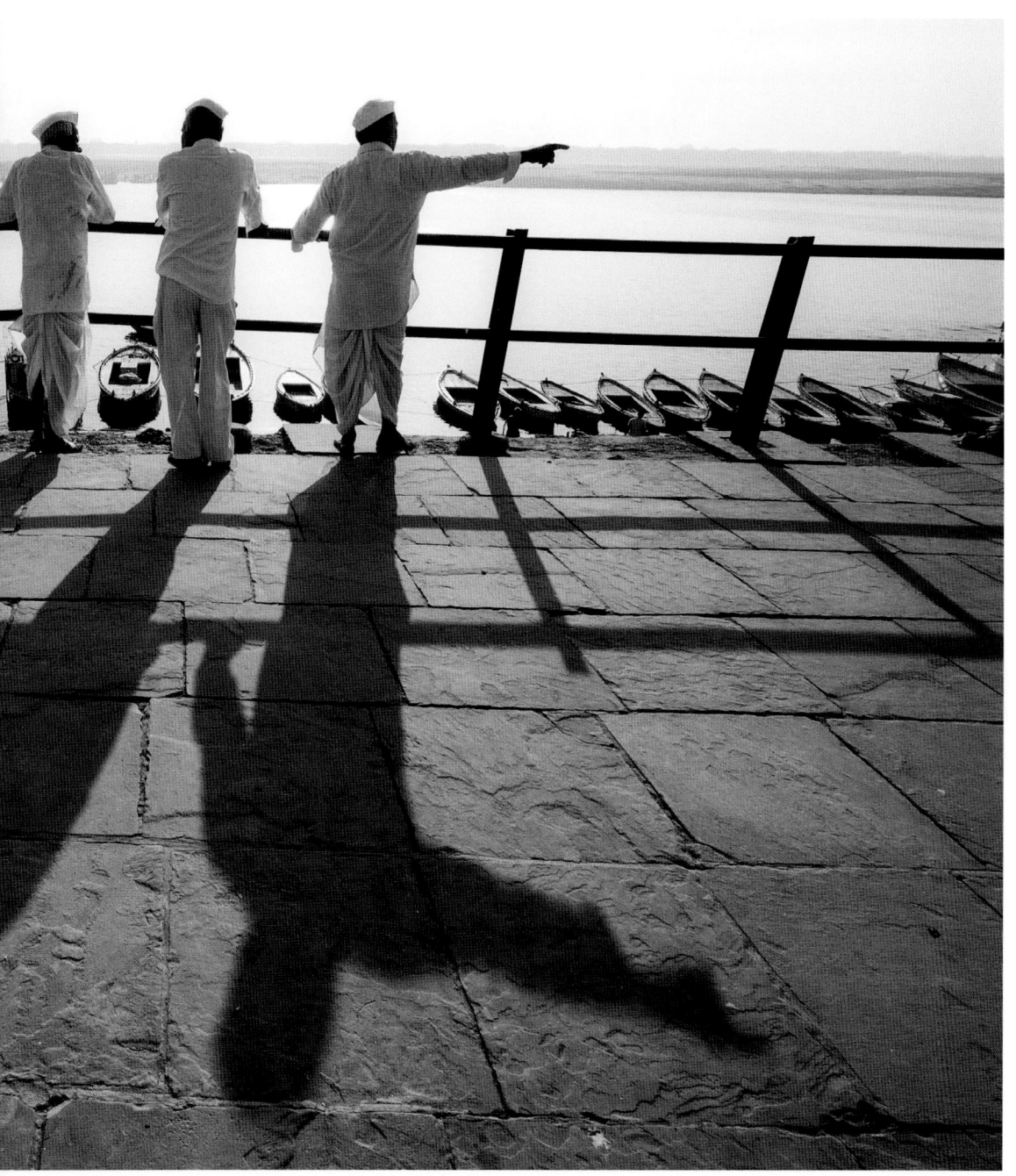

Varanasi, India, 2018

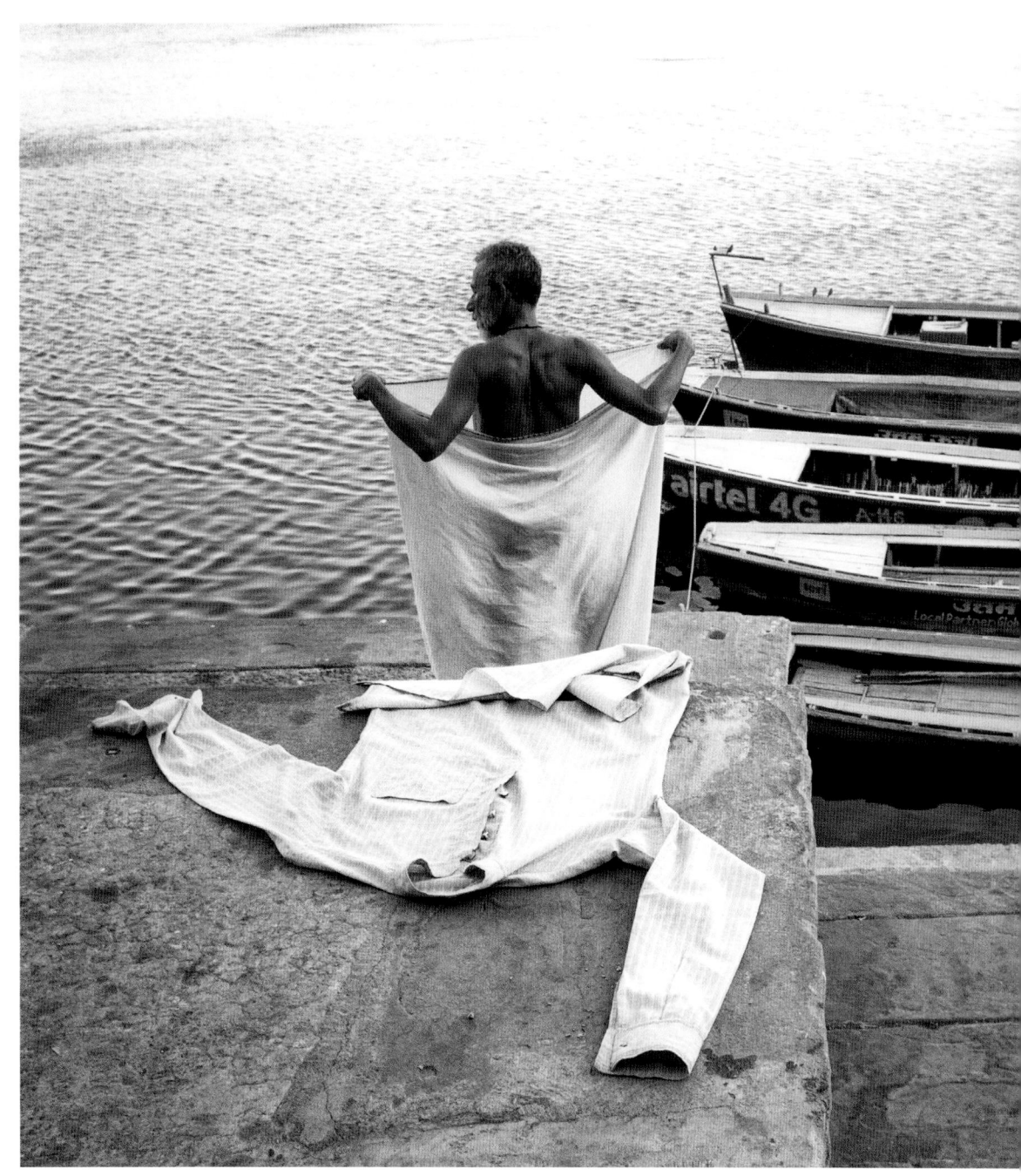

Varanasi, India, 2018

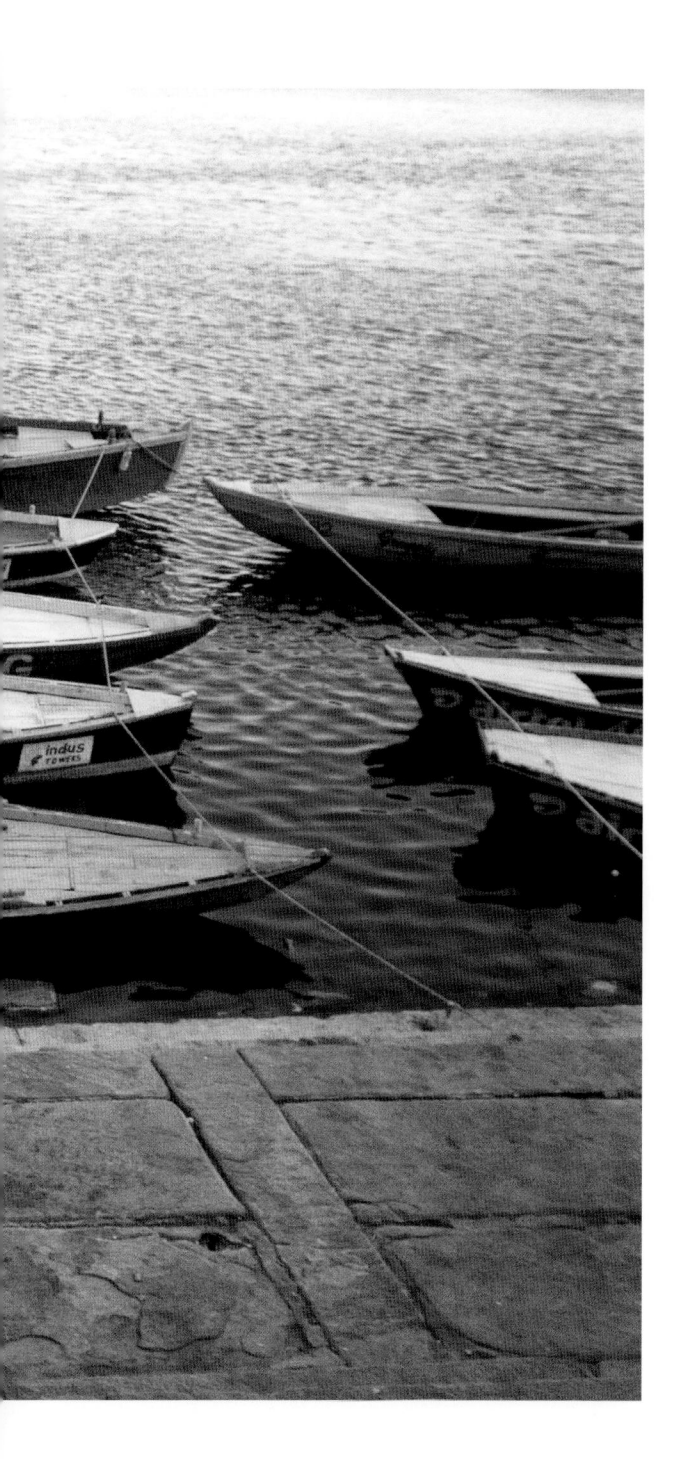

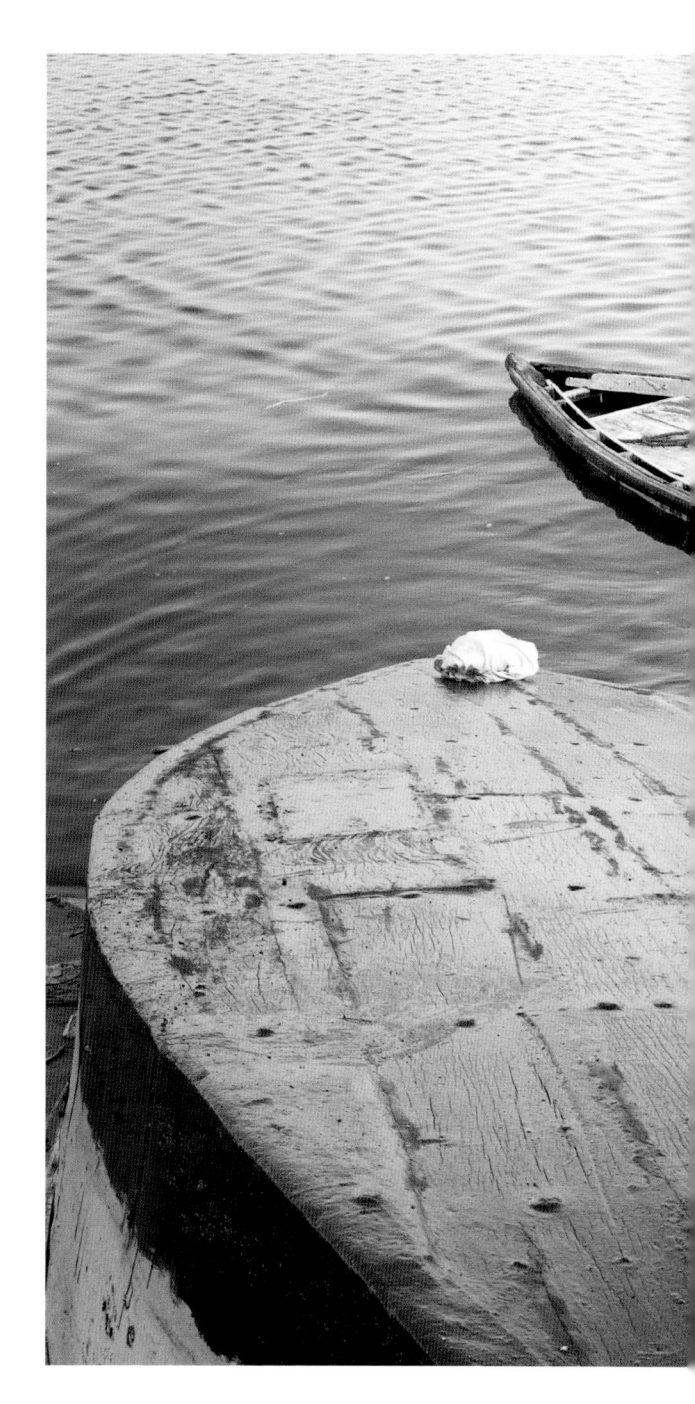

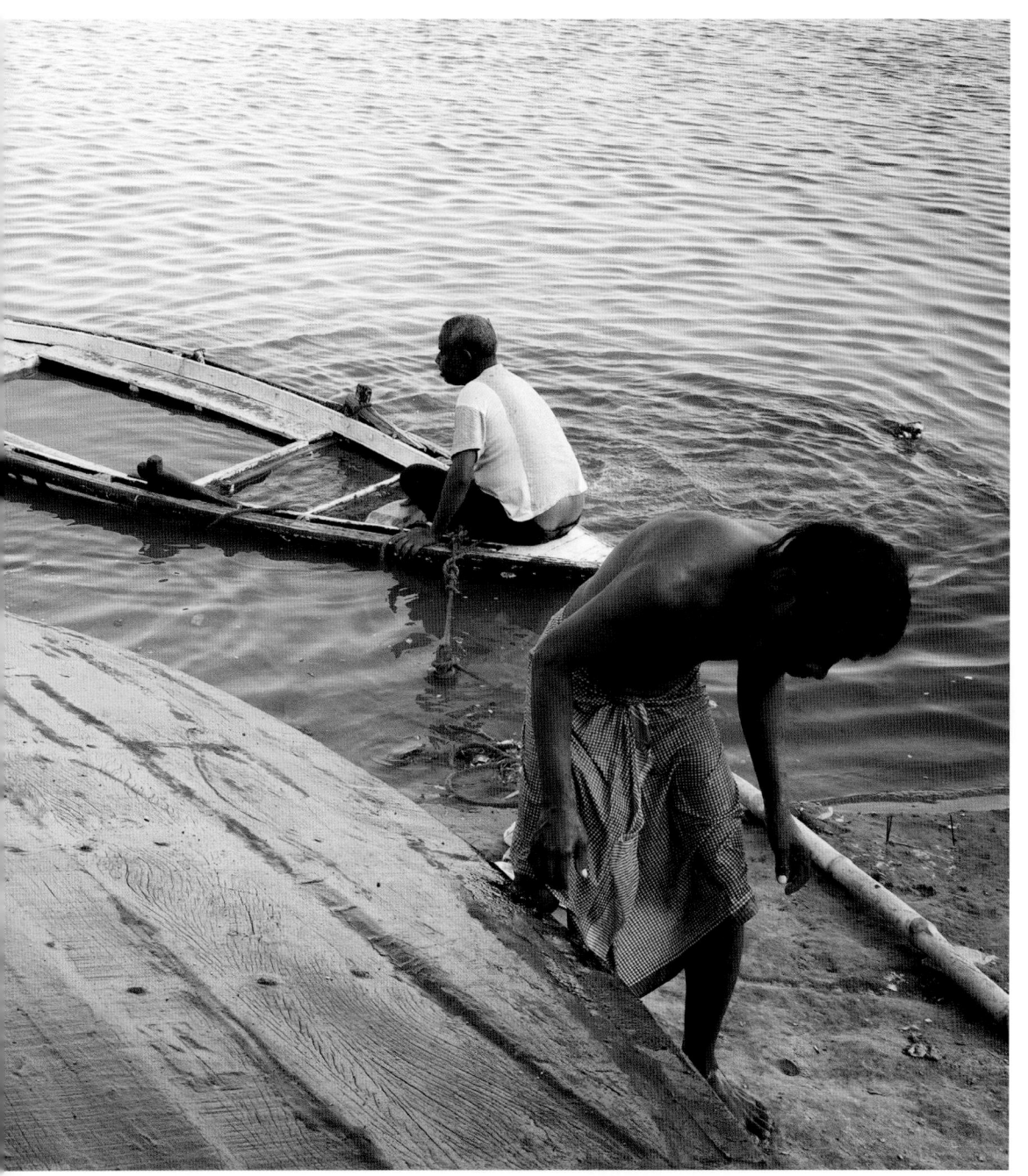

Varanasi, India, 2018

We know what the
world looks like.
Show us what it
feels like.

14
What Is the Energy?

I DON'T RECALL EVER BEING TAUGHT about energy within a photo-graph. I suspect we were all too busy just trying to nail our focus and exposure. But somewhere along the way, it became clear to me that some photographs have more energy than others. At first, I thought the energy in the image came from the subject itself: a fast skier, a running child, or newlyweds on the dance floor. But after seeing many photographs with these kinds of subjects that didn't possess that energy, I began to realize that it is the photographer's choices that put that energy into the final picture. So it's not just an energetic subject, but a subject energetically expressed, that brings the image to life.

If a specific quality, like energy, is key to the subject finding its best expression in the photograph, then are we aware of that and aware that our choices will help or hinder the transmission of that quality into the image? In the case of the

It's not just an energetic subject, but a subject energetically expressed, that brings the image to life.

newlyweds on the dance floor or the running child, what choices (such as a slow shutter or the use of rear-curtain sync on a flash) could give you more motion, more sense of the speed and the joy? Is your fastest shutter speed, which would freeze the action, the best choice? Does frozen action express speed and energy as well as other choices might? How you answer that is up to you, and it's what makes your photographs so potentially creative and authentic.

Another consideration, which we'll explore more in Chapter 17, is your choice of frame: both the orientation of it and the proportions, or aspect ratio, of it. Some frames are more appropriate than others for conveying certain kinds of energy; one frame might exaggerate the energy while another subdues it. A long, vertical waterfall, for example, might be nice in a horizontal frame, showing the context of the surrounding jungle. But if the intention for the image is more about the power of that waterfall and less about context, then a vertical frame allows the vertical movement of that waterfall to increase that energy. And if you wanted to make it feel even more powerful, you could use a longer frame, like a 9:16 ratio rather than the more standard 2:3. Or, of course, you could split the difference: if the jungle is important but you prefer more vertical energy than a horizontal frame gives you, then a 4:5 frame might give you a needed compromise.

When we choose a frame, we choose a canvas on which to place our image. Wider horizontal frames give more energy to wider, horizontal energy, lines, and relationships. A square frame gives equal weight to both the vertical and horizontal lines or energy and can be an excellent choice when you realize that the energy of this particular subject is, in fact, a calm one. Serene. Stable.

There are different types of energy, too. Emotional energy, like the laughter of a child, depends very much on the photographer's choice of moment. Paying attention to that timing and being aware that different moments carry different emotional charges and selecting from among them—both when making the image and when editing and selecting the final frame—will help you choose the strongest expression of that energy. Trust your gut here. Energy is about what we feel, and if you yourself are not reacting to the energy of the scene or the resulting photograph, if it's not grabbing more than just your curiosity, then there's little chance it will grab the emotions of others.

One of the reasons I often choose to exclude colour from my images is because of the energy those colours carry, and the challenge of controlling them. When those colours contradict the energy of the scene—perhaps with too much red in an otherwise calm scene, or by pulling my eye in the opposite direction from the intended journey I want the eye to take—it's best that colour be removed. You may never choose to work in black and white, and that's fine, of course. But you need to find your own ways of managing the energy of the scene. Here are some of the questions I use to prompt further possibilities or creativity:

- How can I use my optics to control the energy? Would a wide-angle lens too far from the subject diminish the energy? Would it give more energy if I got in closer? If I need to subdue some of the energy, would a longer lens used from a greater distance be helpful?

- In which direction does the energy run, and would a different frame or aspect ratio help to increase or decrease this?

- Does the energy depend on choice of moment, and am I being mindful of that timing? What can I do to anticipate a stronger moment?

- How do the lines in my image create energy, and could my point of view be affecting those lines? If I moved my perspective, could I turn static, horizontal lines into more dynamic diagonals? If I wanted to diminish the energy, could moving the camera square up those lines and make them more stable, allowing other areas of the image to dictate the quality of the energy in the frame?

- Do I need to photograph this scene or action from the other side? We read a frame left to right and, generally speaking, action or energy that flows left to right in the frame takes advantage of that visual momentum. Action that goes against that natural reading creates tension, slowing the energy. Could I move the position of the camera to take advantage of the natural left-to-right momentum of the eye in the photograph, so the child runs from left to right, which gives a greater sense of that forward energy?

- Is my use of colour adding to, or diminishing from, the energy, and is this what I want? For a subject charged with sad emotional energy, for example, are my choices of colour helping me express that sadness? Could I use black and white to give the photograph a more sombre feeling?

- Which combinations of shutter speed and techniques like panning, intentional camera movement, double exposure, or rear-curtain flash could I use to give more energy to the photograph?

This is not a heartfelt plea that you begin to make more energetic images; not every photograph wants to be energetic in the way we usually think of the term. Instead, it's a plea that you intentionally consider the energy in your subject and in the way you feel about that subject, and that you make choices to maximize that intended energy. Sometimes the energy will be strong and directional, sometimes purely emotional, sometimes subdued. But remember this: it won't be felt unless you put it there. We need photographs that make us feel, that grab our hearts and don't let go. We know what the world looks like. Show us what it *feels* like.

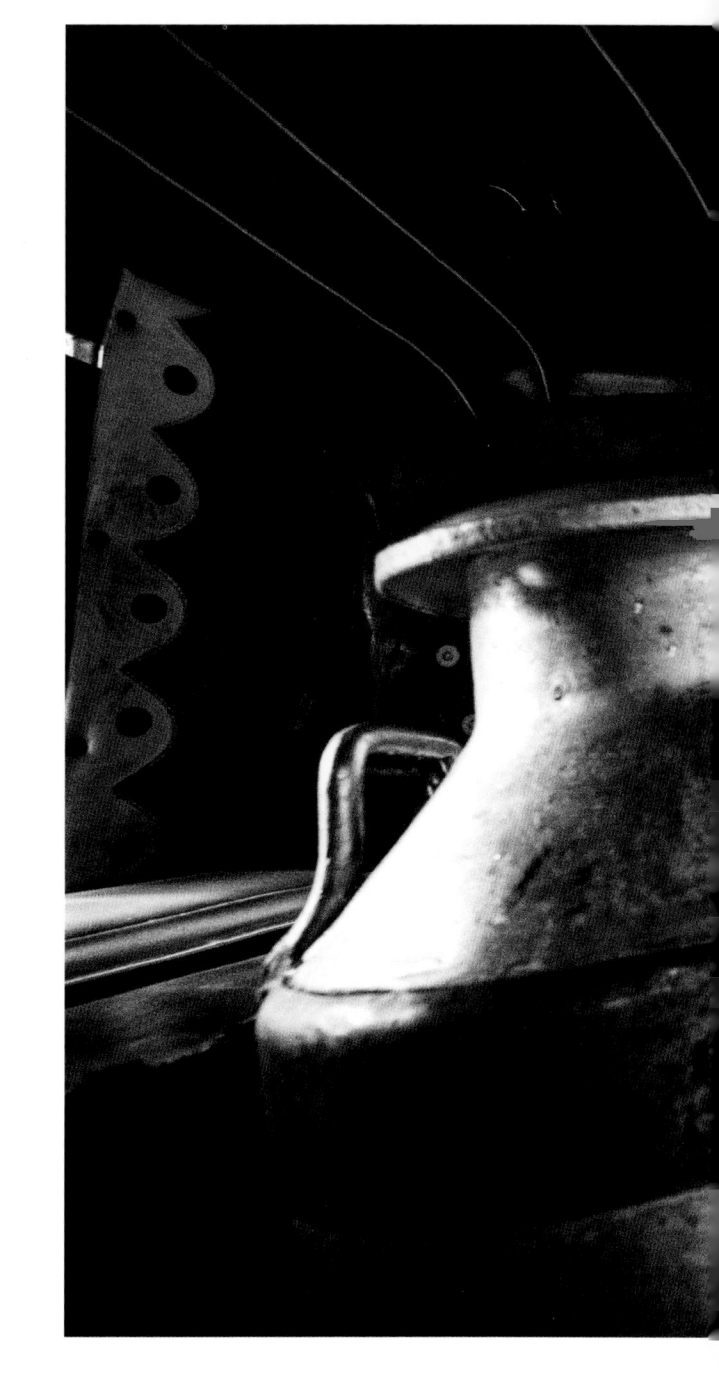

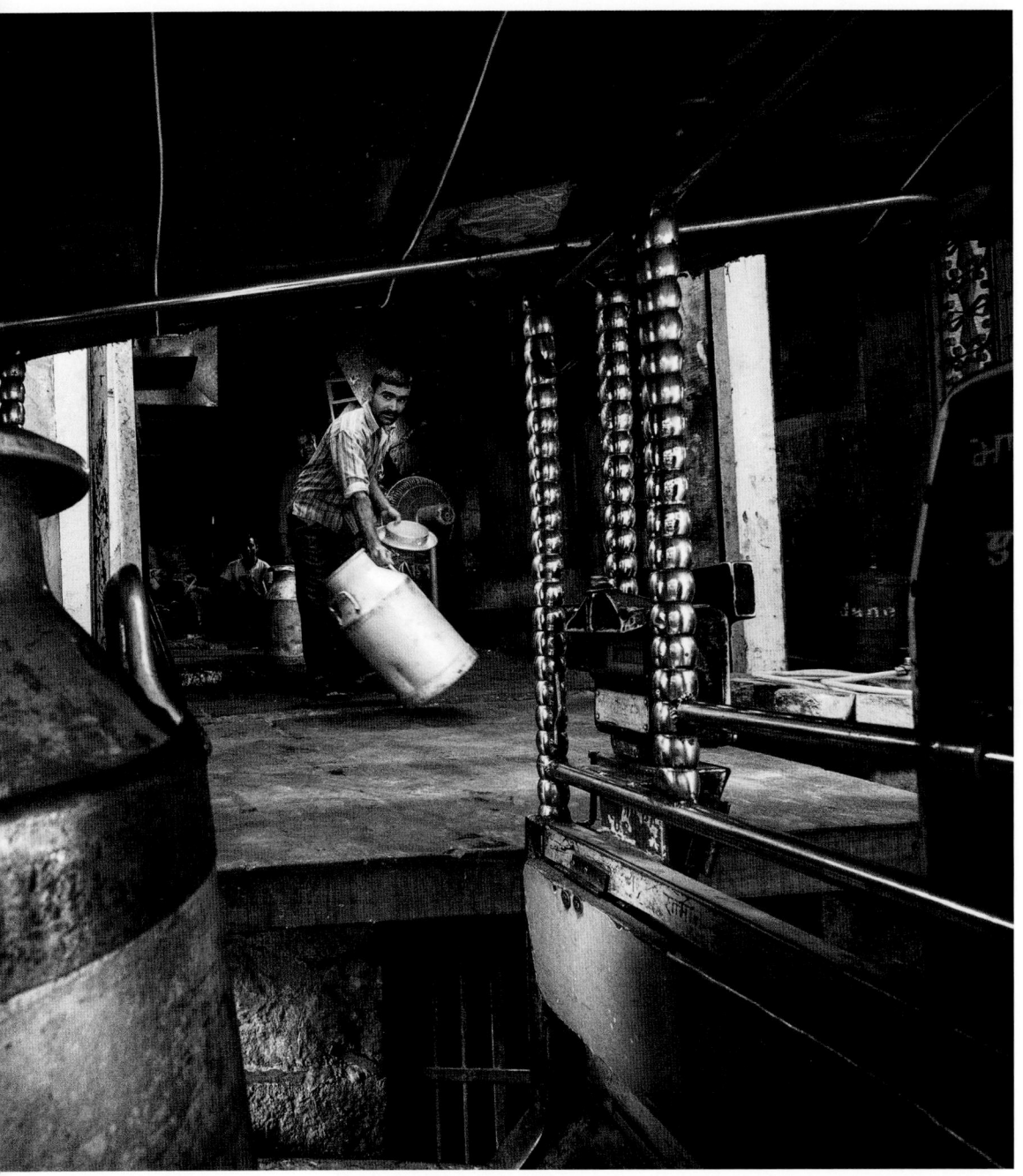

Above and next spread: Jodhpur, India, 2017

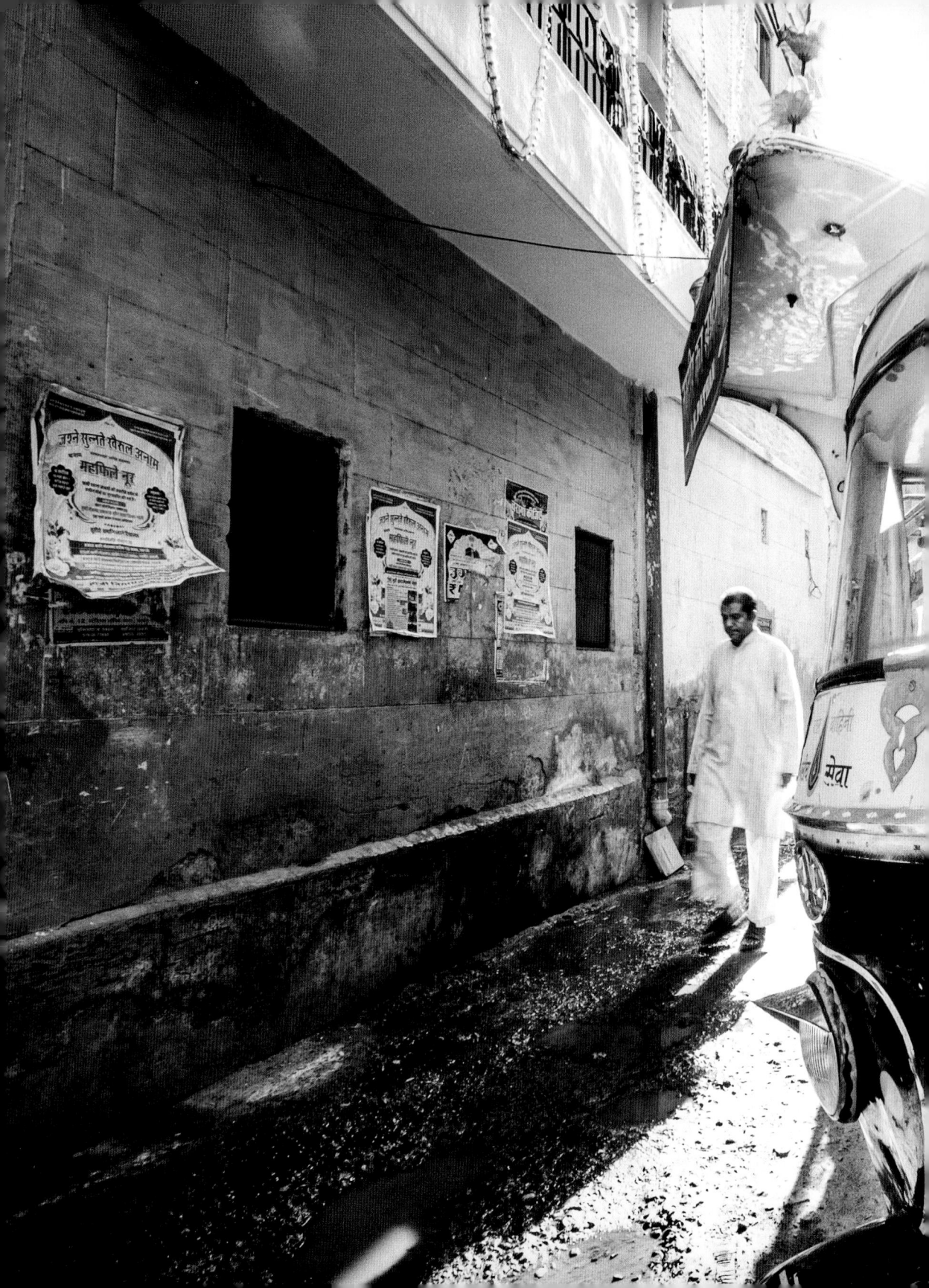

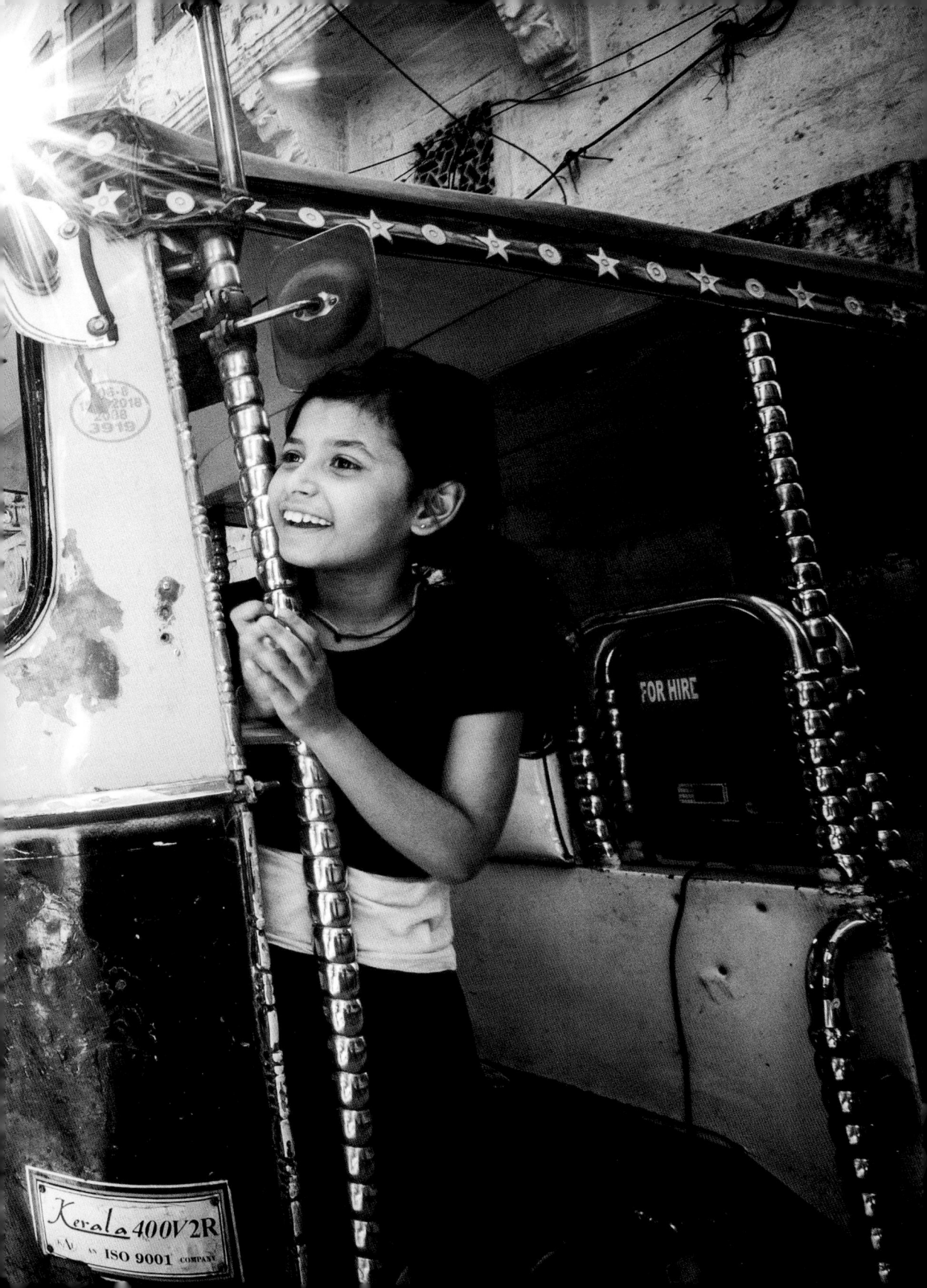

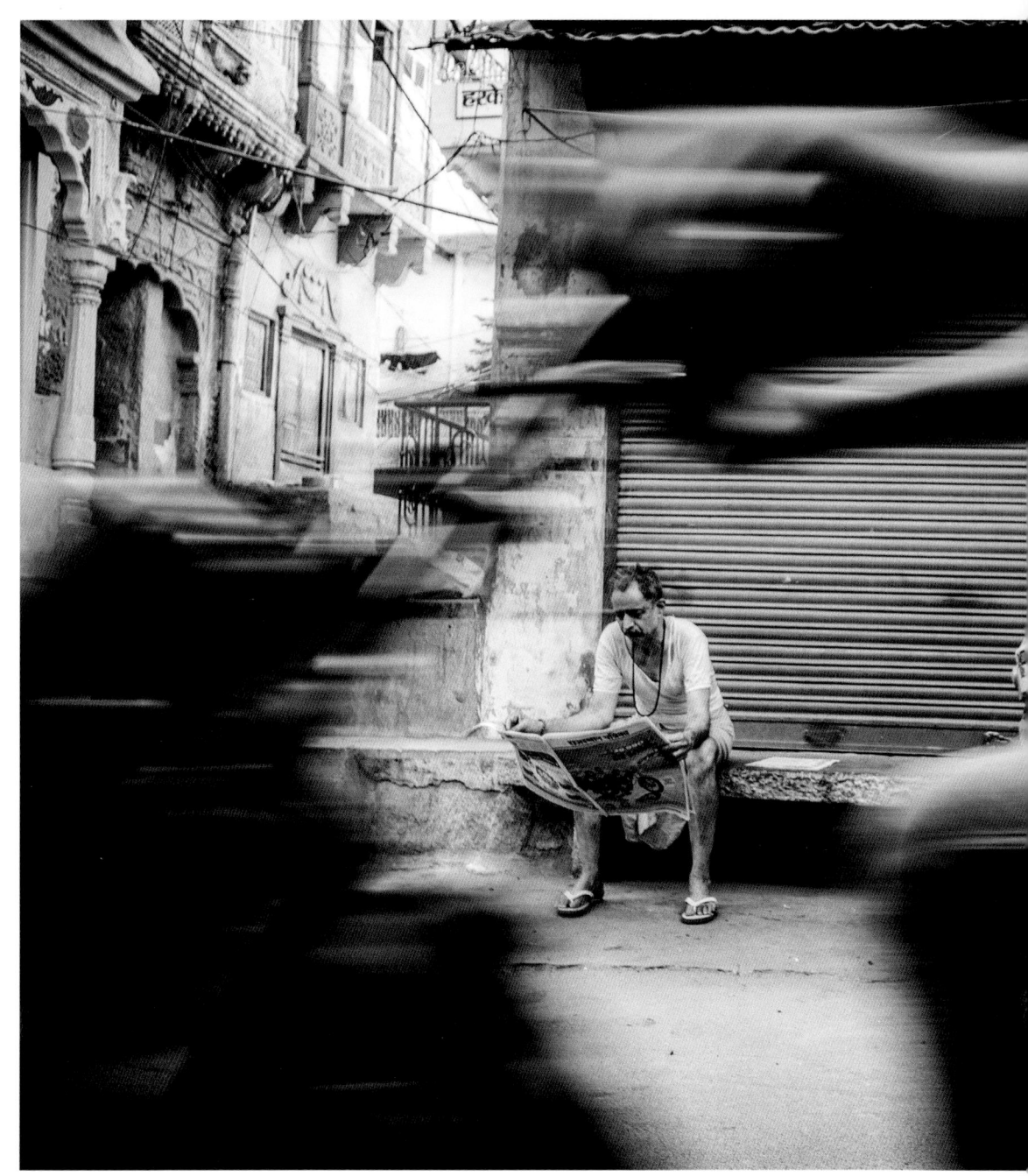

Jodhpur, India, 2017

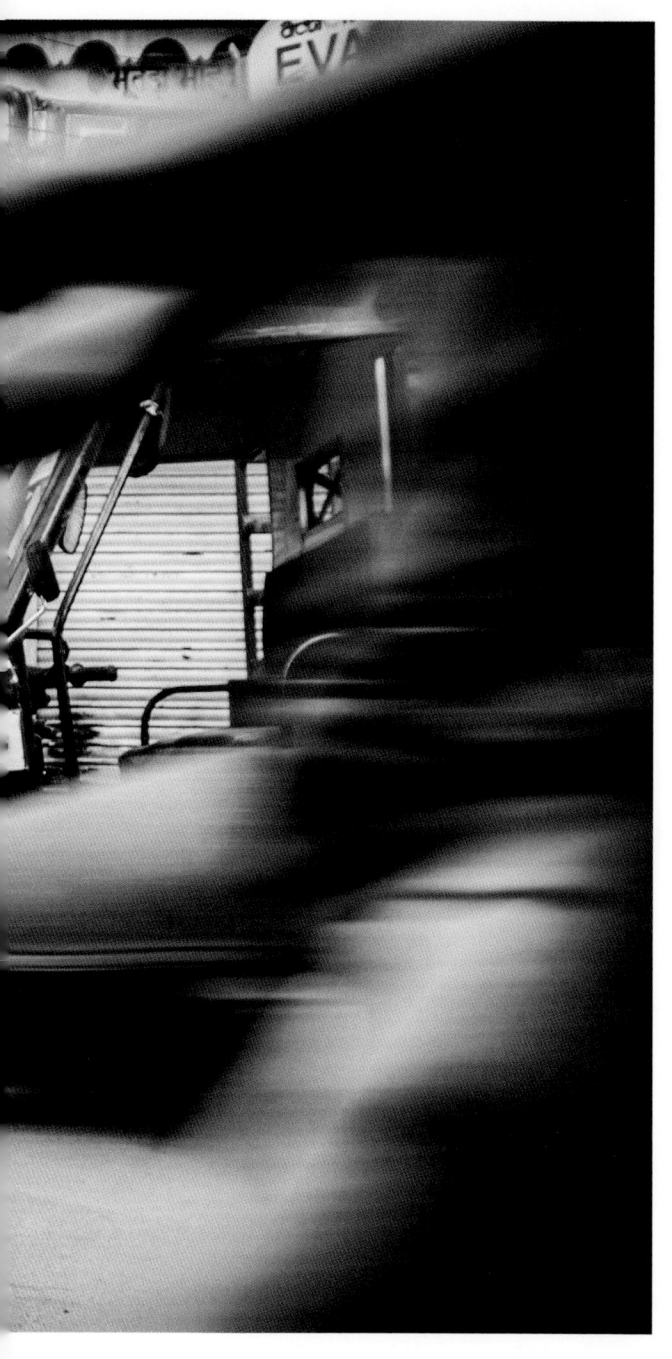

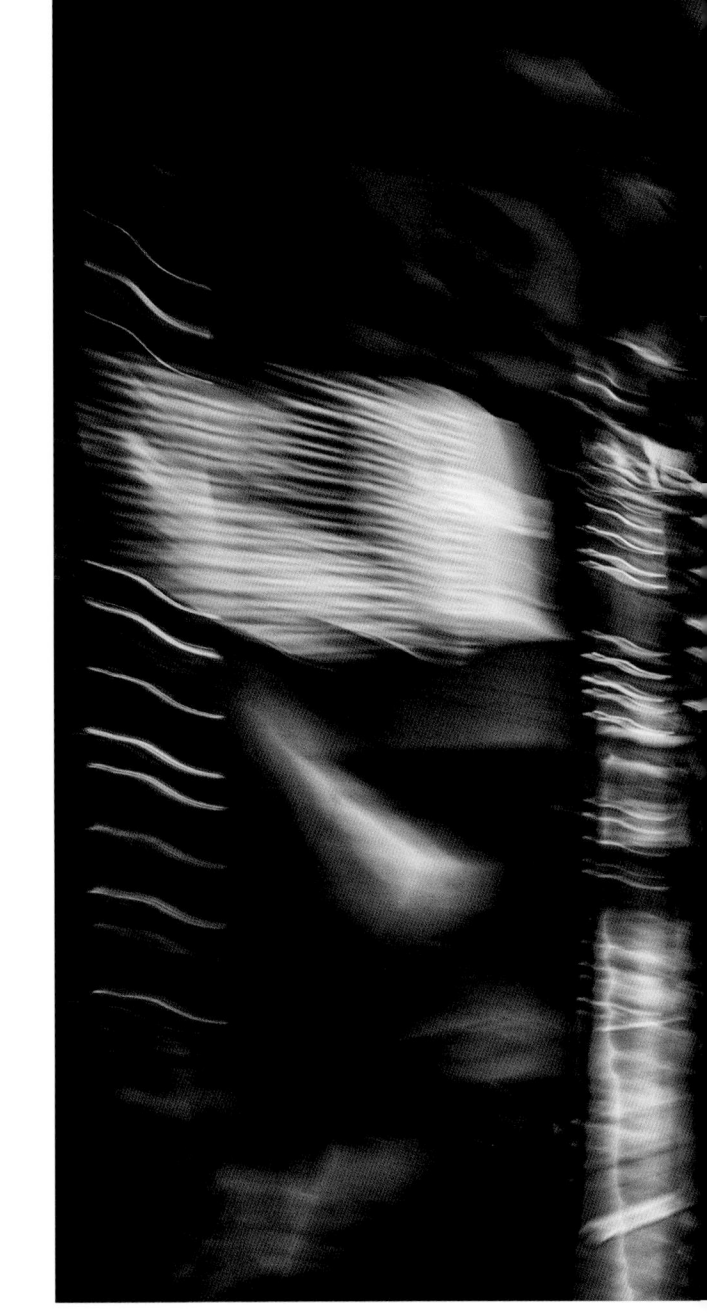

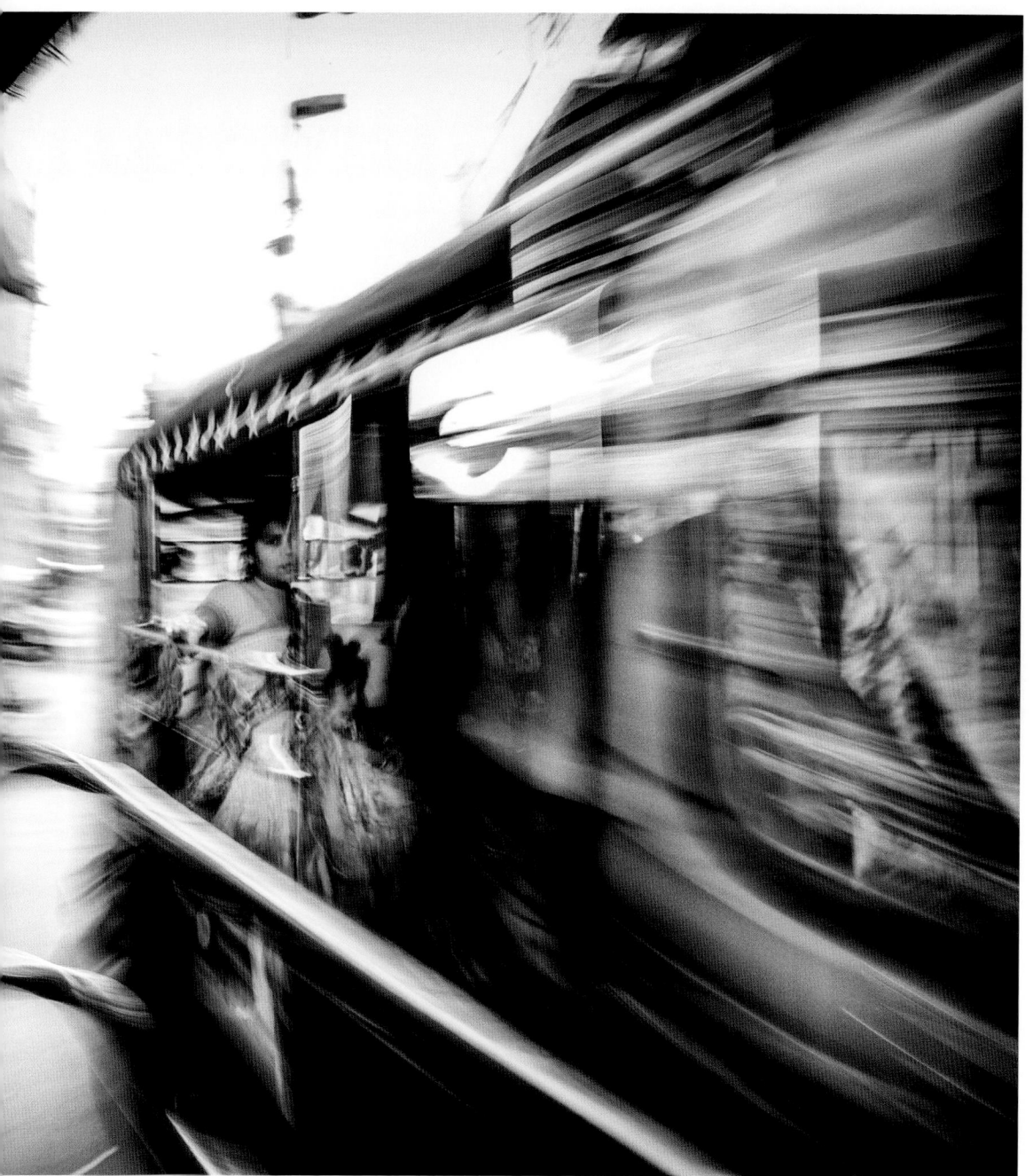

Jodhpur, India, 2017

Isolate the subject
and get as close as
you need to give that
subject its full impact.

15
How Can I Use Space and Scale?

THE EYE MOVES AROUND THE FRAME in much the same way as we move around the physical world: we take a path, we are led by what interests us, and we get trapped or blocked by things that stand in our way. In large, brightly lit rooms with high ceilings, we feel differently than we do in small, dark rooms with low ceilings and no windows. Our experience of a photograph is similar, despite it being only two-dimensional. In fact, I wonder if our experience of photographs can be even more claustrophobic because they lack that third dimension; the elements, all flattened, don't give us as much room to move among them.

If we want to make images that have a sense of space, then we have to be conscious of the desire for that space and learn how to create it. The opposite is also true; if we want to photograph subjects that are cramped and uncomfortable, then a good first step to being aware of the possibilities is to ask how we can use space to create that feeling.

The simplest way to begin thinking about the use of space within a photograph is to remember that the frame is a very real and often impenetrable border. It exerts visual mass, and when we consider the elements within the frame, we must remember not only their relationship to each other but to that frame. An image in which the elements all come right to the edges of the frame will do a couple of things that can make the image a less pleasurable experience to read. And that displeasure or difficulty will either hinder your efforts to express your subject a certain way or help you do exactly that.

An image in which the elements touch (or come close to touching) the edges of the frame feels unwelcoming. It makes us visually claustrophobic and looking for the exit. It prevents the eye from taking the kind of journey around the frame that makes us stay longer and want to take our time with the details. At first glance, this experiential truth seems to fly against the rule so many of us learn in the beginning: fill the frame! The fact that it is *how* we fill the frame and *why* that is important, not just that we do it, should make us all suspicious of any blanket statements that sound overly simple.

The idea of filling the frame is a good one, but I prefer to express it differently: isolate the subject and get as close as you need to give that subject its full impact.

Some ways of doing this are better than others. Imagine you are making a portrait of a woman. You could photograph her so you get the full outline of the head and all the details of the face, with room to move visually between the head and the edges of the frame. Maybe you see a little of the background behind her. It's a nice frame and there is plenty of negative space, which is the space that is not the subject but helps define it and give the eye room to move. That's one way to fill the frame with a portrait. The subject is well isolated, with no distractions, and there is plenty of room to move. It's elegant.

Another option is to get really close. So close that you see most of that astonishing face, but not so much that you see the edges of the head. The subject here is just the face, the details, the expression. It's deeply intimate. You've filled the frame, but even so, there is room between the most visually massive features (like the eyes, the lines that form the nose and the mouth) and the frame. I could stare at this for hours.

A third way is to split the difference. We often take this approach as beginners, and some of us never grow out of it. You fill the frame too much to give me room to move but not so much that you give the face its own role. The line that forms the shape of the head is so close to the edge of the frame that it creates tension. It creates small areas between the head and the frame that trap my eye. My eye doesn't so much move around the frame as it feels tense and wonders why you just crammed it all in. Sure, the frame is full, but to what end? The "rule" has been obeyed, but not such that you've made an elegant, intimate, easy-to-read photograph.

Is that okay? Am I in danger of making a foolish rule of my own? Yes, it might be okay. There may well be cases where you want this kind of tension, when you want to make me feel uncomfortable because the subject itself makes you feel that way and you use every tool available to make me feel cramped, tense, distracted, and claustrophobic. My larger point is this: what we need are not rules, such as "fill the frame," but guiding principles that say, "If I consider this, and do that, it will result in this, or that." Then we make choices according to our vision.

Consider how space in the frame makes you feel. If you want a feeling of vastness, then your use of space in the image will help or hinder that. You might also think of this in terms of scale. We've explored the idea of contrast, and scale is essentially a contrast of size and space. Usually scale is created by showing a contrast between one element and another element of a known size. We feel how small the child is when she's standing beside a giant tree; we notice how large the elephant is when it's standing beside a car. That's scale, and it helps us not only to make sense of proportions but also to feel them.

A sense of scale can also be created by contrasting an element with the frame itself. Yes, the child is at the foot of a large tree; we get it. But go wider, give me more space around that child, and let me see just how large the tree is—make the child small relative to the frame itself—and you'll create a much greater contrast. Of course, there's a point at which going too wide will make the image fall apart, and you'll lose the impact you were trying so hard to create, but there's nothing to be lost by experimenting.

One of my favourite photos from an adventure in the Gobi Desert in Mongolia is an image I made of a photographer on the sand dunes. He's small, not only in relation to the large dunes, but to the frame. He probably fills only five percent of the frame, if that. I have photographs in which he's larger, but they lack impact. And I have photographs in which he's smaller, but they lack information as well as impact. Instead of the viewer thinking about how small the photographer feels in such a vast desert, they wonder what that small dark element in the frame might be.

This is not the end of the conversation about the use of space. We'll explore it further when we discuss depth in the next chapter. For now, think about space on a two-dimensional level, and ask yourself:

- What decisions can I make that will allow the eye to move more freely around the frame?

- Is my subject better expressed with a more liberal use of space, or would a more constricted feeling be more appropriate? Try it! Find out!

- Am I aware of elements intersecting the frame? Are they impeding the movement of the eye?

- Am I filling the frame with my subject but sabotaging that effort by neglecting the idea of negative space?

- Could I use scale, or contrast in size between elements, to exaggerate the experience of that size?

- Could I use the size of the subject relative to the frame itself to imply something about that subject or bring a more spacious feeling to the image? Would the opposite serve me better?

I hope you've taken to heart my suggestion to study both your images and the images of others in connection to all the questions that I'm putting forward here. The way to learn all of this—to really make these ideas your own—is to ask the questions, to think about them for yourself. And while you must eventually do that with the camera to your eye, it can begin with photographs in front of you. How did the photographer use space? What decisions did the photographer make with negative space or scale? What would this photograph look like if the photographer made different choices? Would it feel the same way? Why?

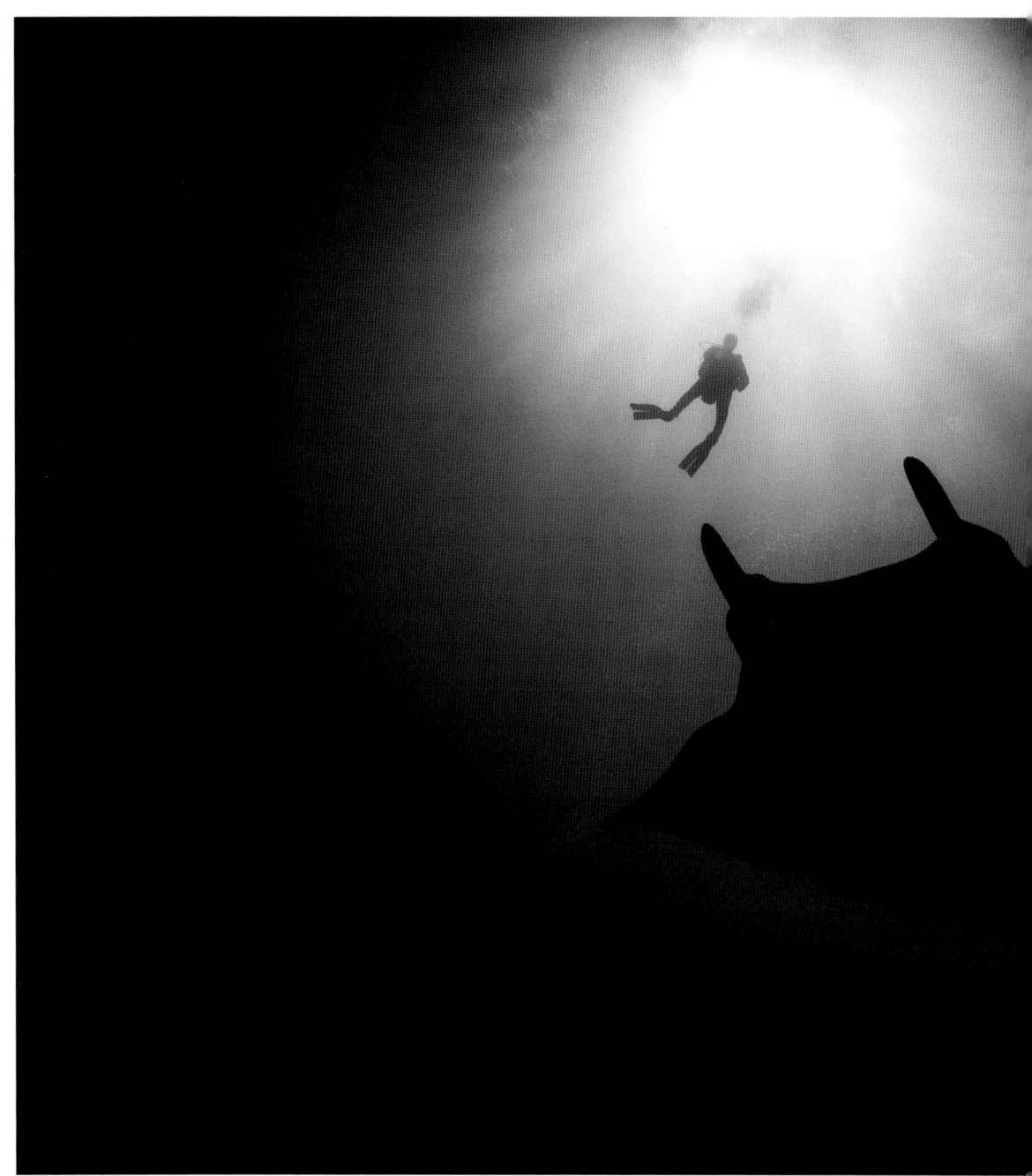

Revillagigedo Archipelago, Mexico, 2017

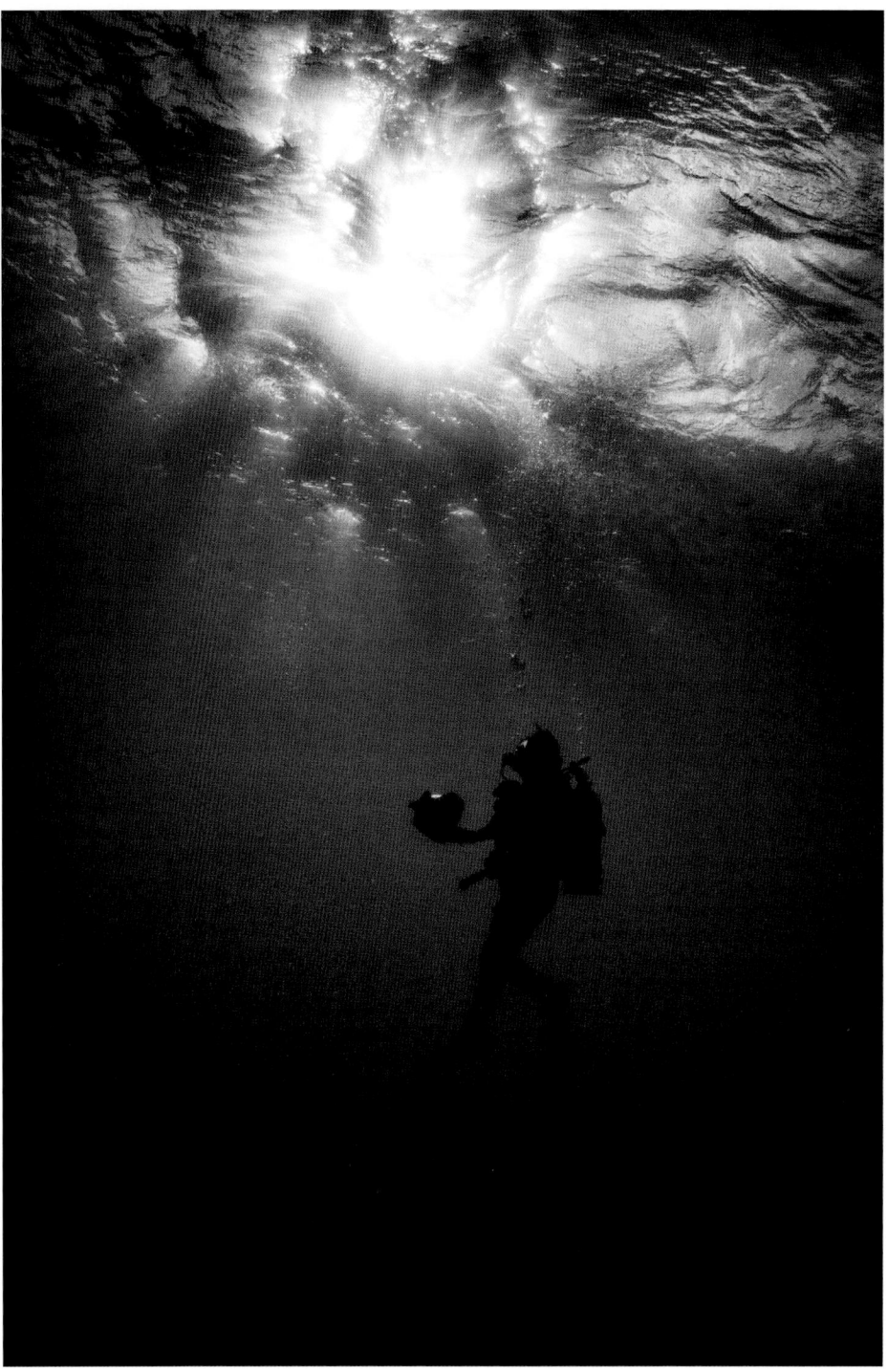

Revillagigedo Archipelago, Mexico, 2017

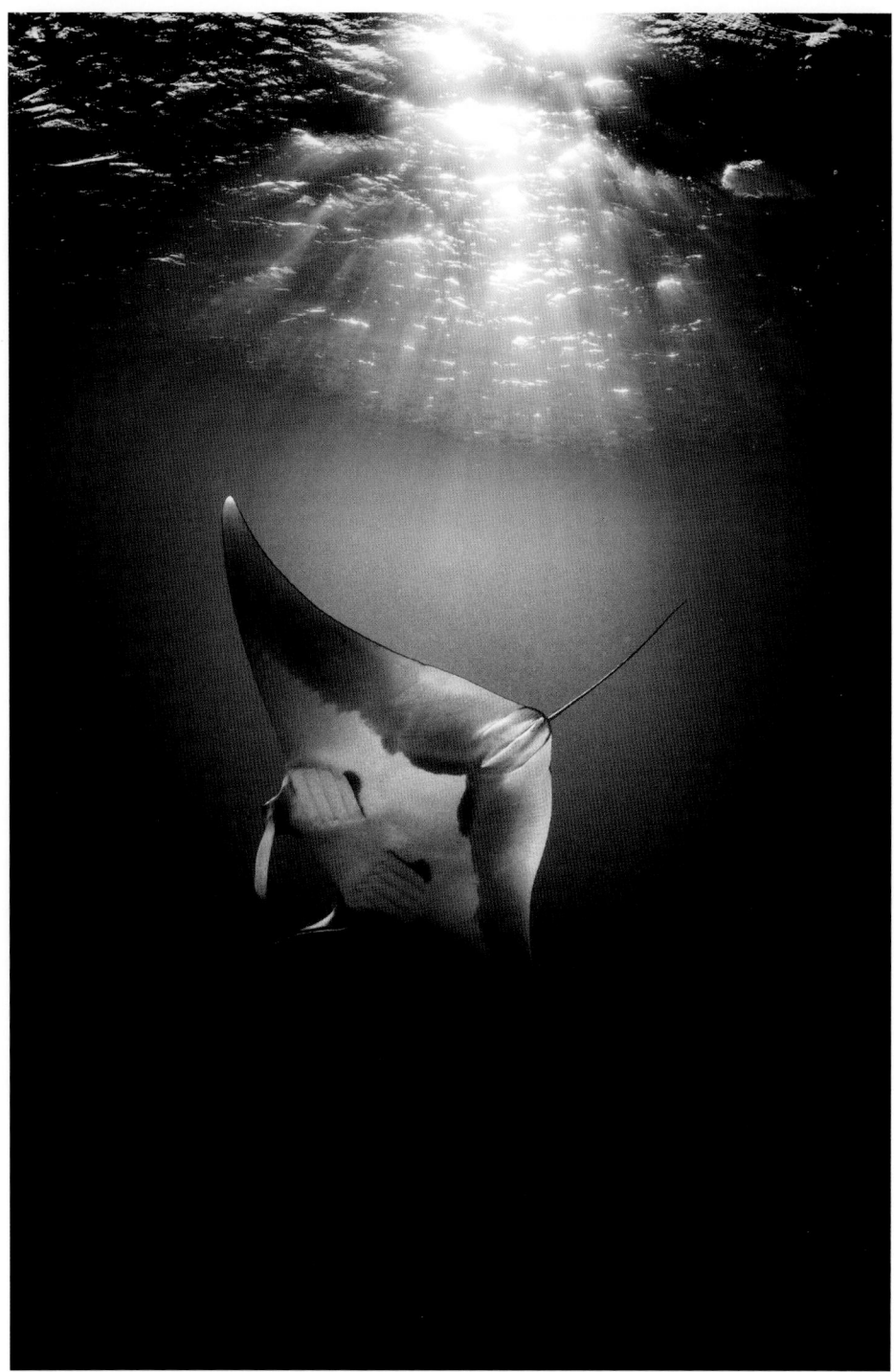

Revillagigedo Archipelago, Mexico, 2017

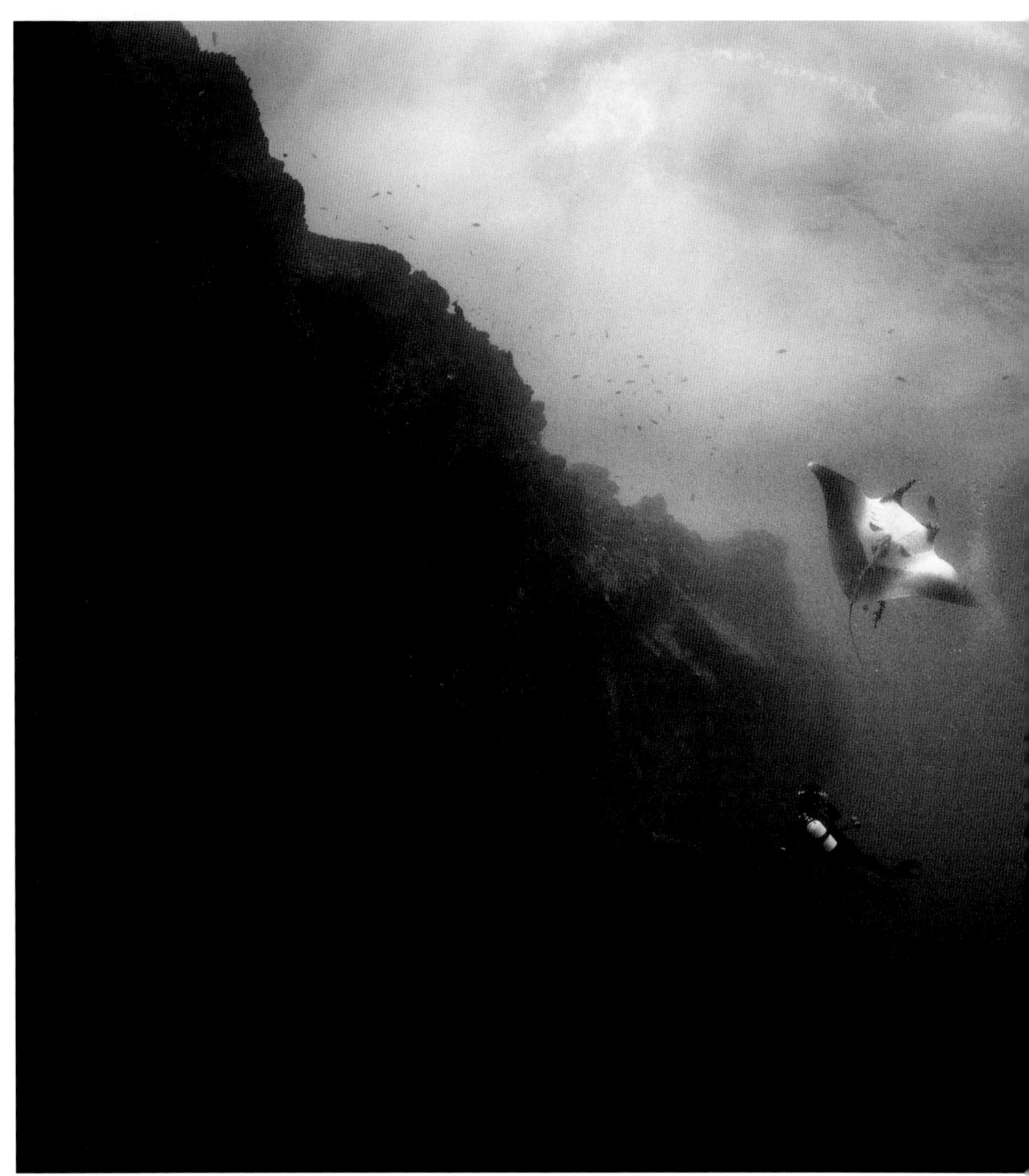

Revillagigedo Archipelago, Mexico, 2017

One of the reasons
we photograph is
to be more engaged
with this world.

16
Can I Go Deeper?

DESPITE BEING A TWO-DIMENSIONAL IMAGE, a photograph can have tremendous depth—or at least the illusion or feeling of depth. This feeling depends on the choices you make as the photographer, beginning with a recognition of whether or not a sense of greater depth serves your vision of the subject. Some images succeed not because of a sense of immersion or depth, but for the very lack of it. Some depend entirely on removing any perceived depth, and on pushing elements against each other to create forced connections or implied relationships that they would not have if there were more perceived space between them.

I have spent the last few years pursuing greater depth in my images because one of the reasons I photograph is to be more engaged with this world. The act of photographing pulls me into experiences I wouldn't otherwise have, and how I do that determines how engaged I am. To a great extent, I have done this with an exploration of wide and ultra-wide lenses. Wide lenses pull elements apart; they make closer foreground elements larger and background elements shorter. They recreate a sense of peripheral vision, and of being immersed in the scene. For me, they are often the tool I need to give my subjects the intimate, interactive expression that I chase. If I am to create a frame with energy and impact, wider lenses demand that I get in close, and closer still. They force my interaction and participation. This is true with landscapes, portraits, street scenes, and as much as possible, with wildlife.

Wider lenses allow me to create depth that no other tool can. They do this largely by manipulating the experience of perspective. When they make the foreground larger relative to the background, we feel close to that foreground element. When they make diagonal lines seem longer and more diagonal, they make us feel that change in energy, pushing the vanishing point further into the distance in a more dynamic way. With smaller movements on my part, they allow me to shift elements around in the depth of the scene, which doesn't necessarily change the sense of depth but does allow me to control what happens in the space that depth creates.

I am in the middle of a portrait project right now, photographing the people in my life who are most important to me. I am using nothing longer than a 35mm lens (full-frame equivalent), and often closer to 20mm. This is not the "preferred" focal length at which we are often told to make portraits. A 20mm lens won't make the list of the ten best portrait lenses anytime soon. It's unconventional because we usually want our portraits to be flattering—to make our big noses look smaller, our features a little less prominent. But is that the only reason we make portraits? To flatter? Do we not sometimes want something much closer to our usual experiences of people: close, intimate, flaws and all? Do we not sometimes want something more honest, more representative of the experience of sitting face to face? The depth created with wider focal lengths, especially when used close up, can do this in ways that longer, more flattering lenses can't. They just feel different. So the question is, how do you want this photograph to feel?

I've encouraged you many times already to consider what the best expression of your subject is and to make choices that explore the possibilities leading to that final photograph. I think this portrait project is a good example of that. My subject is not only the individual people I am photographing, but in a deeper sense, the intimacy between us. It's the emotion and the honesty. On some level, it's the vulnerability I'm asking of them. For this project, I sat across from my friends, very closely—the lens usually no farther than 16 inches from them—and asked them not to pose, not to smile or mug for the camera, but just to look into the lens. Sometimes they did just that. Sometimes they looked around the studio because being so close is awkward. Sometimes they took a drink of the whisky I put in front of them. And, after some initial failures, what has resulted is an ongoing series I call The Treasury, because these are the people who make my life richer. I needed an intimate feeling. I needed the depth that a wide lens can create.

Optics are not the only thing I used to create depth in these images. Light has always been used to great effect to create depth, or dimensionality, in photographs. When we use directional light—from the sides, top, or bottom more than from the front—the light hits every bump and feature and casts a shadow. This is one of our visual clues to three-dimensionality in an image, and an awareness of this and a willingness to control it can create more depth in your photographs. You can do this by waiting for different light, positioning your strobes off-axis to your subject rather than directly at them, or by changing your position relative to the scene itself.

Light has always been used to great effect to create depth, or dimensionality, in photographs.

You will have your own sense of what your subject is and how you want to best express it. Depth won't always be the right tool; for you, it might never be the right tool, in which case you'll do whatever you can to remove a sense of depth. You will favour long lenses and forced perspectives. You will take advantage of the way those longer focal lengths apparently compress space and the relationships among elements. It's not that one lens is better than another; it's that lenses do different things, and it's up to us to decide what to use based on what our vision or intent is. Some questions to consider:

- Would my subject benefit from the greater depth, or greater separation among elements, that a wider lens can create?

- Would a flatter, more graphic feeling be stronger?

- Would my subject benefit from the tighter relationships among elements that lenses over 50mm can imply?

- Is it important to me that the image feel immersive, as if the viewer were part of the scene, or would a feeling of detachment be a stronger expression of my subject and my intent for it?

- Could I use the effects of light and shadow to create or diminish the depth in my images by waiting for different light, using a different placement of my strobes, or simply moving the camera to better see and feel the shadows that create texture and dimension?

Just because we work in a two-dimensional medium does not mean we should, or really even that we can, ignore the third dimension. Our choices allow us to use and manipulate that perception of depth, and these choices have a strong impact on whether the subject that we intend to be the very heart of the photograph gets its strongest interpretation or not.

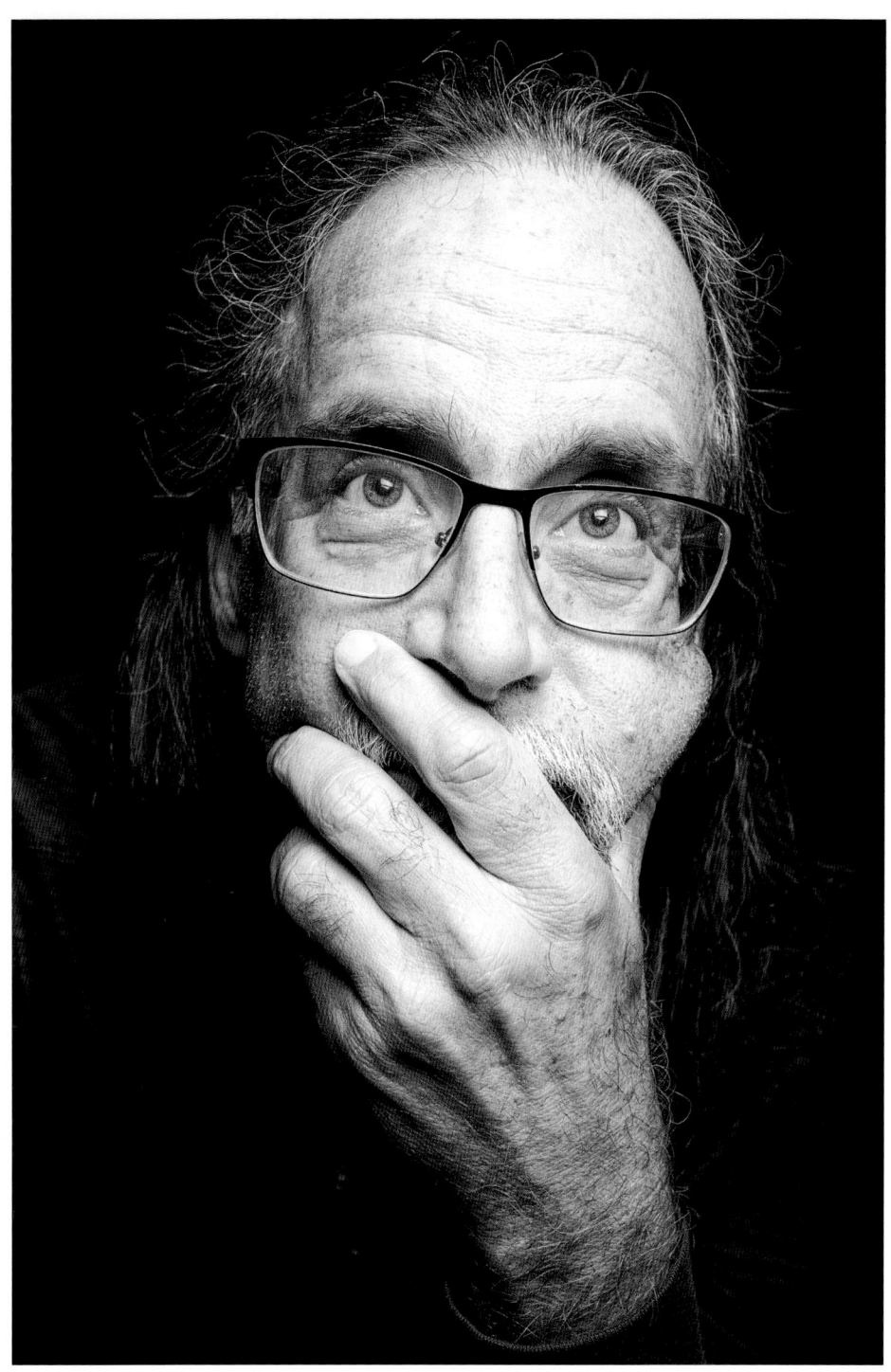

Andy Wallace, 2019

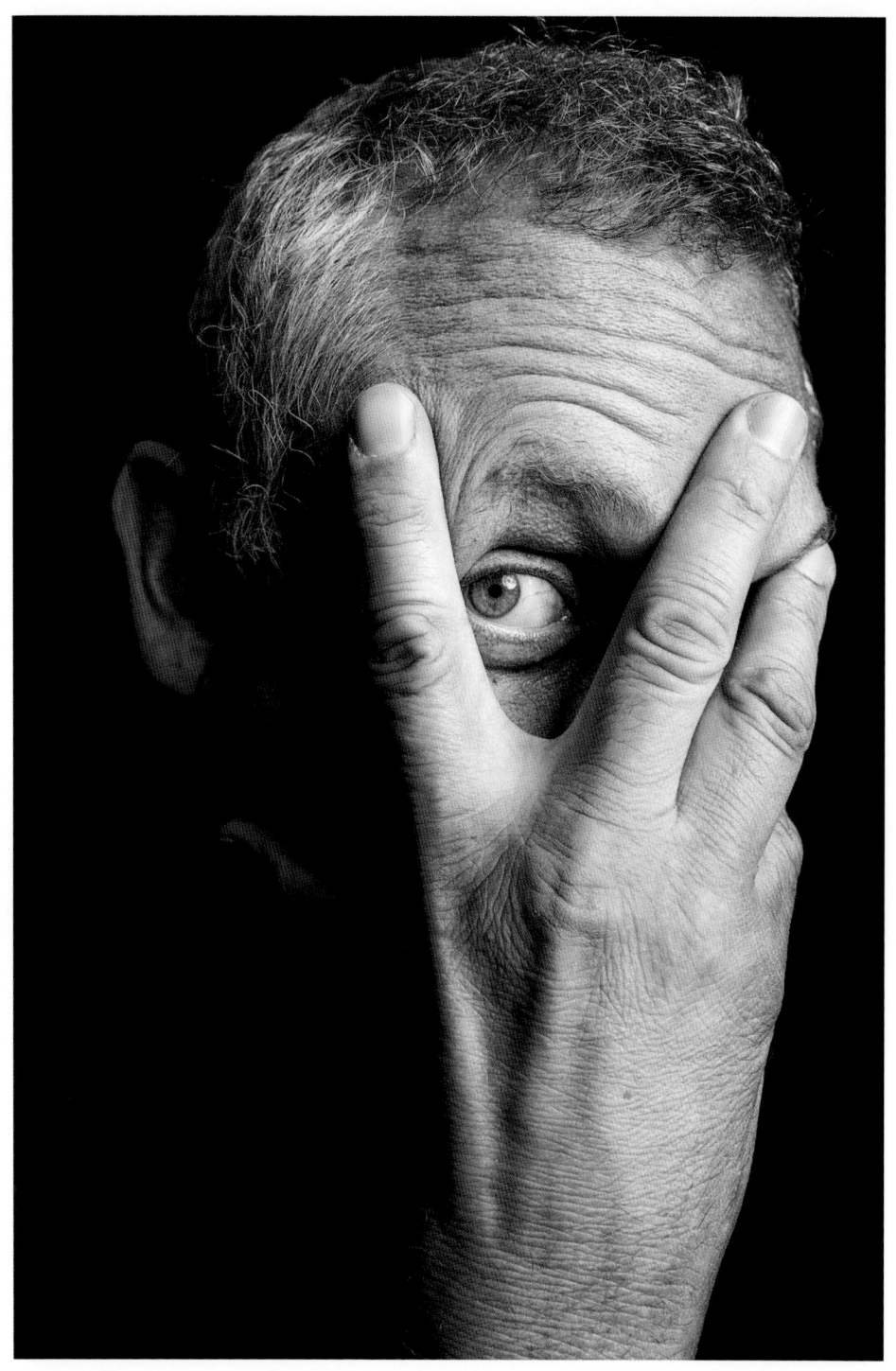

David Adam Edelstein, 2019

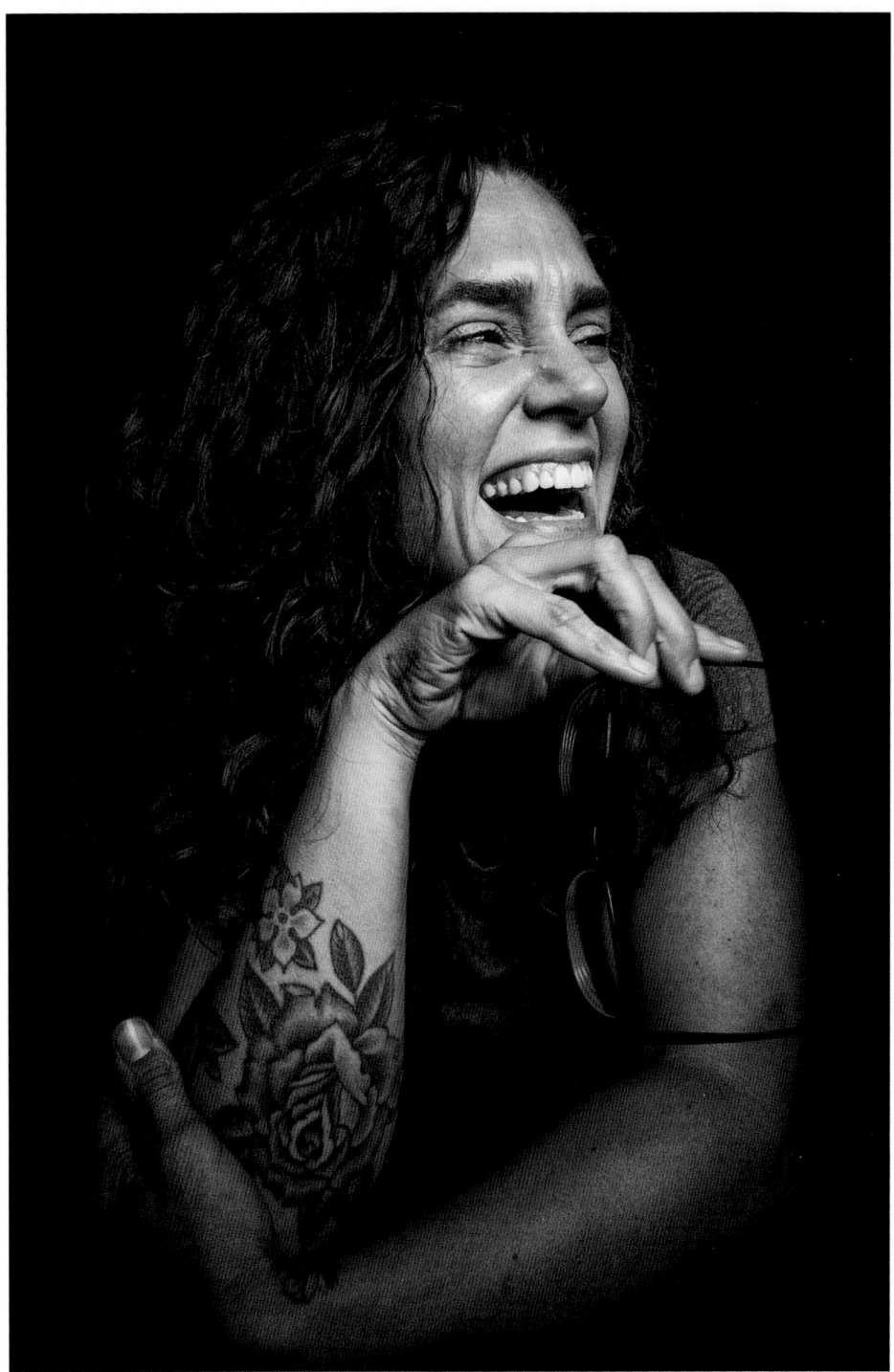

Kate Siobhan Mulligan, 2019

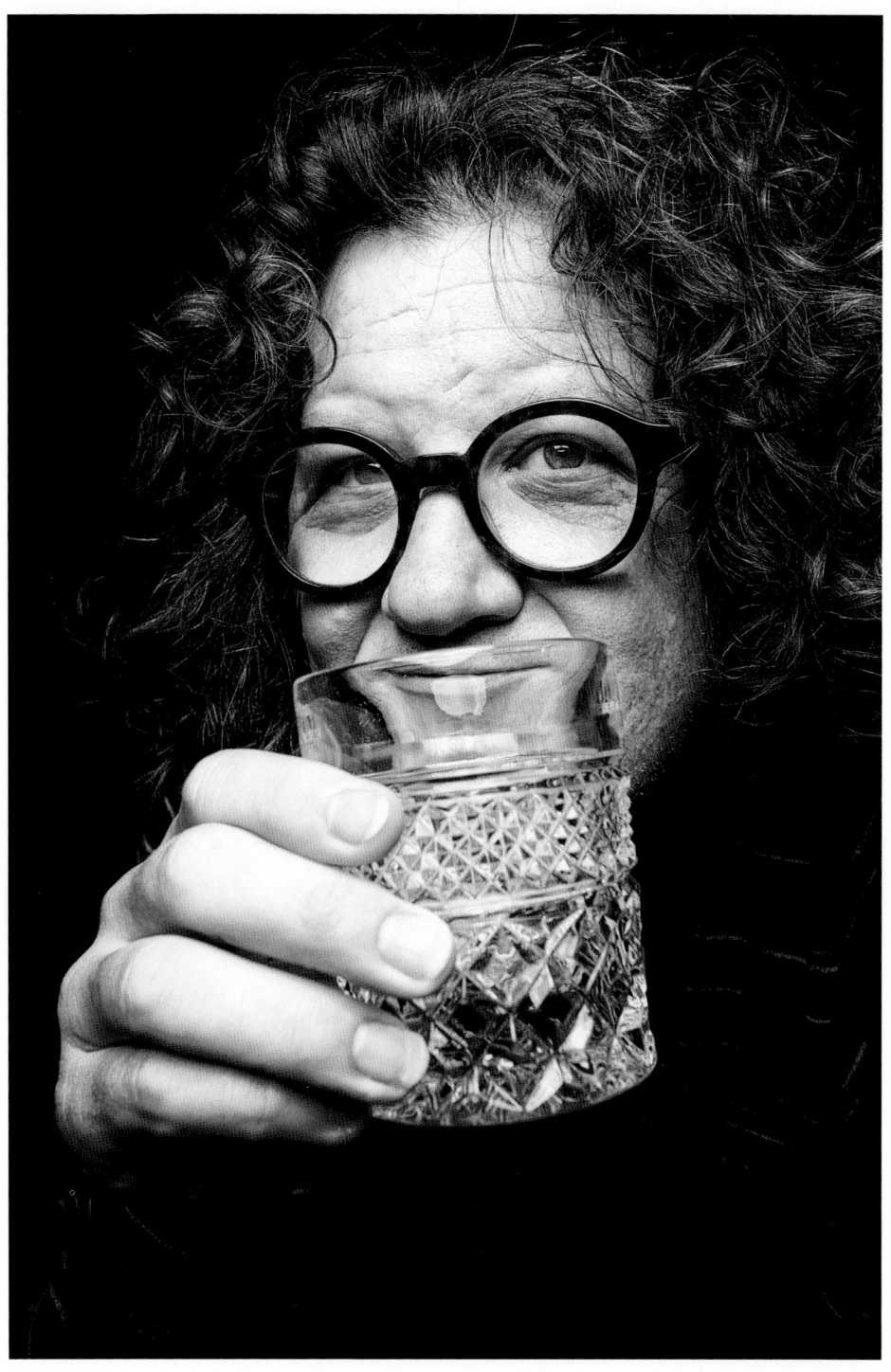

Jon McCormack, 2019

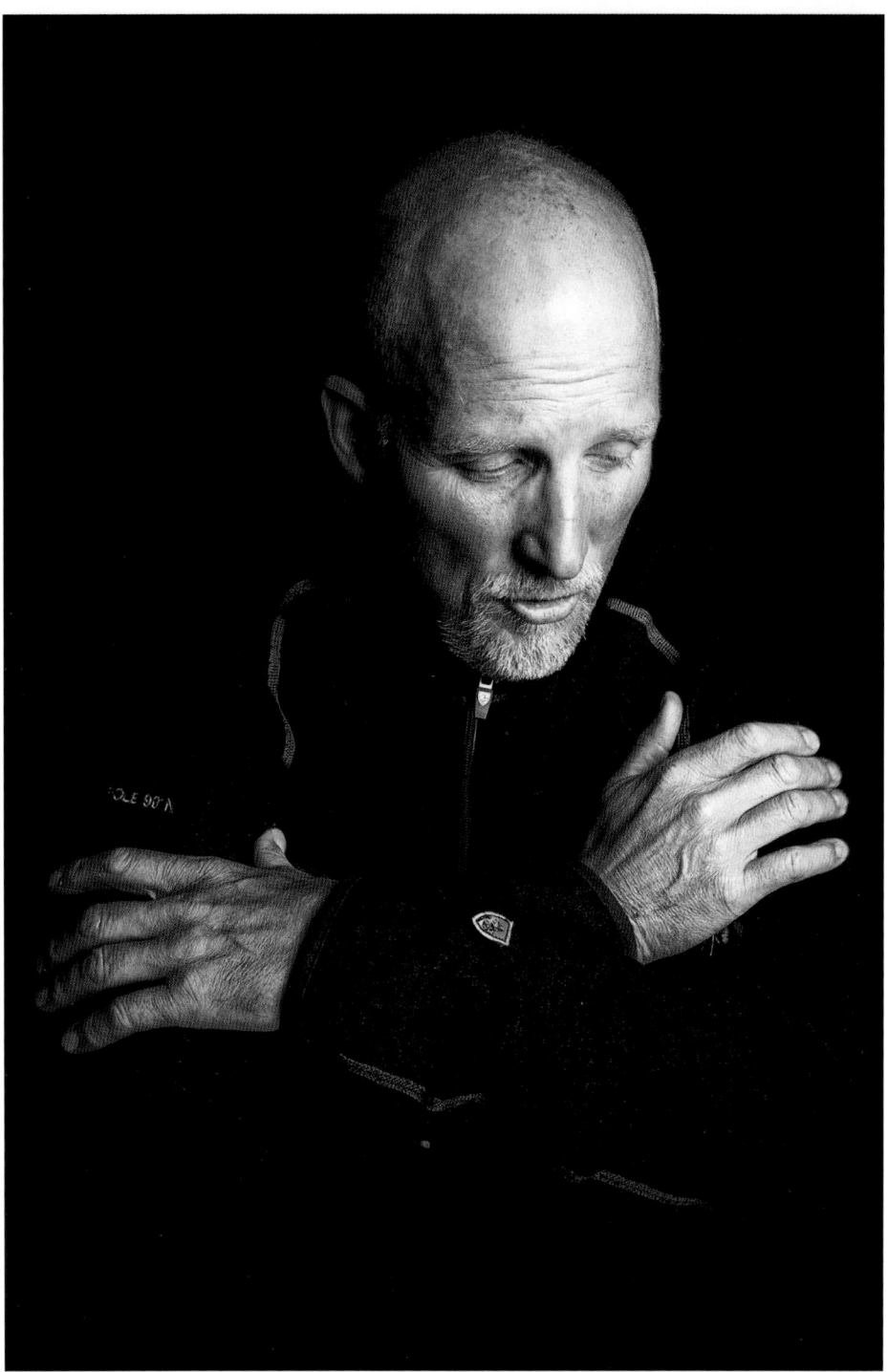

Paul Nicklen, 2019

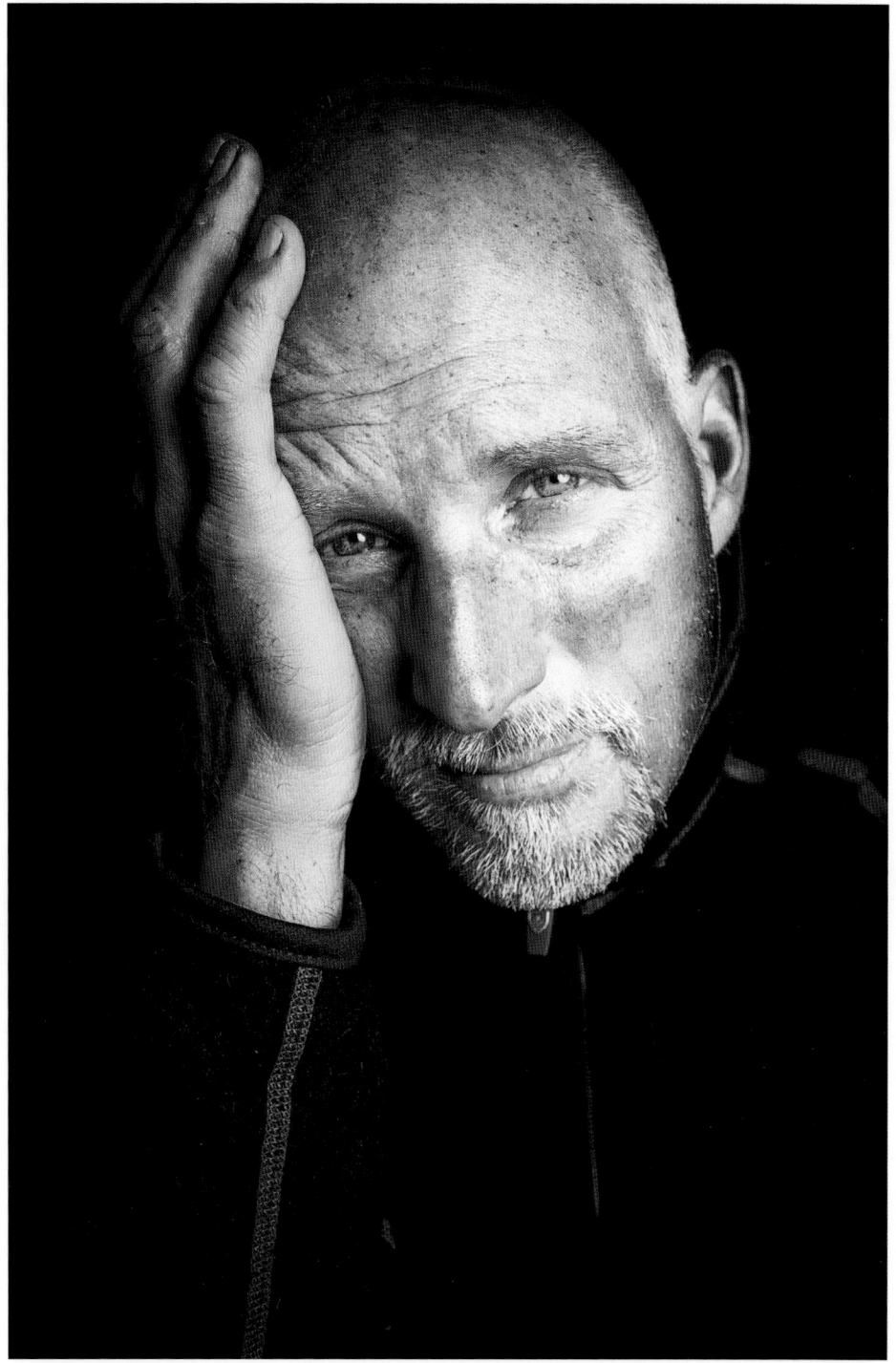

Paul Nicklen, 2019

The more you
cram unnecessary
information into the
frame, the more you
dilute the impact of
the photograph's most
important elements.

17
What About the Frame?

IF IT SEEMS ODD TO DISCUSS FRAMING so far into a book that is essentially about compositional choices, remember that these ideas are not intended to be taken sequentially. Most of the choices we make in the creation of a photograph happen in a reactionary way, depending on what first draws us to a scene and what other priorities and constraints impose themselves on the process. These decisions are interdependent, but they don't happen in any particular order. You might need to make ten decisions before you know what you need to do with the frame, or your choice of frame might be the first decision you make, but be open to reconsidering it any time.

When we choose a frame for our photograph, even if that choice is to always photograph horizontally with a 3:2 aspect ratio, we must be aware of the way the frame itself informs our reading of the image. I touched on this in Chapter 14 when discussing the energy within a photograph. Our choice of frame pushes those who will read the picture to read it in a certain way. Simply put, and in general terms, when we make a long horizontal image, we are saying that the horizontal relationships are more important than the vertical relation-ships, that the picture should be read horizontally. The same is true of a vertical frame, which places an emphasis on vertical relationships, shapes, and energy. A square frame gives equal weight to both the horizontality and the verticality of the elements, relationships, and energy within the image.

The big question that begs to be asked is this: Is my subject primarily vertical or horizontal? Or equally both? Remember, the subject is not necessarily the person or the tree that might seem to indicate a vertical frame. It could be the gesture of the person, wide and horizontal, or the relationship between that person and another, from left to right, forming an implied horizontal. In what direction does the story flow? How do you want me to read the image? If my eye wants to go up and down but you force it into the limited verticality of a horizontal frame, then you're going to frustrate me and create dissonance between the subject and its best expression. Not only that, but you'll probably also have to include other unnecessary elements or background on the left and right in order to fill the frame, and the more you cram unnecessary informa-tion into the frame, the more you dilute the impact of the photograph's most important elements.

There are other considerations for framing, including the appropriateness of the proportions of the frame—for example, whether you want not only a hori-zontal image but also one that feels *much more* horizontal, as a 16:9 frame does, though I think the earlier discussion about energy within the frame is sufficient to help you understand the impact of aspect ratio on the image. Asking yourself not only if your subject is best expressed horizontally or vertically but also *how horizontally* or *how vertically*, and knowing that these decisions are entirely yours to make, should be enough to encourage experimentation and creativity.

For some of us, it just comes down to taste. You may prefer a standard 3:2 horizontal frame, in which case you've made your choice. But the questions that inform that choice remain and should be considered:

- How do I place the elements within this specific frame in order to create balance and tension appropriate to the subject and what I want to say about it?

- Where do I stand in order to establish the relationships among elements and the frame itself?

- What choices do I need to make to maximize the movement or energy in the frame?

- Have I given the eye the room it needs to move?

- How does my choice of moment, my choice of lens, and the position I take relative to the scene itself affect the way I answer these questions?

This is not a complicated idea, but it's too often overlooked. It's easy to get into the habit of holding the camera one particular way, or to get into a groove with our compositions and see the frame as merely the edges of the photograph and not part of the photograph itself, part of the image that determines how it's read and what importance we give to certain relationships, dynamics, and stories. Ask yourself if you've made the strongest match between your true subject and the frame itself, and you'll make more intentional choices and photographs that better express that subject.

The eye sees it all,
but the mind is what
gives a thing meaning.

18
Do the Elements Repeat?

PHOTOGRAPHY HAS MUCH IN COMMON with graphic design. In fact, photography *is* graphic design—the arrangement of graphic or visual elements to say a certain thing. That we do not learn more from that discipline continues to baffle me, though I wonder if it's because in popular photography culture we tend to rely on the quality of our cameras for the quality of our images, whereas graphic designers have never had the luxury of believing their tools had much to do with the arrangement of elements on the page. That's a whole other sermon, but it highlights an opportunity for the photographer who is willing to study how graphic designers use basic design principles like contrast, alignment, balance, and repetition.

Repetition of elements can be as useful a tool to the photographer as it is to the graphic designer, though it should be acknowledged that the latter has more ability to move elements around, duplicate them, or remove them, while the photographer is often limited to recognizing the presence of repeated elements and then maximizing or minimizing them with their choices. First, however, it's important to know what repeated elements bring to the photograph.

When you look at a scene and see lines, shapes, gestures, or colours repeating, there is an opportunity to create a visual echo in the image. Just as contrast allows us to point to something and call it out by comparing it to what it is not (a small child made to look even smaller in the presence of something much larger, for example), repeated elements allow us to point to certain things by putting them in the same frame as other things that are *similar*. The more similar they are, the more we notice them and find them interesting. A red ball is echoed by a red hat and a red sign on a nearby building. Those repeated elements draw us through the frame and give the eye shapes and paths to follow in the same way certain lines do. They naturally provide a point of interest.

When repeated elements are observed and placed creatively within the frame, they can tie an image together, pulling the disparate elements into a unified whole. When there are enough of these elements that they create a perceivable pattern, they can also provide another means of creating contrast when that pattern is broken. When there are many circular shapes in the frame but only one prominent triangle, we notice that triangle all the more. When there are many red elements in the frame but only one blue one, it is the blue element we notice because it's different. Questions to consider:

- Are there elements in this scene that echo each other in shape or colour?

- What choices can I make to maximize or minimize these repetitions according to my intent for the photograph? Could I include or exclude more of them, for example?

- Are there enough of these repetitions to make a pattern, and can I find a way to break that pattern to create contrast and stronger visual interest?

- Can I use these repeated elements to create a unity in my frame that might not otherwise exist?

- Can I move my point of view or use a different lens to make a clearer path for the eye with those repeating elements?

What you do with the repeated elements in the scene depends on what you're trying to accomplish, but it always begins with seeing them and the possibilities they present.

I'm often asked how we can learn to see better—how to more easily recognize repeating elements or any other photographic element—and my answer is always this: to see something is not a function of the eye but of the mind. The eye sees it all, but the mind is what gives a thing meaning.

We don't need to see better; we need to recognize elements and possibilities for what they are. The word *recognize* means "to know again." To do that, we have to know that particular thing to begin with. As with other topics and elements we've covered, if you begin to consciously look for and recognize repeated elements in strong photographs, you'll begin to do so when making photographs.

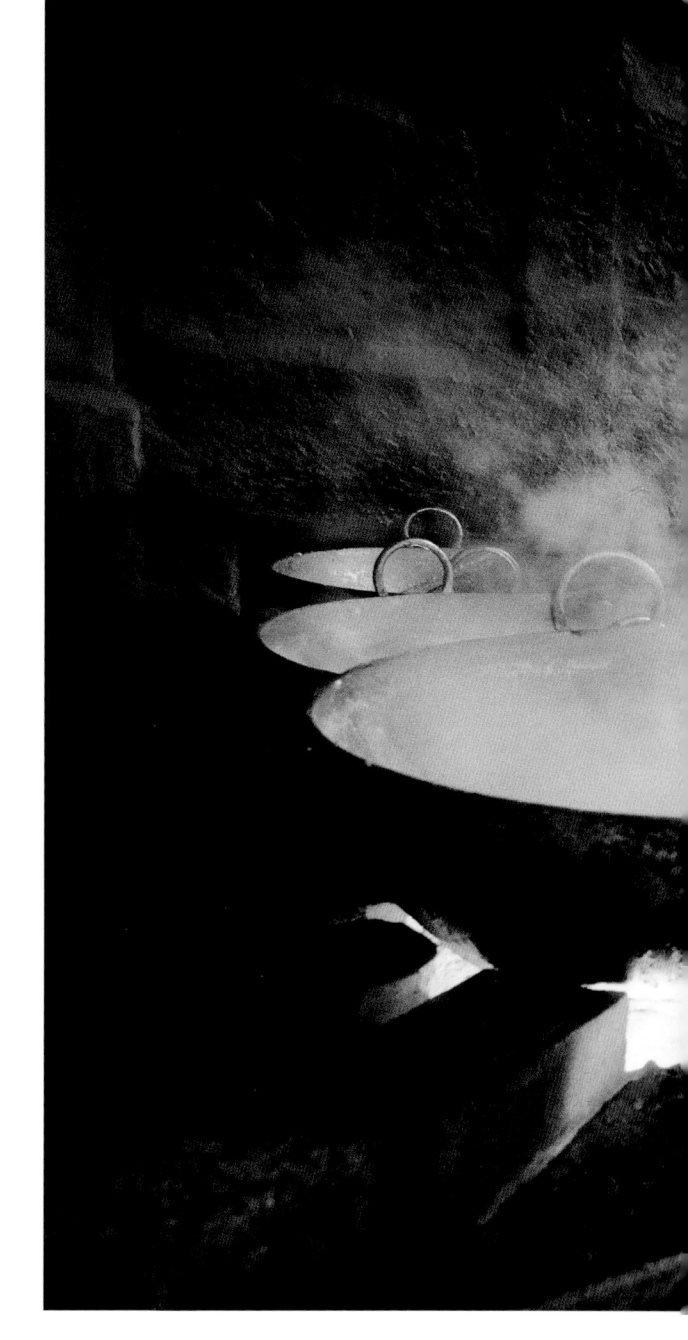

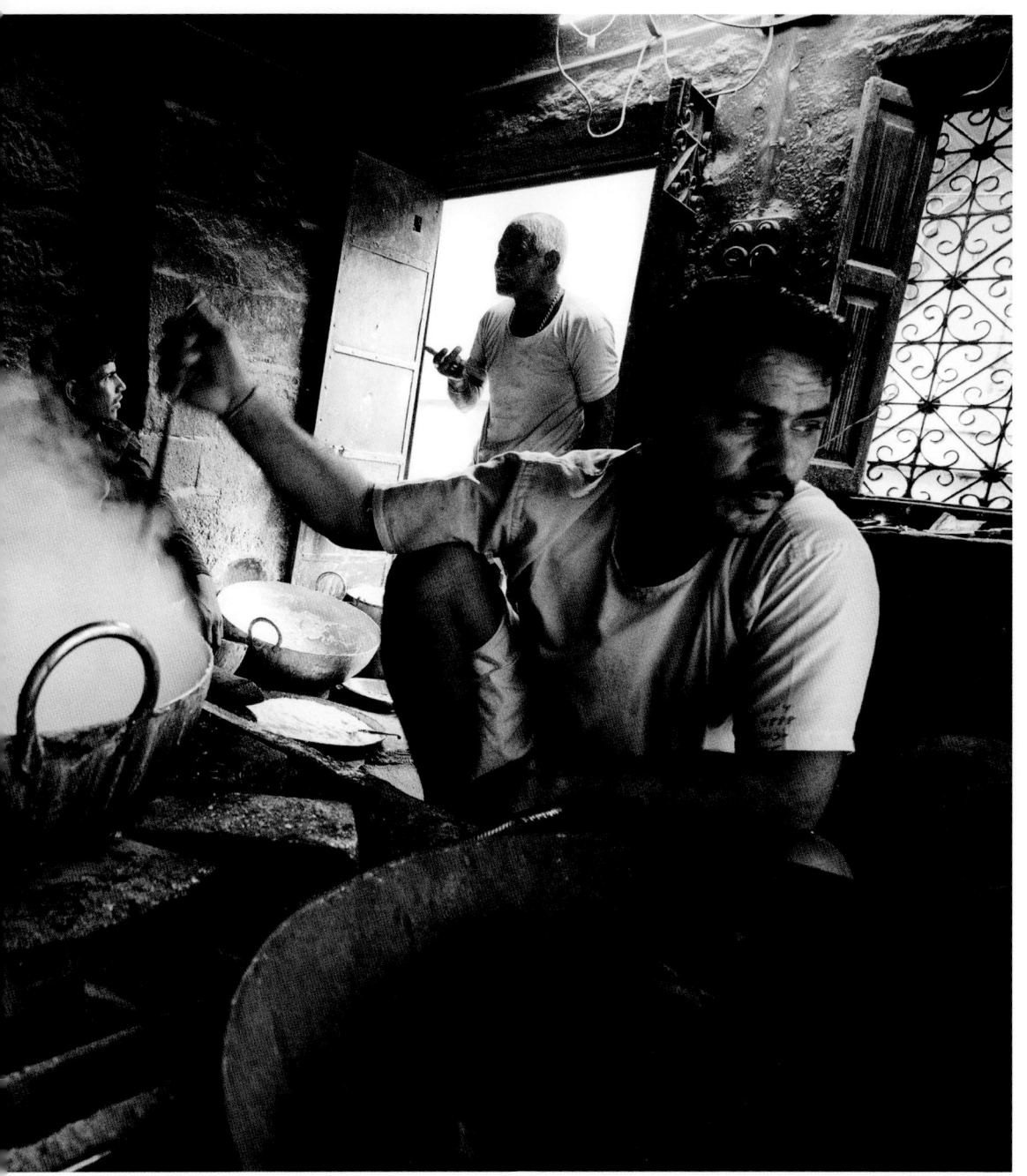

Jodhpur, India, 2017

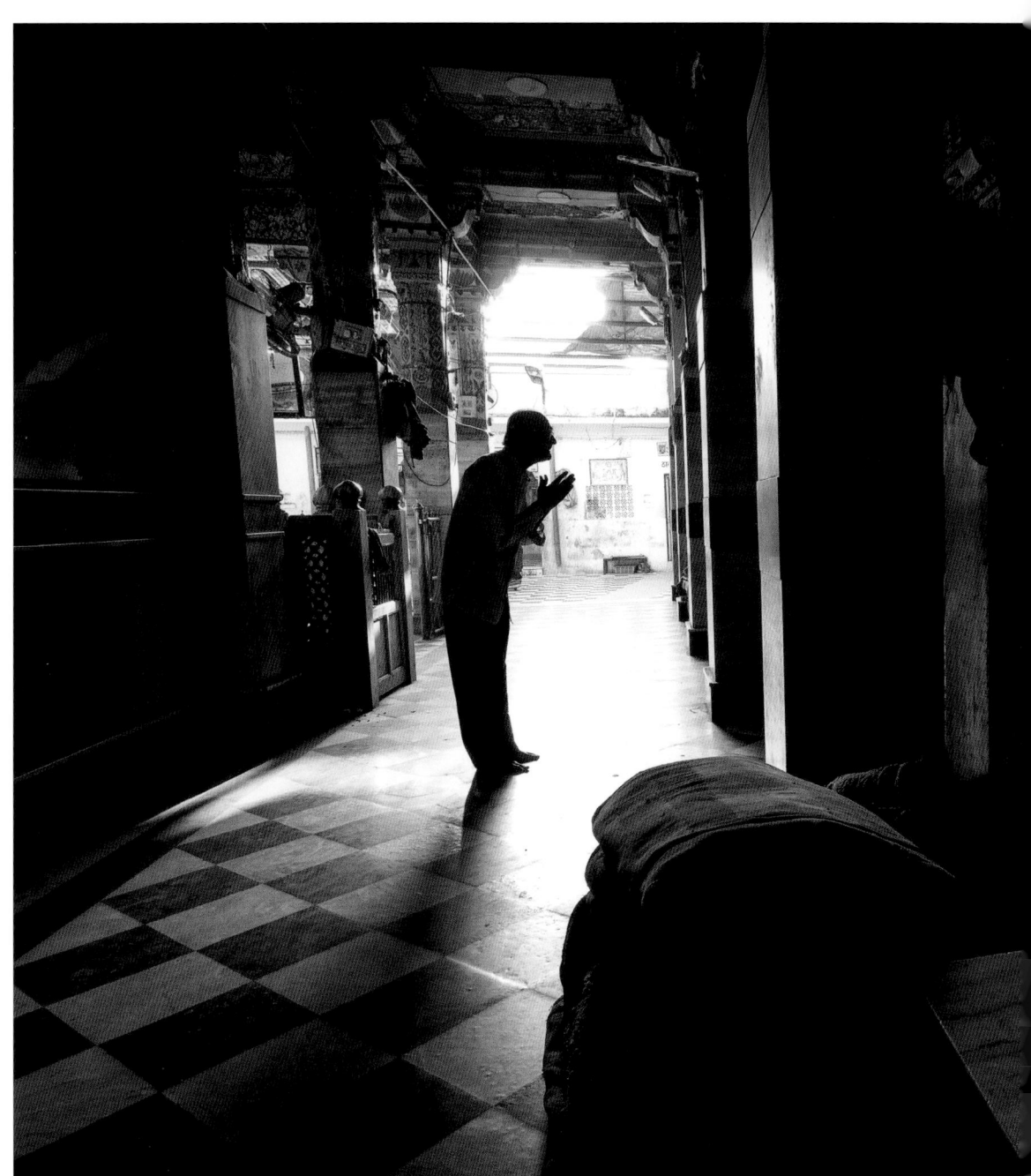

Jodhpur, India, 2017

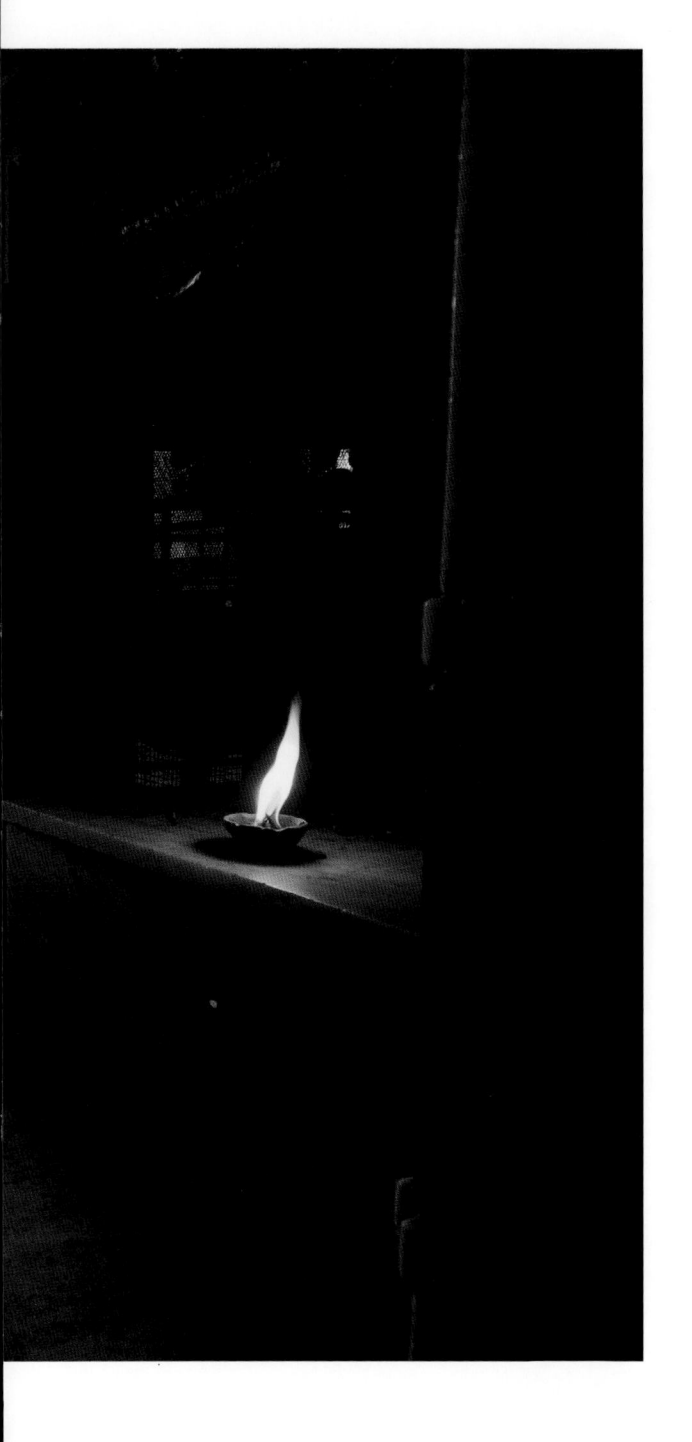

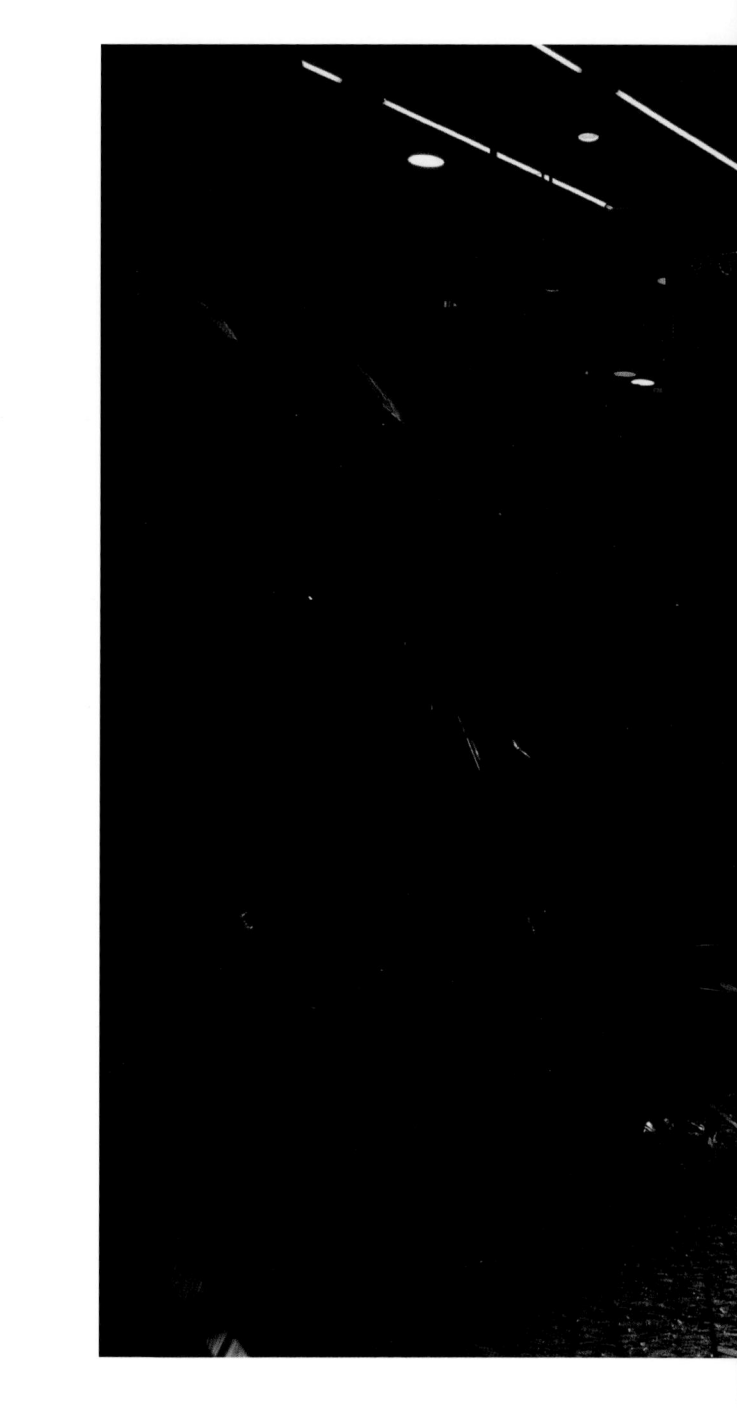

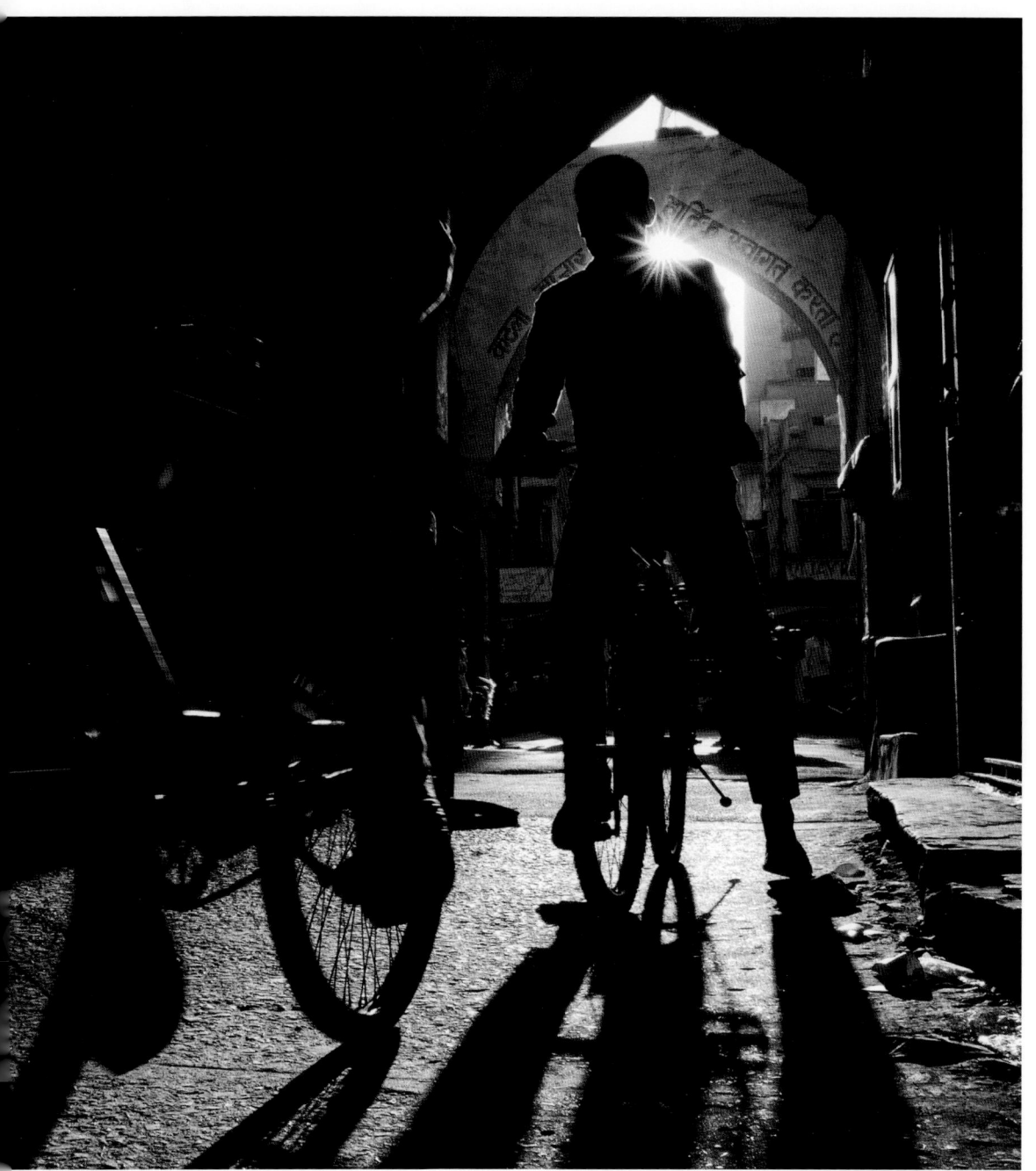

Jodhpur, India, 2017

Harmony is achieved when everything in the image is working together.

19
Harmony

ONE OF THE MOST COMMON REACTIONS I have to images of photographers first beginning their journey (and which I have to my own early work) is that the image lacks harmony. It lacks unity. There are a lot of elements in the frame and they don't all work together to create a single, cohesive whole. It's as if they're all there only by the force of the frame holding them together.

My central premise for this book is that the heart of the photograph is not just the subject of the image, but *the best expression of that subject*, as the photographer chooses. Harmony is the agreement of all the elements to support that goal. When you say you want the image to be about the relationship between two people, or the chaos on a street in India, or the way the light hits the land and sea on Scotland's Isle of Skye, harmony is achieved when everything in the image is working together to that one end, and no element is fighting your intent.

How can I use colour, repeated elements, or thematic reference to create or maintain harmony in the picture?

When we look at an image and say, "This element or that element is distracting," what we're saying is that it lacks harmony. Because of choices made about what elements to include or exclude and how those are arranged, we feel instinctively that the image is about *this*, but there are other elements fighting against that; it's the lack of harmony we're reacting to.

So what about contrast? How do we use contrast to support that harmony and not fight against it? Balancing harmony and contrast is important to a good photograph, and while I think it's something you need to feel and test in the image, the most helpful question is this: Does this contrast support the idea of the image? Without variety, harmony can become monotony, and it's contrast that can help you avoid that. The idea of a pattern being broken is exactly this.

Three of the more obvious and powerful ways to create harmony in an image are the intentional consideration and use of colour palettes, repeated elements, and thematic reference. Using an intentionally chosen colour palette, so that the hue, saturation, and luminance values within the photograph work together, creates a visual whole. Throwing in an element that contrasts with that palette can disrupt or call attention to that palette and be used to good effect as long as it doesn't steal the show. We've already explored the idea of repeated elements, but thematic reference is worth a deeper look.

Thematic reference is about the visual support of the main idea. Do the chosen elements support the expression of the subject? This is important, particularly the recognition that we do, in fact, choose the elements in our frame. Photography is the art of exclusion, and the strongest photographs contain no more than they need to. Fight to keep the unnecessary out of the frame.

We'll look at how that's done in Chapter 21, but for now grab onto this idea: if it doesn't belong, if it doesn't serve a function—specifically, to be part of the expression of the subject—exclude it. Be merciless about this.

- What is my one idea or subject? Does everything in the frame support what I am trying to say, explore, or express in this image?

- How can I use colour, repeated elements, or thematic reference to create or maintain harmony in the picture?

- How can I use contrast to provide interest or a counterpoint to the rest of the image without that contrast derailing the image's harmony?

Harmony is something we don't talk about as photographers. But we experience that harmony, or the lack of it, in every photograph we study or make. That harmony helps the photograph work, or its lack weakens the image. The photographer who is constantly aware of and asking themselves about harmony, or visual unity, will begin to make stronger, more intentional decisions to create that harmony and photographs that powerfully express their chosen subject, undistracted by unnecessary elements.

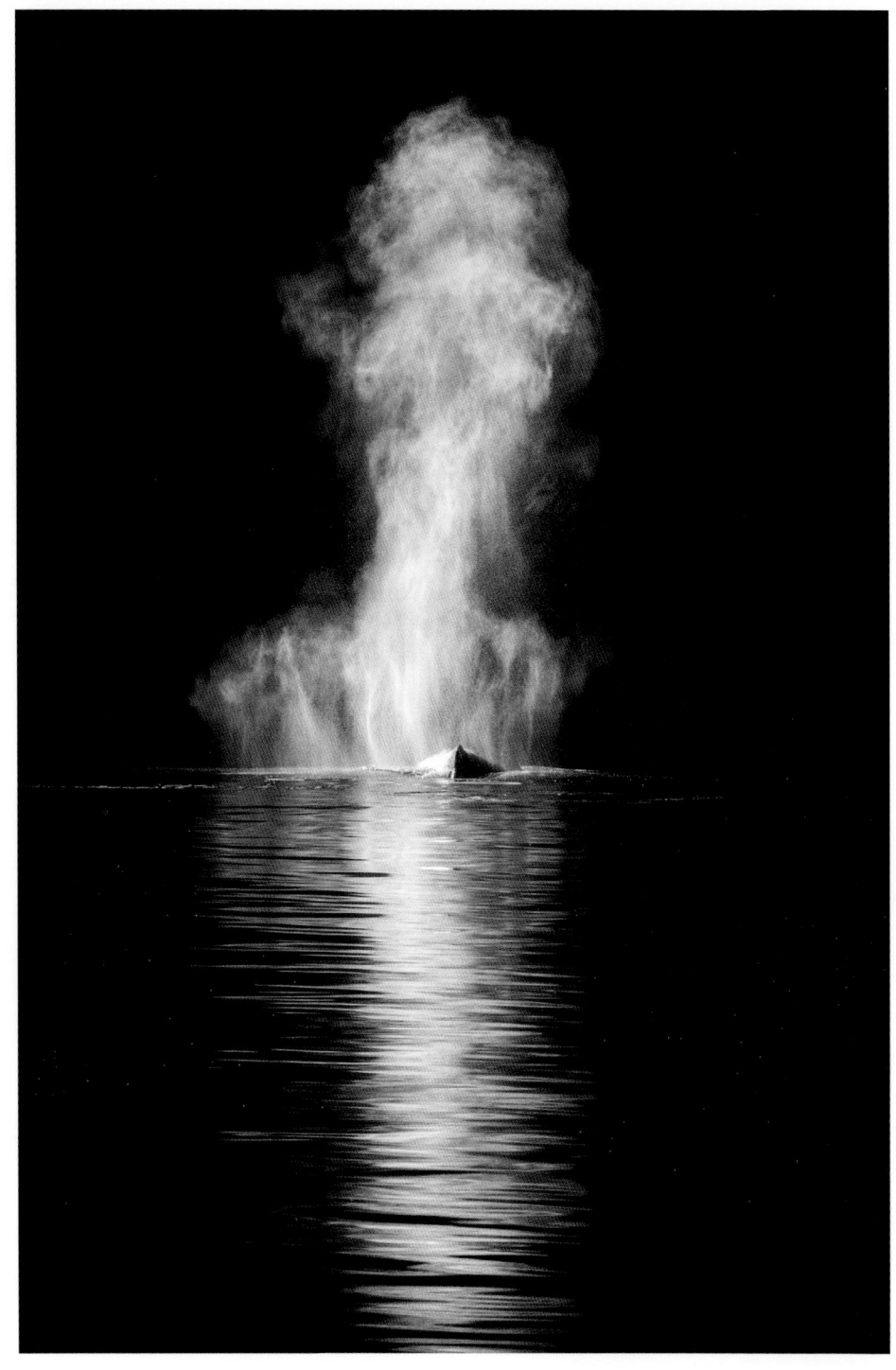

Coastal Waters, British Columbia, Canada, 2017

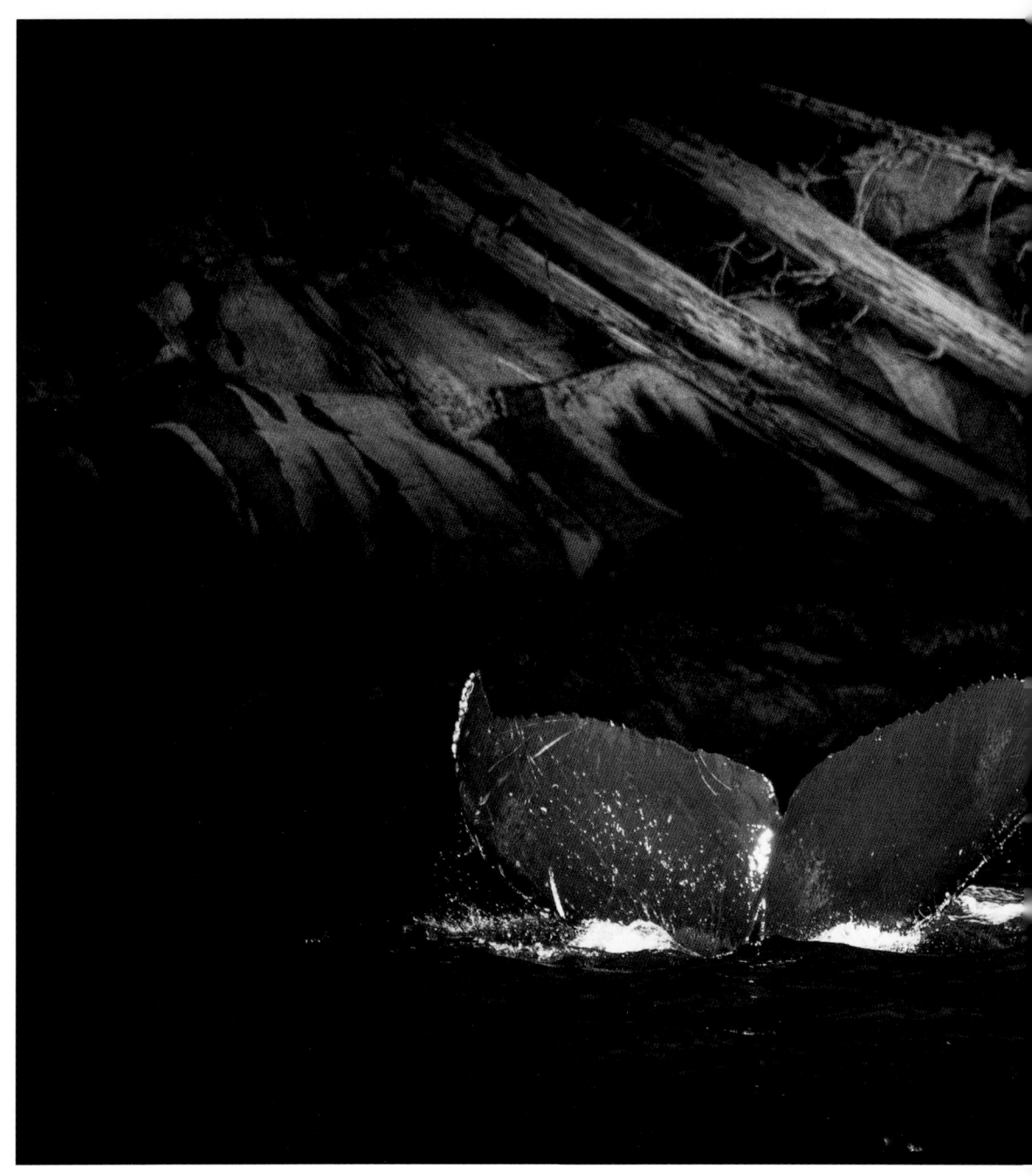

Coastal Waters, British Columbia, Canada, 2017

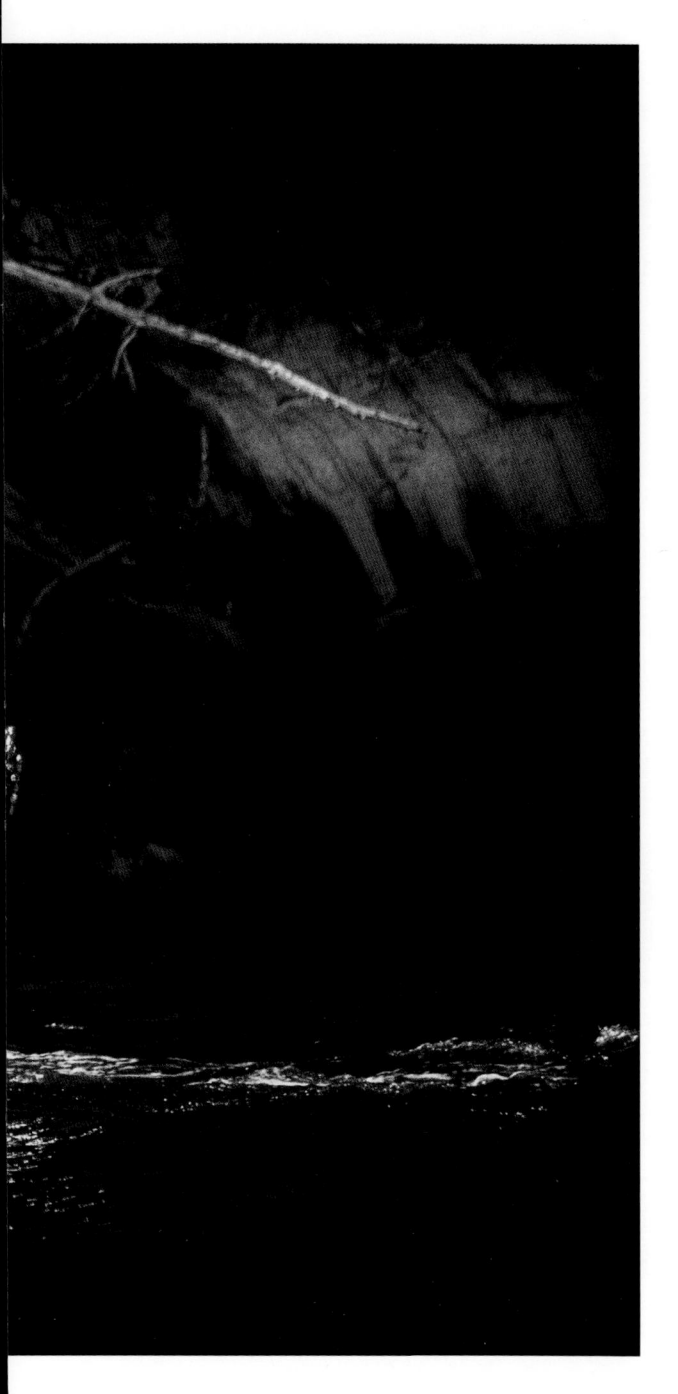

Coastal Waters, British Columbia, Canada, 2017

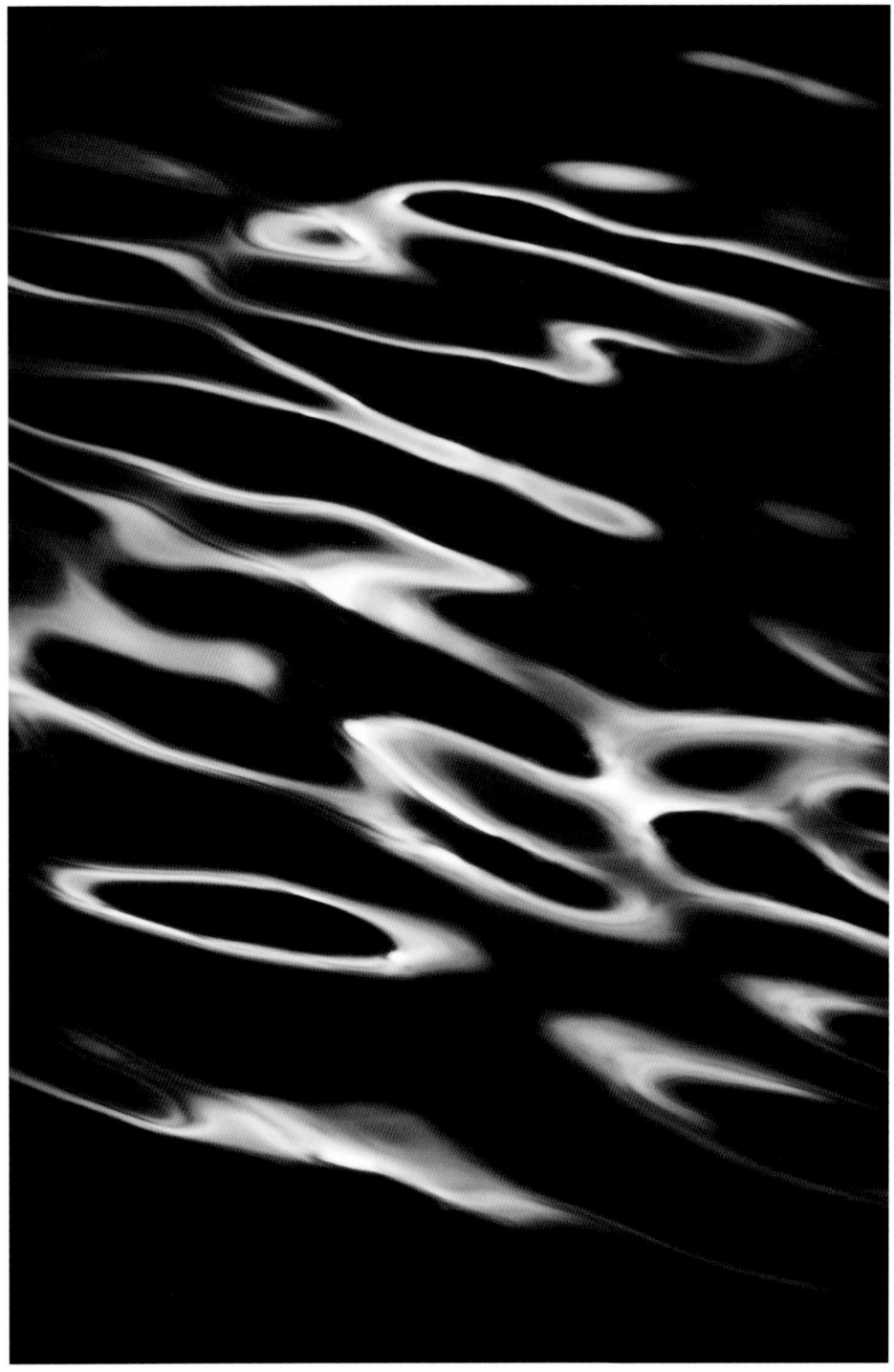

Coastal Waters, British Columbia, Canada, 2017

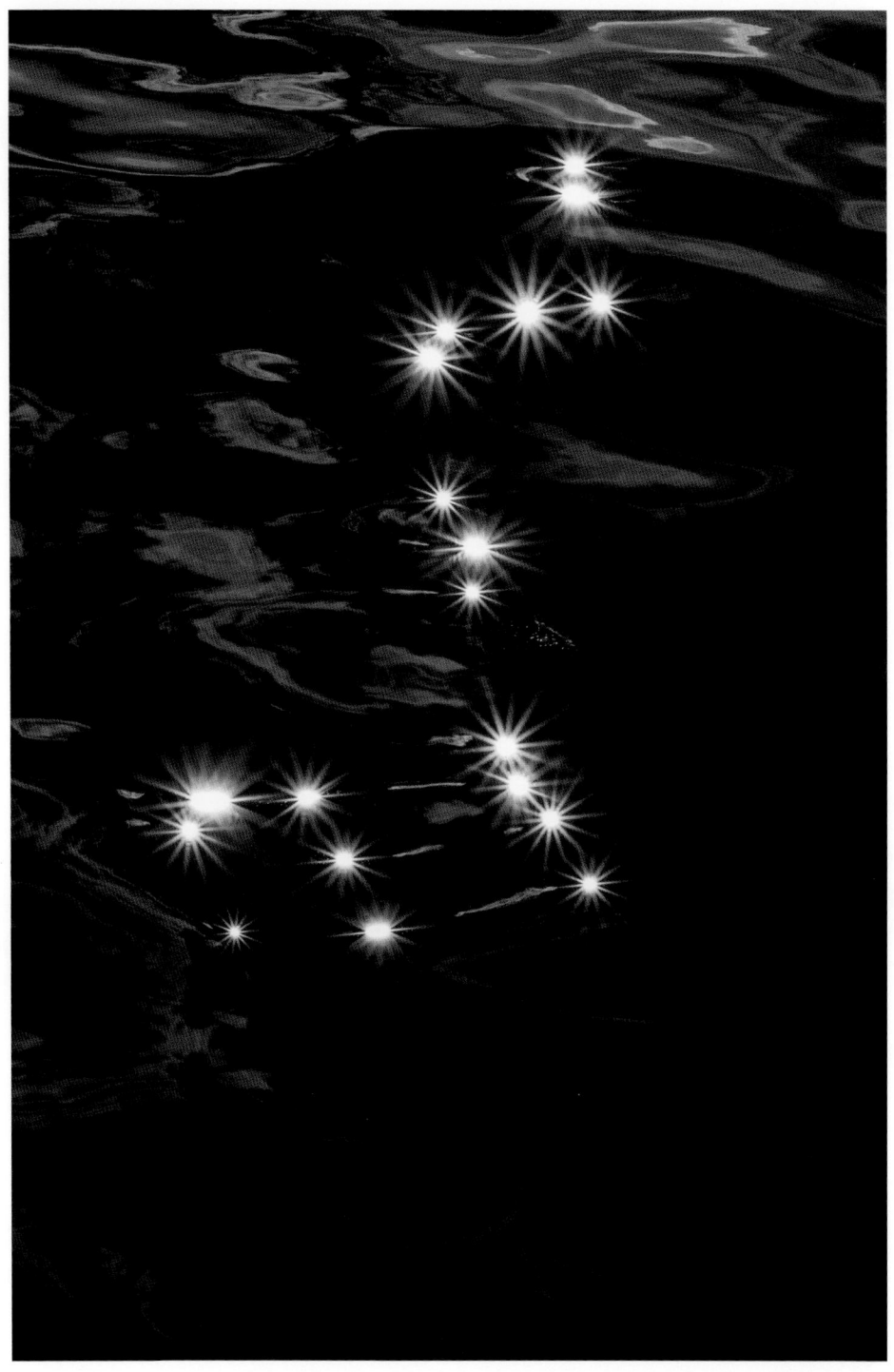

Coastal Waters, British Columbia, Canada, 2017

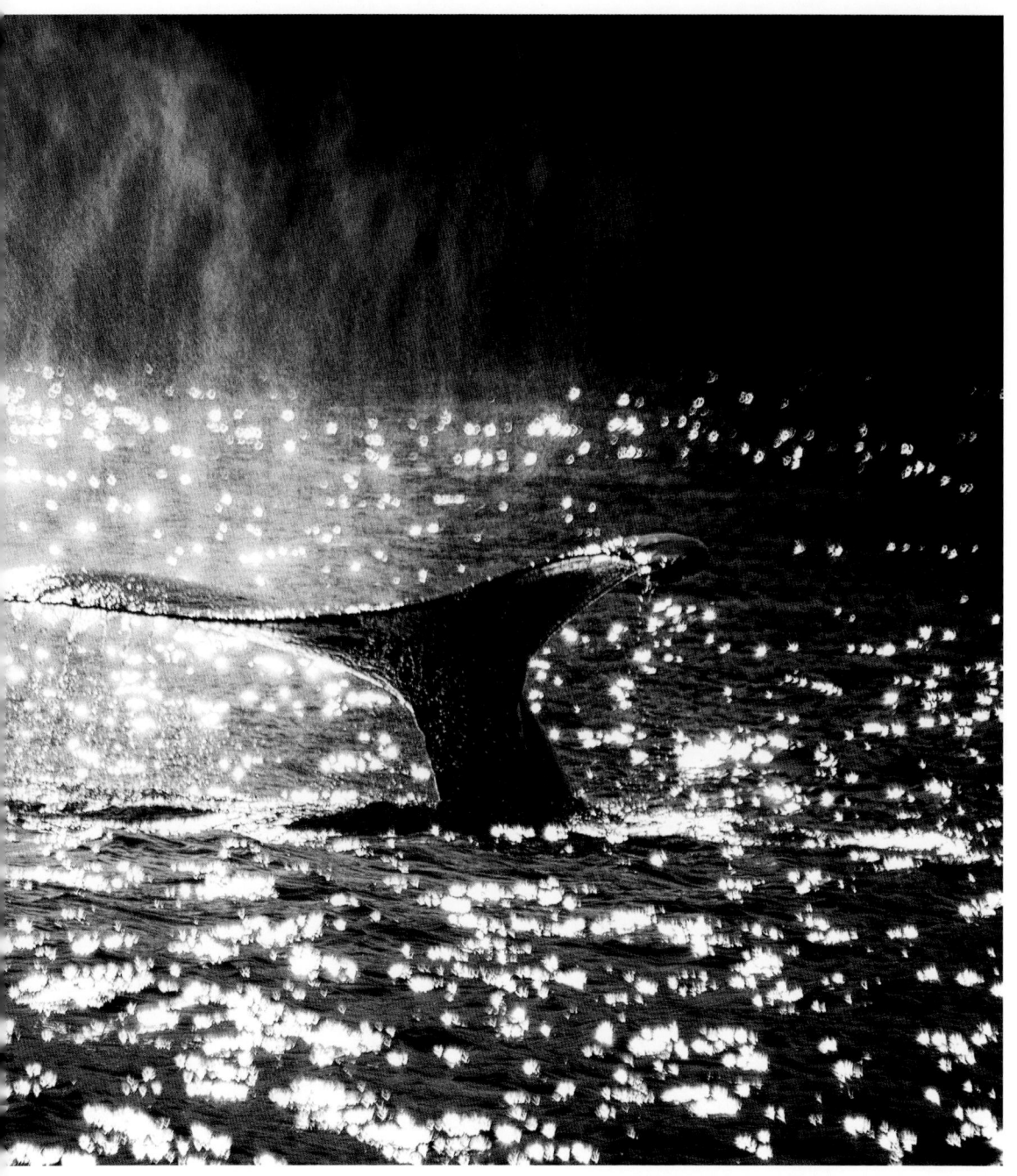

Coastal Waters, British Columbia, Canada, 2017

Anything that does
not help express our
vision of the subject
has a diminishing
effect on the power
of the image.

20
Can I Exclude More?

IF HARMONY IS ABOUT THE WAY in which elements work together within an image, then asking ourselves if we might achieve better harmony by excluding more from the frame is a helpful question. I prefer to focus more on what I am trying to maximize rather than just asking if there is more I can leave out of the photograph, so I look at this task as one of isolation. How can we use the tools of our craft to best isolate the true subject of the photograph by including only those elements that carry the most information or impact in expressing that subject?

This pursuit is important because the more we put into the frame, the more those unnecessary elements compete for our attention and dilute the impact we hope the photograph will have. Anything that does not help express our vision of the subject has a diminishing effect on the power of the image and its ability to hold our attention or communicate clearly.

The most obvious means of exclusion comes from the frame itself and our mindfulness regarding where we point the lens. A little to the left, and we exclude elements on the right, and vice versa. A little closer, and we begin to exclude elements on all sides. Add to this the isolating or exclusionary effect of longer lenses and their restrictive angles of view, and we have the powerful ability to limit what goes into the final image. But these are not the only tools in the photographer's toolbox.

We can isolate one moment or action by choosing to photograph one particular sliver of time—*this* 1/60th of a second rather than *that* one. Time can be used to isolate in other ways as well. When we choose to use a 30-second exposure, we isolate or exaggerate the softness of moving water, and in so doing, we exclude the particular details of the waves. Alternatively, we can use a longer shutter speed to isolate a stationary object if it's surrounded by moving objects; that slow shutter allows the moving objects to blur while keeping the stationary object still, effectively excluding the individual moving elements.

Depth of field has long been used to intentionally isolate or exclude based on the plane of focus and how much you choose to keep sharp and how much you allow to blur, often very effectively reducing the visual mass of a cluttered background and isolating the foreground.

Using the behaviour of wider lenses and pushing them in nice and close takes advantage of the foreshortening effect of perspective, making the foreground element larger, the background elements smaller, and effectively isolating the former against the latter. If you recall our discussion of visual mass, this is simply an application of those ideas.

If you want to better isolate one element from another, give the one greater visual mass and/or decrease the visual mass of the other. One sharp element will be isolated against the blurred elements; those blurred elements might not be completely excluded, but their presence can be diminished. Elements that are made larger relative to elements made smaller will also be isolated. These same considerations can be used in post-production as well, the eye being pushed and pulled around the frame with careful dodging and burning.

Questions that guide us toward better use of isolation include:

- Does everything in the image provide either needed information or important impact? No? How can I exclude it?

- Are there elements that would, by their exclusion, give the picture greater clarity of message or emotional impact?

- Can I use a longer lens to tighten up the scene and compress some of the distance between elements?

- Can I use a wider lens pushed in close to give more impact to the foreground?

- Would less depth of field help isolate the subject, or do I need more depth of field to better tell the whole story?

- Would creative use of my shutter speed allow me to give more impact to the subject?

- Would a different choice of moment better isolate this event in time, excluding other moments that are less clear or powerful?

- What can I do in post-production to further isolate and draw the eye to the most important elements?

Twelve images with impact will always be better than one image that tries, but fails, to say everything.

It's easy to understand the desire to include more, to tell a bigger story, to see details that you really want to photograph, but that is often best accomplished not by including more and more but by making more than one image, each of which focuses on giving the most impact to the one subject in each of those images. This is one reason why photographers, such as those who work with *National Geographic*, work in a multi-picture format. They know that twelve images with impact will always be better than one image that tries, but fails, to say everything. With everything crammed into the frame, nothing would carry more weight than anything else, and the power and clarity would be lost. Asking ourselves if we've isolated the subject well, and excluded all else, is a step toward saying what we want to say about our subject without confusion or a loss of impact.

There is a vast difference between focusing the lens and focusing our attention.

21
Where Does the Eye Go?

EVERY ELEMENT IN THE FRAME pulls the eye to one degree or another. If we've been aware and intentional about where those elements are placed, then the eye of the reader has a journey ahead. Where the eye goes, how it gets there, and in what order all have an effect on how we read the photograph. And as much as we talk about where the *eye* goes, it is more a matter of where the *mind* goes; specifically, to what is our attention drawn?

As far as I can tell, it was my friend and photographer John Paul Caponigro who said, "There is a vast difference between focusing the lens and focusing our attention." If I'm wrong about that, then it is certainly the kind of thing he might have said, and the kind of thing I would nod my head at and shamelessly misquote in one of my books. The idea resonates strongly with me—I think that's because we spend so much time and effort talking about how we focus our optics and we obsess over the sharpness of those same optics, but then we become very sloppy indeed when it comes to making choices that direct the attention of the viewer within the image itself.

In Chapter 20, we discussed this very thing, though in terms of isolation and exclusion. I want to elaborate on that important discussion by adding a further notion: the path of the eye. If you only make images in which there is a single element right in the middle of the frame and with very little space around it, not only are you likely going to have boring images (though I'm open to being proven wrong about this), but you will also have no use for this conversation. The viewer's eye will go to that single element and stay there. The rest of us who tend to rely on several elements to, for example, tell a story, provide counterbalance or tension, or create contrast need to consider how the eye moves among those elements and around the frame itself.

To consider this at all, you need to have a sense of visual mass. If you understand what elements the eye goes to first, second, third, and so on, you can plot points on the journey that the eye takes. No photographer I know would think quite so analytically about this, but if asked, most of us could trace our finger along a photograph and say, "My eye goes here, then there, and then here again." Doing so with photographs you admire is a good visual literacy exercise.

The question we need to ask is this: "Is that where I intend the eye to go?" From there, other questions and considerations make themselves available:

- Does the path of the eye imply certain relationships?

- Does that path take me around the frame or into the depth of the image, or does it lead me out of the frame, cutting short my reading of the image?

- Is that path a pleasant one that encourages a second or third reading, or is it frustrated by clutter or a lack of intentional design?

- Does that path possess the kind of energy I want the image to convey (see Chapter 14)?

- Does my attention land on the most important element first, or does it get there quickly?

- Is there a way to trick the eye into thinking the most obvious element is the most important, only to provide a surprise that is less prominent but crucial to understanding or experiencing the image?

- Is it possible that I've given too much visual weight to elements that should, in fact, be secondary or tertiary?

I want to remind you that what is important here is the value of the questions themselves. It is not important that you know the answers but that you ask the questions.

Nor is it important that you find only one answer. What's important is to keep asking and answering the questions by experimentation and a willingness to say, "I don't know. Let's find out." Some of the ideas we're exploring in this book are not often talked about among photographers, at least not with the kind of enthusiasm or insight that we seem to have about the mechanical tools of their craft.

These questions I'm proposing are questions of discovery designed to help you become more familiar with the other tools of this craft: creativity, composition, storytelling, and an awareness of your own vision and voice. I would argue these are at least as important as the physical tools we hold in our hands, if not more so, and they will not be discovered with the same kind of mathematical, precise approach that our cameras and lenses can be.

Every element in the frame pulls the eye to one degree or another.

Don't be discouraged if your first efforts to answer these questions feel clumsy. When we learn a new language (which isn't far from what many of you reading this book are doing), the words and ideas feel wrong on the tongue. They are unfamiliar and lack the depth of meaning that they'll acquire once we use them for a while. What is important is that you ask the questions, that you be okay with the uncertainty, and that you be open to surprising yourself with the answers.

The world has enough photographs that show us what something looks like. Show us how it feels.

22
How Does It Feel?

MAGNUM PHOTOGRAPHER DAVID ALAN HARVEY has been quoted as saying, "Don't shoot what it looks like, shoot what it feels like," a plea to not only shoot from the heart but, it seems, to *interpret* the subject rather than capture merely a literal representation of it. That interpretation, if it's going to have any kind of feeling, must include a consideration of the mood of the scene and our available choices for conveying that mood in the final photograph.

With few exceptions, the world has enough photographs that show us what something looks like. We're drowning in them. Cameras are more present in our lives than ever before, which has led to a flood of pictures *of* things rather than pictures *about* things. Here is a building. Here is a duck. Here is another picture of a kitten. And it may be the most incredible building, the most beautiful duck, and the cutest kitten. But the qualities of those things don't come across in the photograph unless we make it so. That is true of mood as well. If you want mood in your image, you've got to make the decision to put it there.

It would be easy to overthink this and to dive deep into an inventory of proven mood-enhancers, such as backlight, lens flare, or warmer colour temperatures. But I think the strongest approach is to go with your gut. Mood is about feeling, so how do you feel about this scene? What one word or sentence best describes what's going on emotionally for you that makes you want to photograph this experience? Is it warm and bright? Is it cold and rainy? Does the scene feel lonely or nostalgic? Maybe you can't put it into words, but your awareness of the mood drives the search for a way to express it. There's nothing wrong with thinking, "I'll know it when I see it," as long as you go looking for it.

There are more questions about mood than perhaps any of the other ideas we've discussed. I think this is because so many of those ideas represent possible ways of bringing mood to play more powerfully in our images. Two of our first big questions—"What is the light doing?" and "What does colour contribute?"— can be repurposed here. What is the light doing to establish mood, and how can I best use that? What does the colour contribute to the mood, and how can I amplify it?

Here are further questions to nudge forward your exploration of mood:

- Could shooting into the light, rather than with it, give me silhouettes or lens flare, and how would that amplify the mood?

- Could over- or underexposing contribute a greater sense of mood that is darker or lighter? Sometimes all you need to do is stop listening to the camera and go darker or lighter.

- What does the weather contribute to the mood? Should I photo-graph this subject in weather that is, itself, atmospheric and carries emotional weight?

- What can I do to make the most of that weather? Could I photograph through the raindrops on the window? Would it be so bad if I got some rain on my lens and shot through that?

- What does my colour palette contribute to the mood? Am I aware of the possibilities within my camera or in post-production to warm or cool that colour palette and increase the emotional pull of the image? Setting the camera's white balance to Shady or Cloudy, for example, will warm the scene, which will have an effect on how the image feels.

- Would black and white create a stronger mood, perhaps attaching the subject to emotions of nostalgia and memory? Should I subdue a colour palette that runs against the emotional charge I'm trying to create?

- Can I recognize dark shadows and use them as compositional elements to create mystery?

- What kind of mood would candlelight or soft window light create?

- Would a slow shutter speed and some motion blur contribute to a more emotional and less literal interpretation of the scene?

- Would a shallow depth of field and out-of-focus highlights (bokeh) help establish a softer, more romantic mood? Would a little dust on the lens exaggerate this?

- Would the image feel different if I used a much different point of view? A safari photograph shot low and through out-of-focus grasses will go a long way toward creating a feeling of empathy with predator or prey. A portrait shot from outside a window might feel creepy and voyeuristic. A photograph made in the water, with the lens half in and half out of the water, would feel immersive. It's all about the feeling.

Learning how to answer these questions begins with awareness of the mood itself, then a willingness to take risks to convey that mood. Most images with strong mood require us to break the so-called rules, to try something new: move the camera, photograph in inclement weather, over- or underexpose relative to what the camera wants, or use white balance creatively to make something emotive.

The big question that remains is, "Is it appropriate?" Does the mood work with or against the subject? Is there alignment between the subject and the emotional weight, or mood, that you're conveying? Some subjects just aren't happy. Some aren't nostalgic or mysterious or romantic, and trying to make them so won't be giving them their best expression. It'll just cause confusion and dissonance.

The best way to learn about your own preferences in mood and the tools to express that mood is to study photographs with this in mind. Look at photographs that have, for you, a sense of mood. What is that mood? How did the photographer accomplish that mood visually? What choices did they make about light, moment, colour, point of view? Becoming aware of these possibilities, as well as your own tastes, will give you a new visual vocabulary with which to write emotion and atmosphere into your photographs.

Most images with strong mood require us to break the so-called rules.

Next spread: Varanasi, India, 2018

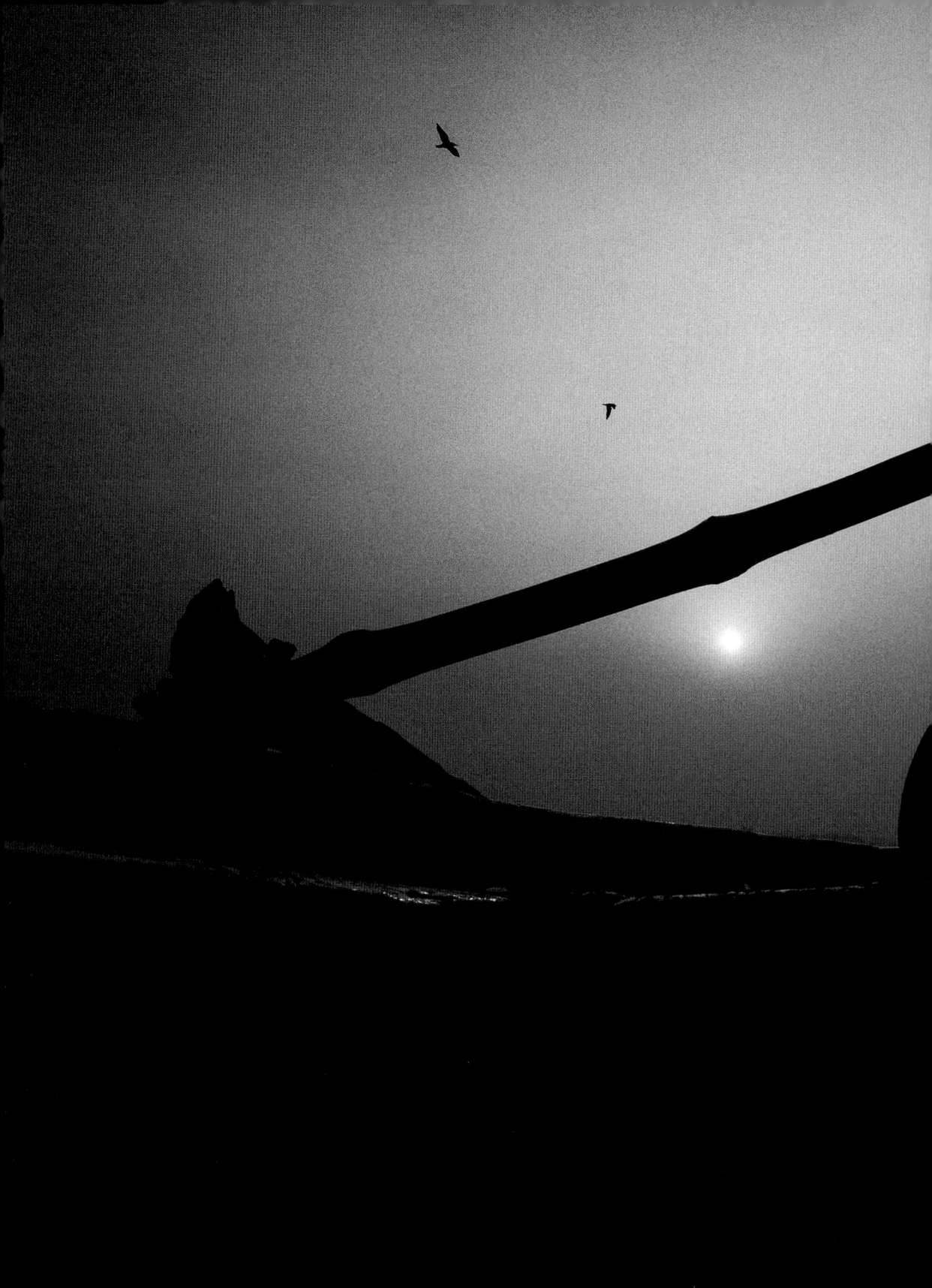

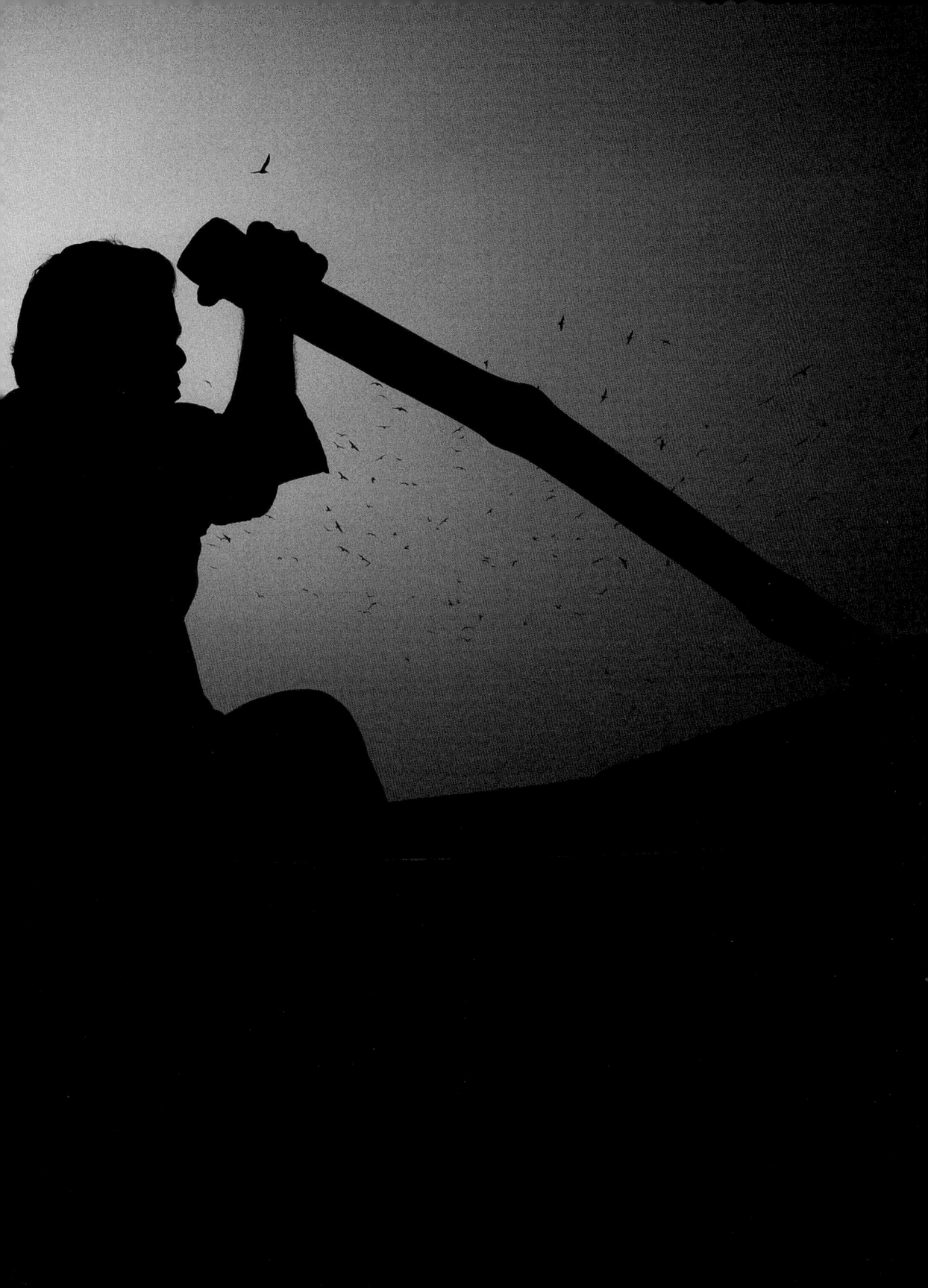

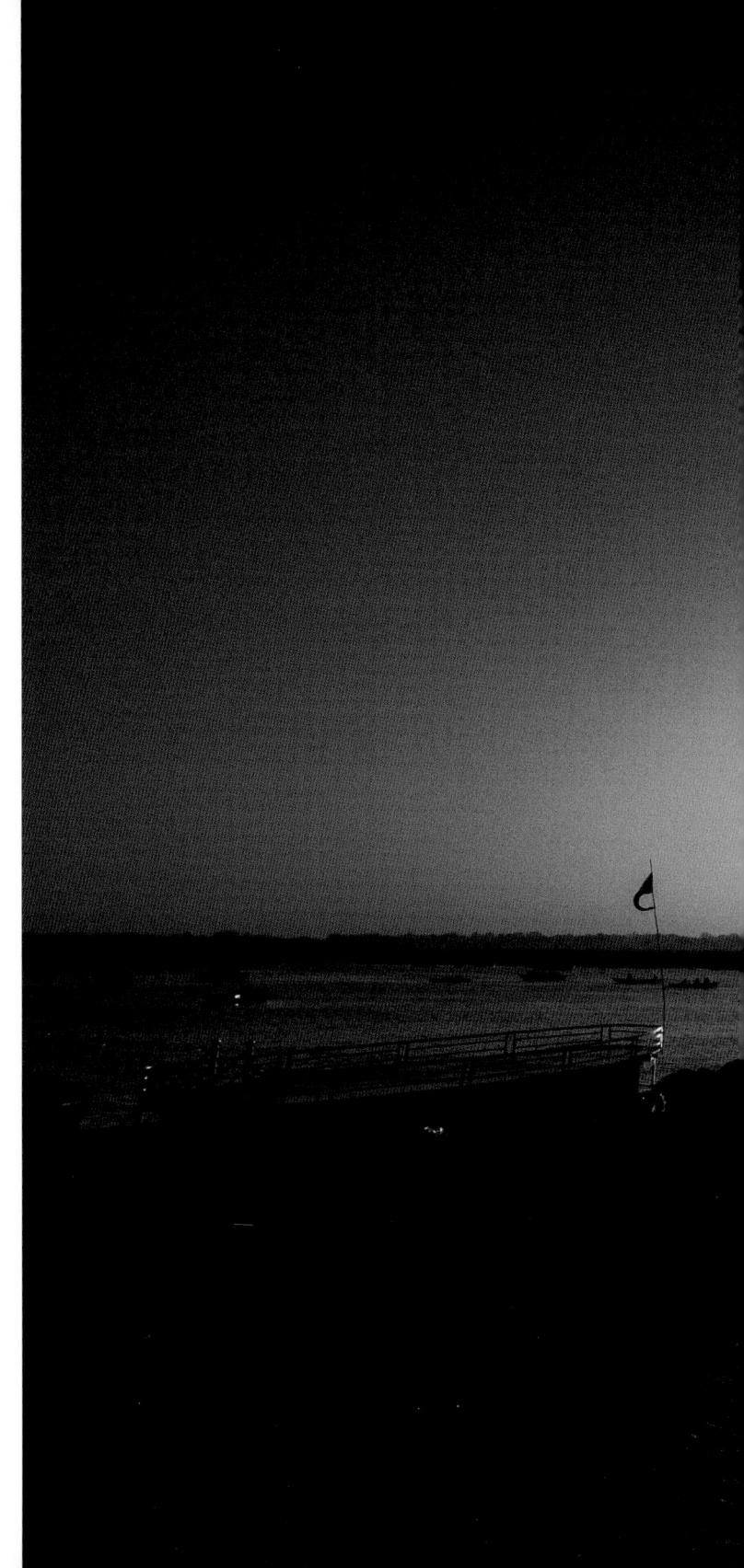

Varanasi, India, 2018

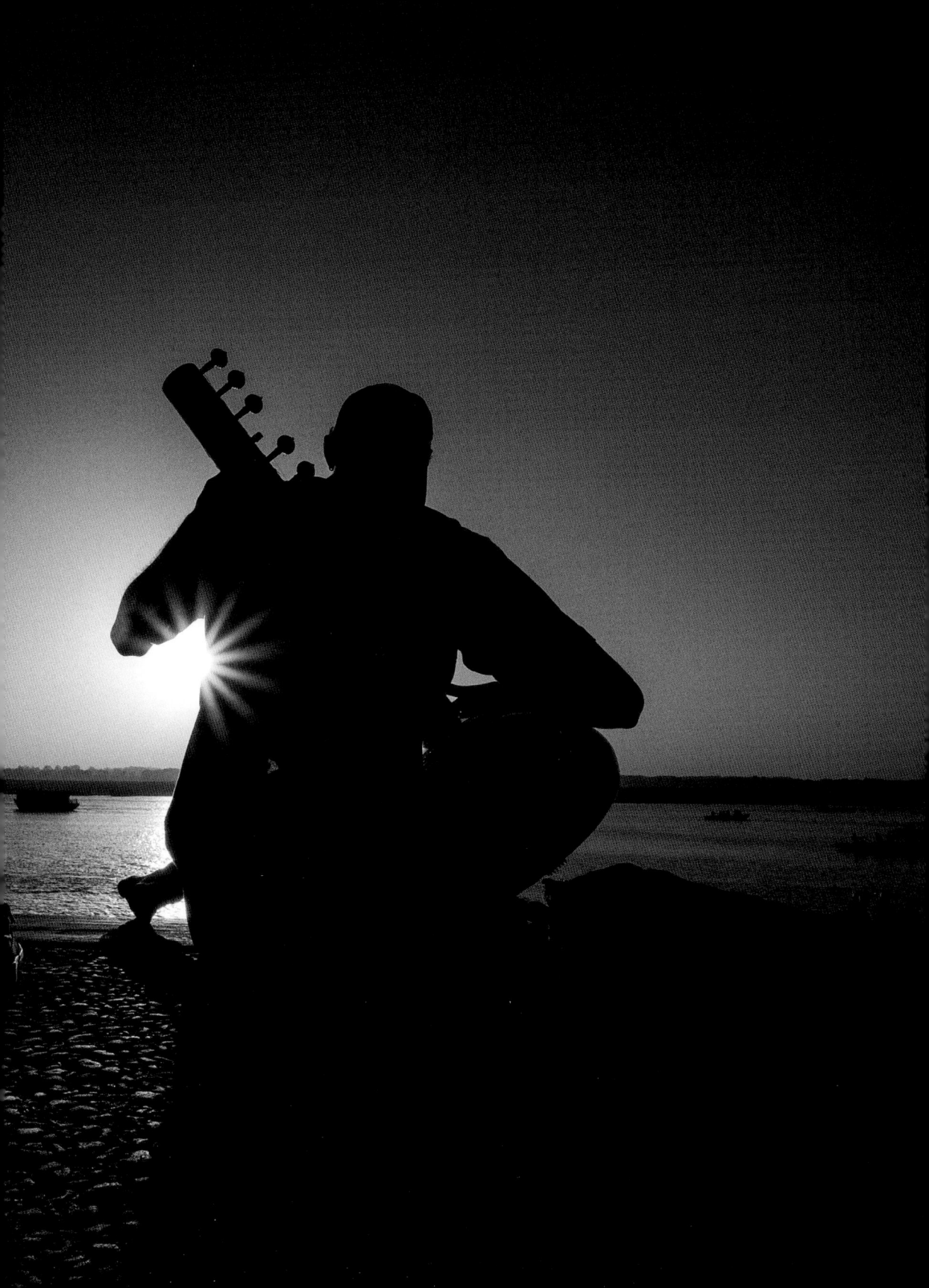

Mystery relies on something more powerful than any camera or technique: imagination.

23
Where's the Mystery?

THERE'S A TENDENCY TO WANT TO SHOW IT ALL in a photograph. To capture all the details, to show what lies in the shadows. But what if so much information comes at the loss of impact? What if the photograph succeeds most powerfully in the absence of detail and the presence of mystery?

Mystery relies on something more powerful than any camera or technique: imagination. The human imagination is hardwired to fill in the blanks. We seem incapable of leaving things unresolved, so our minds try to solve the problem, to make connections. We fear the unknown, and that fear has evolved into a powerful need to understand what we don't know and to peer into dark corners. The power of mystery is its ability to engage the imagination. It's why good filmmakers don't show the monster right away, and it's why magicians don't tell their secrets. The experience is in the not knowing. The monster is never scarier on the screen than what our own imagination can conjure, drawn from our fears. The magic trick always loses its wonder when the secret is told— from the miraculous to the mundane with just one new detail.

Could leaving part of your story untold make that story stronger? Perhaps not always, but there is room in our photography for a little more mystery and ambiguity. Any image that prompts questions—unless there is a strong need for clarity, as is the case in journalism—is likely to be explored further in the search for visual clues and remembered longer as the viewer's mind works to resolve it.

There are a lot of ways to engage the imagination in a photograph. Here are some questions that can spark ideas for incorporating mystery into your own work:

- How can I use shadows to hide details, perhaps by seeking out high-contrast scenes and deliberately exposing for the highlights?

- Could I use the same technique to represent people in silhouette, hiding the details of their identity?

- Could I tell only part of the story by intentionally excluding part of the subject from the frame? Would an arm sticking into the frame and pointing at something make the viewer wonder to whom the arm belongs and why it is pointing, more than if I included the whole person? Would just the back half of the horse leaving the frame make the viewer wonder where it was going?

- Can I leave room for the unexplained with my choice of moment, making the viewer wonder what that person is doing because of an odd gesture or expression?

- What juxtapositions or contrasts might create an implied non sequitur? Drawing attention to elements that are out of context is one way to do this.

- Would leaving key elements unfocused or blurred by motion have more impact than a sharper representation?

- Could I use composition and my ability to control the placement of elements by moving the camera allow me to block the view of other elements, hiding some detail I might otherwise have shown?

- Could I abstract the subject by getting very close or by using multiple exposures?

In 1979, the first of a best-selling series of kids' books was published. The series was called *Choose Your Own Adventure*, and it gave kids like me a chance to be part of the story. As a reader, you were not only the main character, but you had agency—a chance to determine the choices and destiny of that character. You would get to a point in the story at which the protagonist had a choice to make. If you chose to do one thing, you were directed to page X; if you chose the alternative, you were sent to page Y. You had no idea what the result would be, and each book gave you enough alternatives that for several readings, the story was different.

It's a long shot to suggest that our photographs can do this, too, but the effect can be similar. Resist the urge to tell it all, to answer my questions completely. Leave a gap that invites me to fill in my own story. Leave a moment unresolved. Let the shadows invite me to explore them.

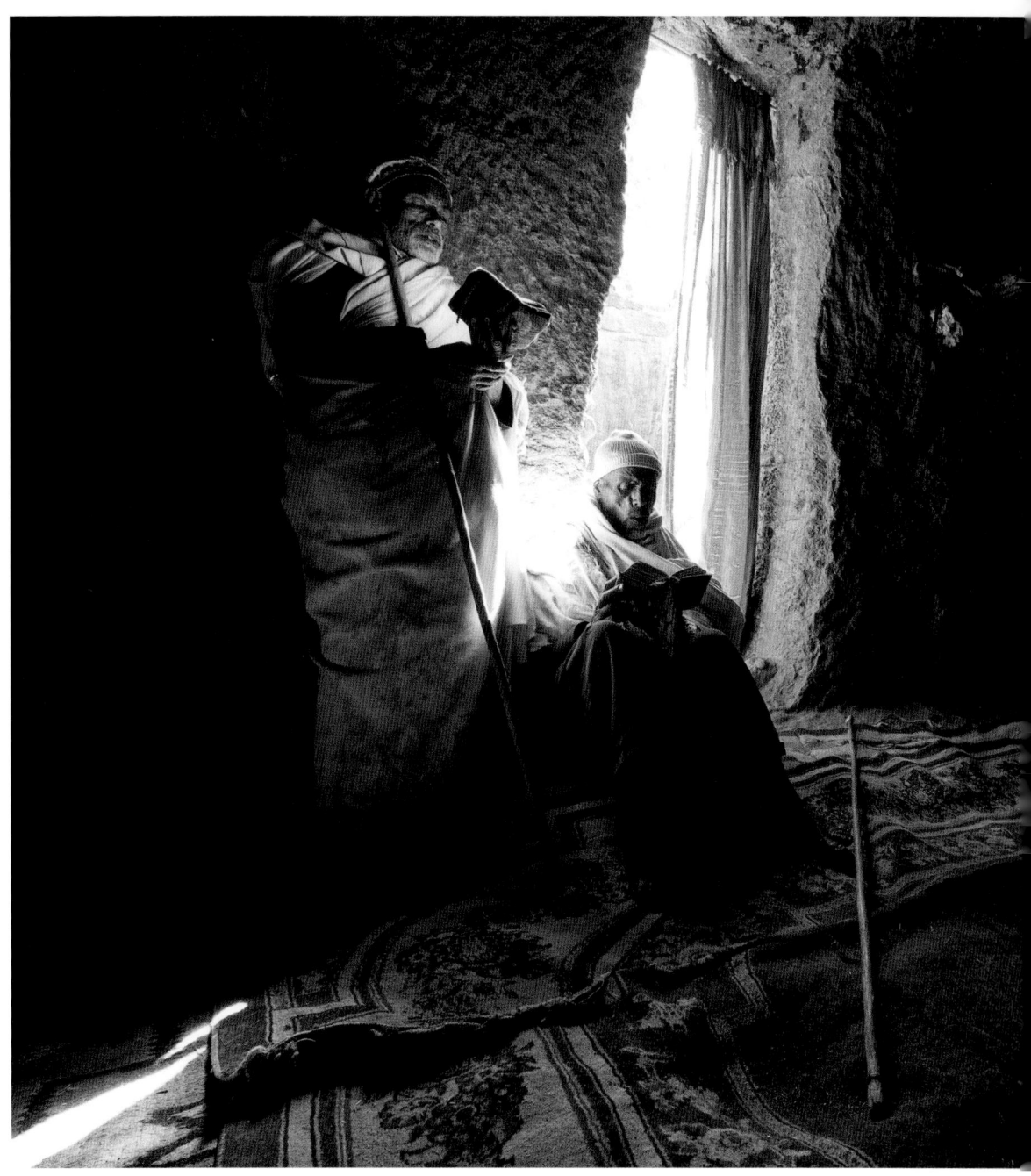

Lalibela, Ethiopia, 2017

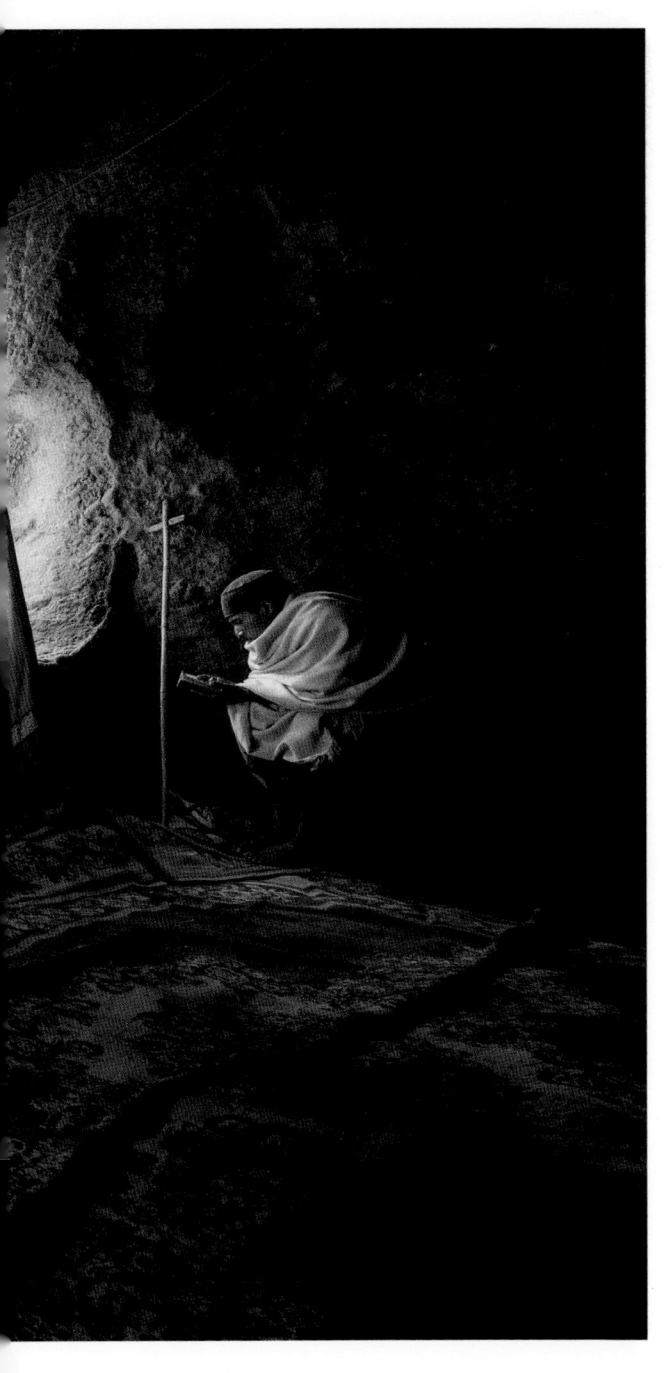

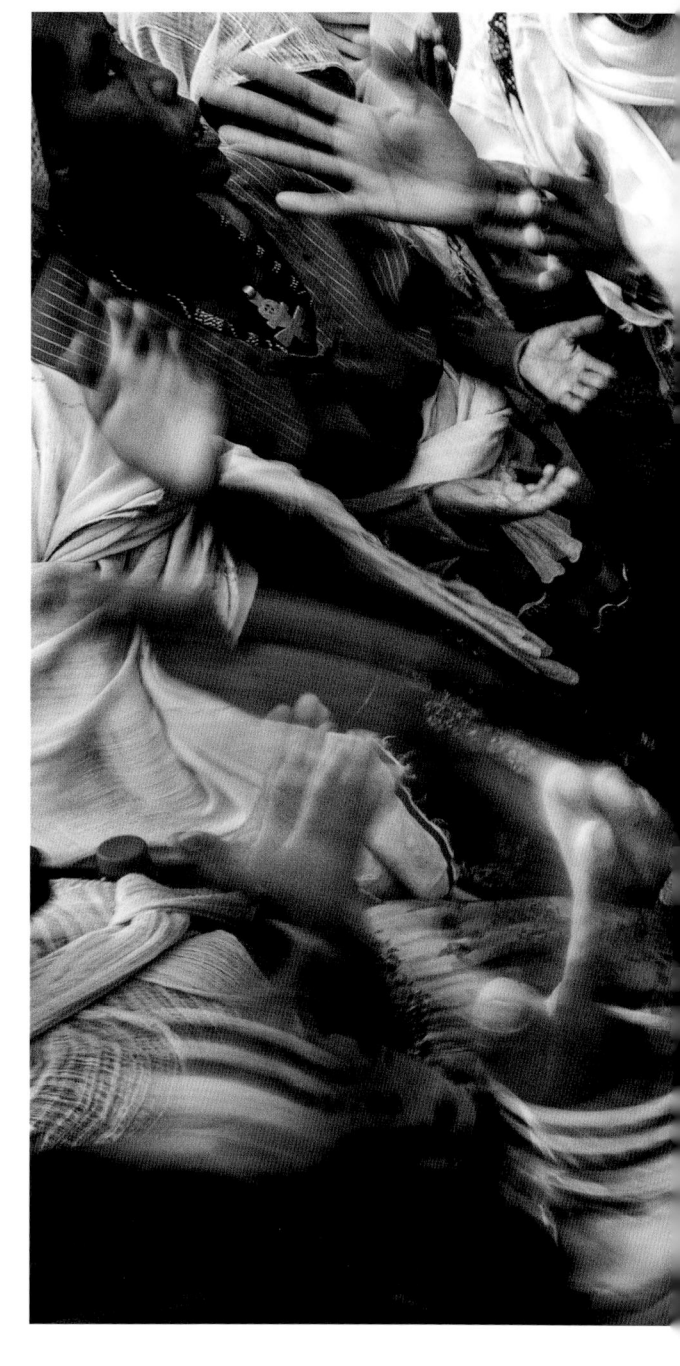

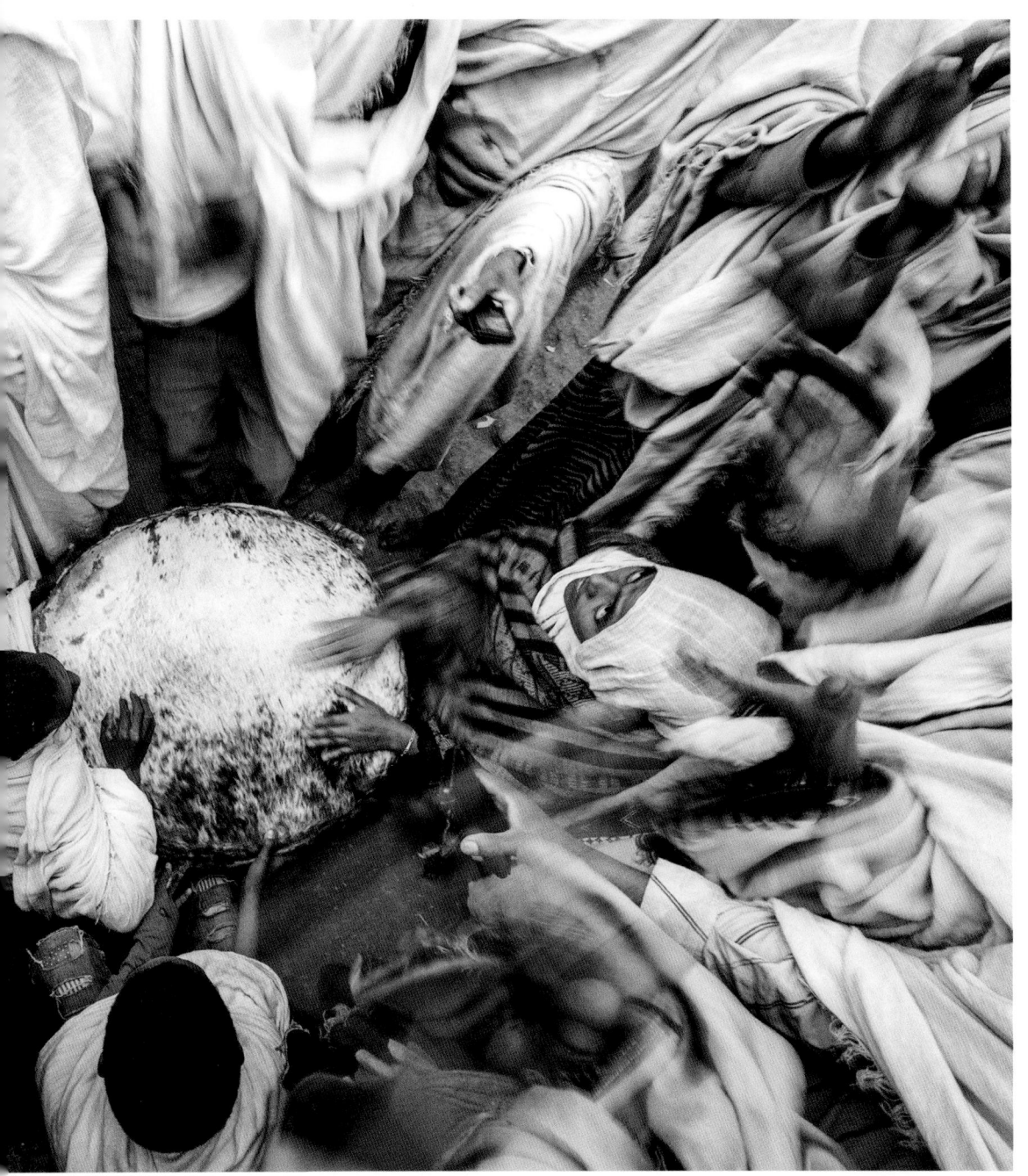

Lalibela, Ethiopia, 2017

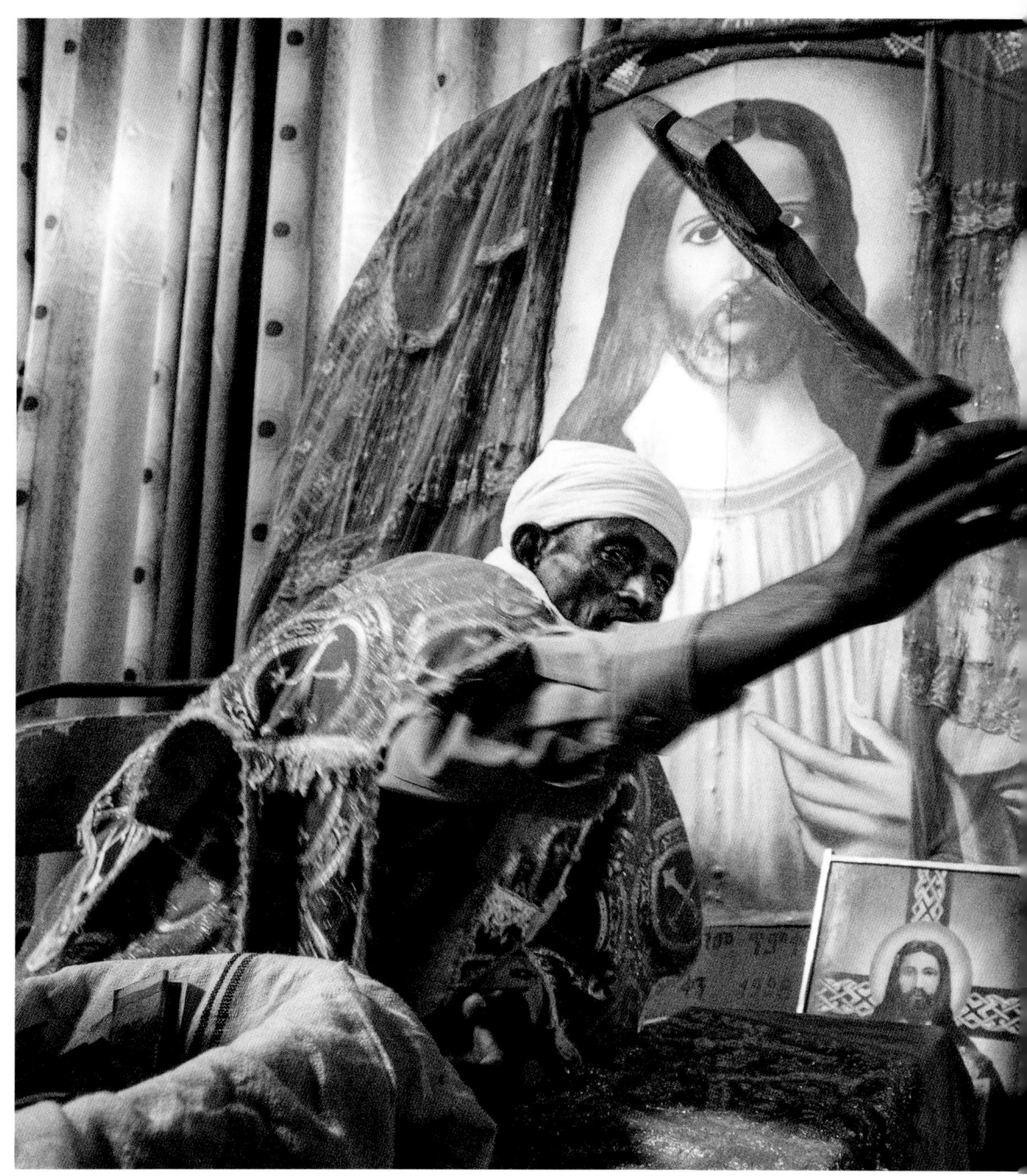

Lalibela, Ethiopia, 2017

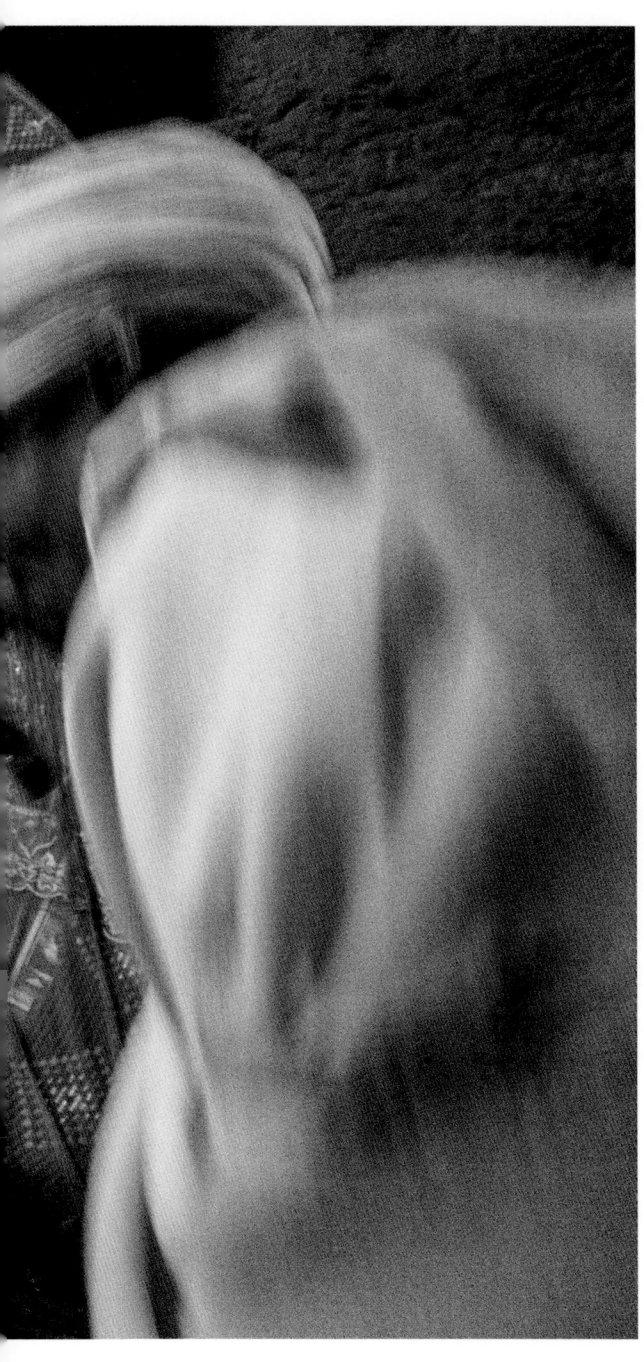

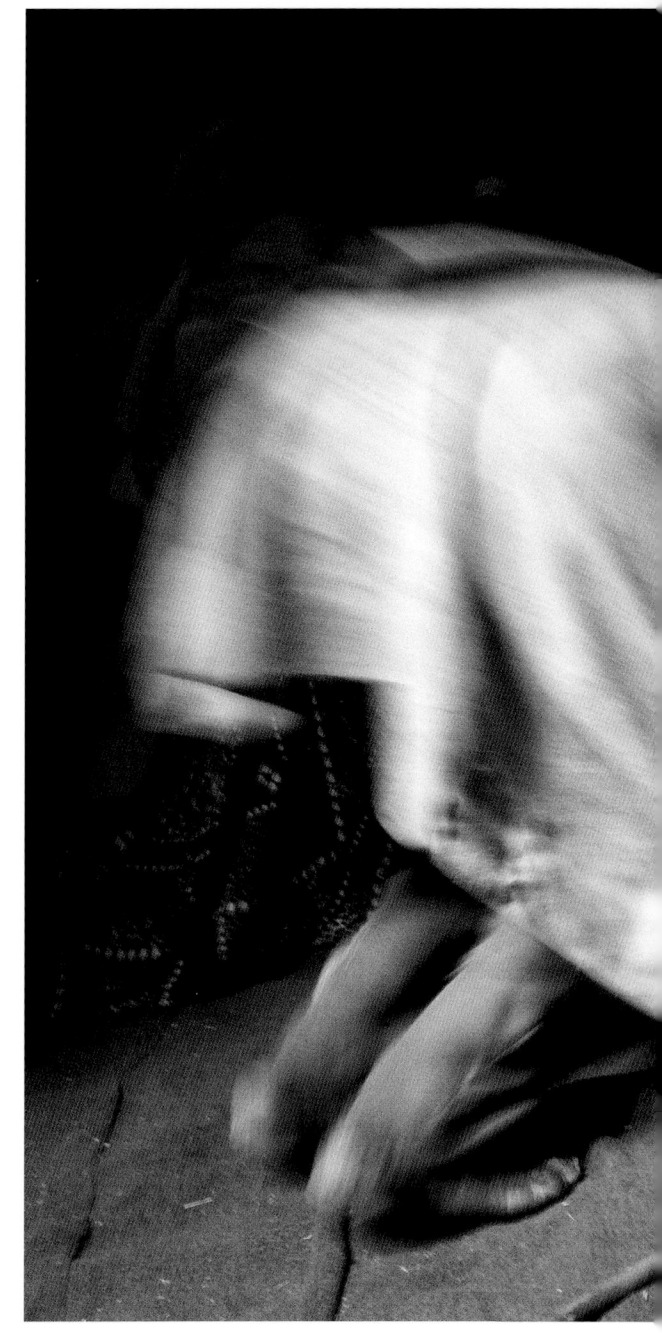

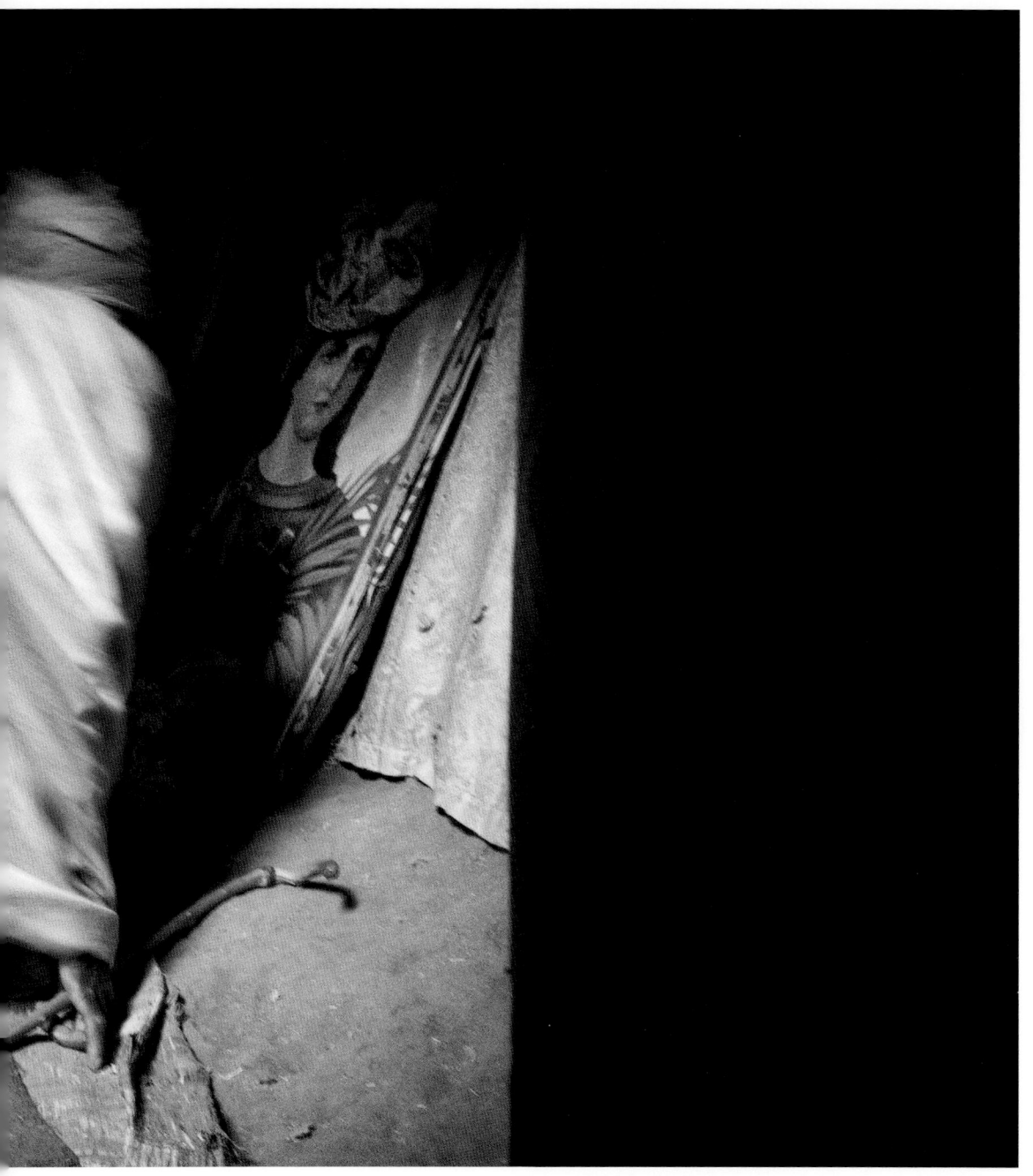

Lalibela, Ethiopia, 2017

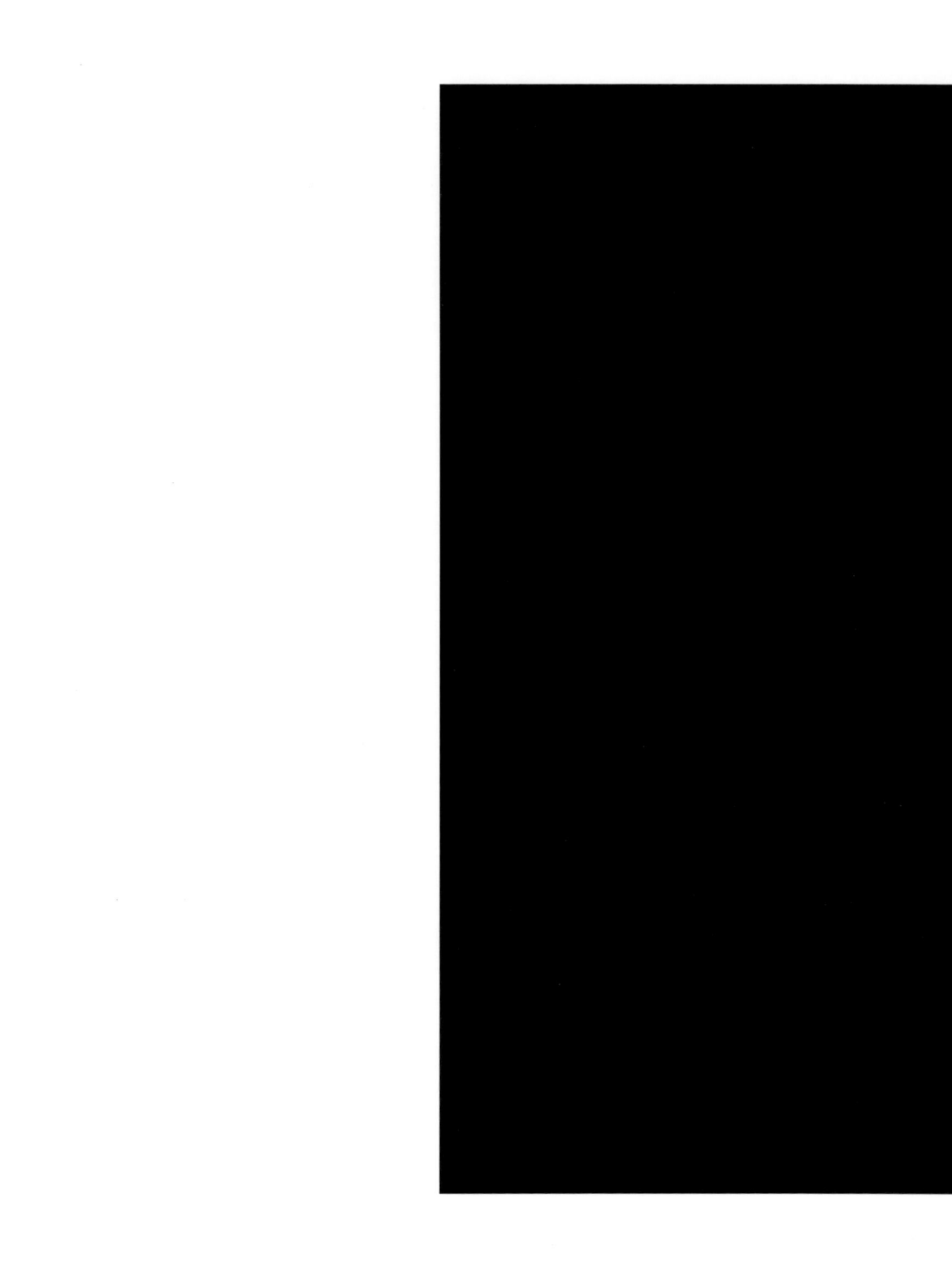

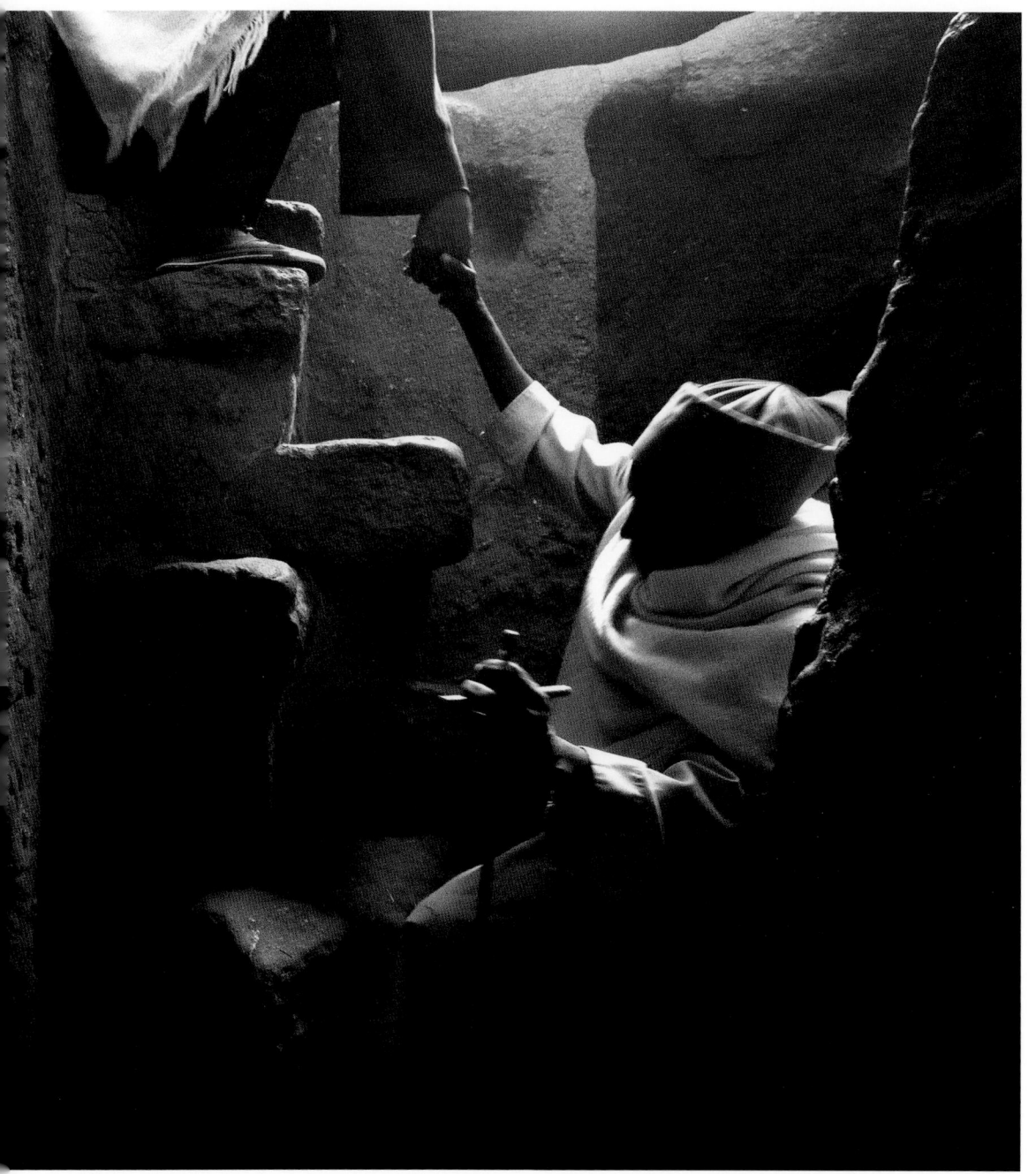

Lalibela, Ethiopia, 2017

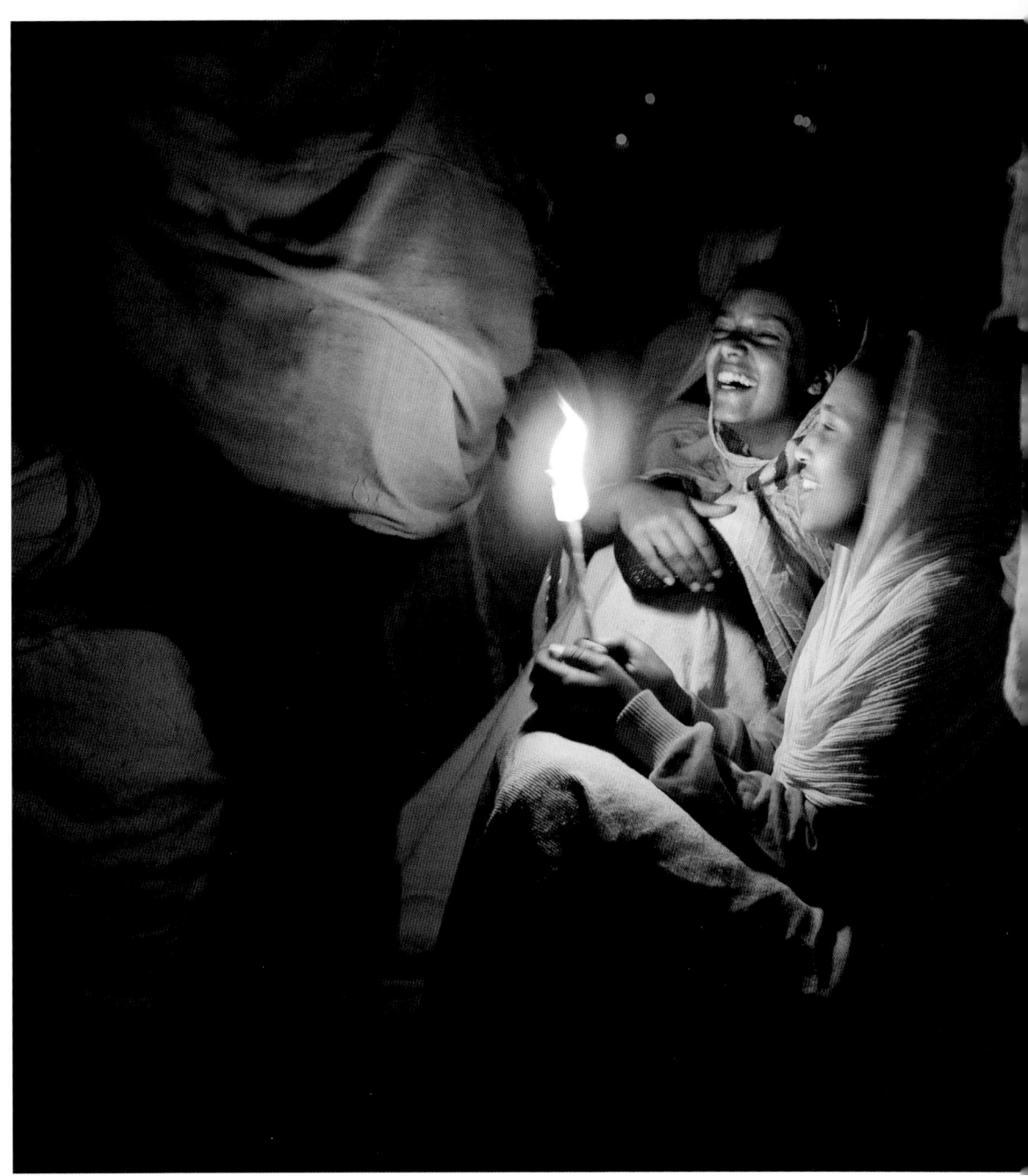

Lalibela, Ethiopia, 2017

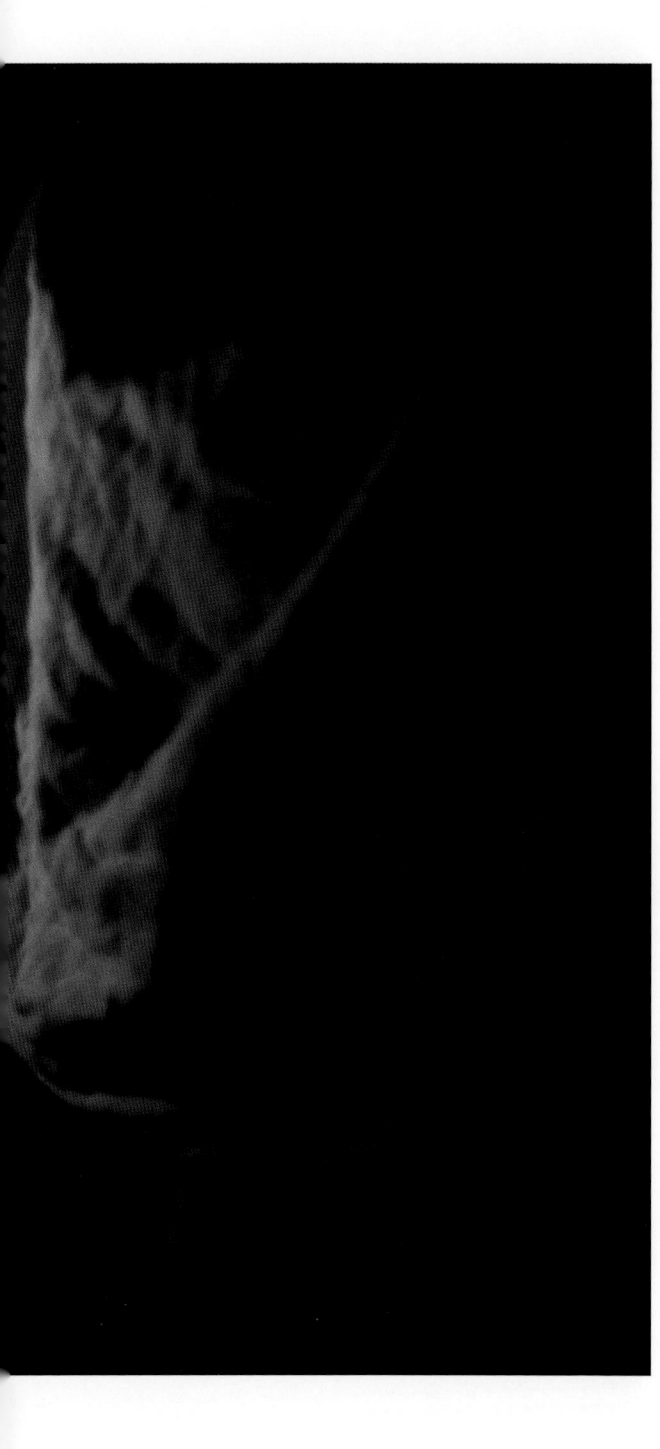

Our memory makes some photographs stronger because it draws from what we believe was.

24
Remember When?

SOMETIMES WHAT WE RESPOND TO in a photograph isn't as much a matter of artifice as we would like to think. A photograph of Marilyn Monroe may not be well-composed or well-timed, but we respond all the same because, well, Marilyn Monroe. Of course, we know that the photograph could be more cleverly composed, that there are better photographs of Marilyn out there, but it's irrelevant because we aren't, in that moment, really looking at the photograph. And we're not really looking at Marilyn.

We're looking at memory.

Many of the best photographs we make will be much more than the sum of their parts. They will be more than the lines and the moments and the colours, though of course these all have their part in making the photograph what it is. They will be powerful because nostalgia and memory are powerful. In the same way that mystery and imagination make a photograph stronger in our minds than it is on paper (because they draw from what we believe could be), our memory makes some photographs stronger because it draws from what we believe was.

I word it that way because memory is a tricky thing. It's unreliable, for one. It's unreliable because memory isn't really about recalling events with objective accuracy; it's about retelling stories that we create based on our own shaky and subjective recall of those events—stories that change with the telling.

Why this matters is that photographs can tap into something powerful when they hint at these deeper memories. It's the reason there is a booming industry in the retro or vintage plug-ins for Photoshop or Lightroom that allow us to emulate certain film stocks from eras that make us feel a certain way. As far back as when George Eastman was making and selling film at the turn of the 1900s, certain films had different characteristics—some with more grain, some with different colour casts and contrast. Different cameras and lenses had certain characteristics, too, and when someone now imposes a white vignette on an otherwise beautiful image made with a $5,000 camera that couldn't make a white vignette if it tried, they are usually doing it to anchor the aesthetic of the image to a certain time period. They are hoping nostalgia will kick in for the viewer. The same is true of the borders some photographers put around their images—borders that were only present because of a certain kind of film. It's a subtle nod to the nostalgia of predigital days.

Whether you choose to use techniques that are this heavy-handed or not, what is important to ask is this: "As powerful as nostalgia can be, is it enough?" Is the nostalgia of a white vignette or the colour cast that replicates a Kodachrome slide sufficient to carry the image?

Before you answer, let me remind you (and myself as I write this) that it may well be. For some people, that is enough. But the images from back-when, the ones we love from our youth or even an earlier era for which we wish we'd been alive—they didn't succeed or find a place in our memories because of that vignette or colour cast. The substance of the photograph was still the subject. So when we rely on these effects, when they are not authentic to our means of working and are merely a style, we risk the possibility that people are not responding to the photograph itself, but only to their memories of similar snapshots; a copy of a copy that reminds them of something else. That's not usually enough for photographers hoping to find and express a vision of something authentic.

That doesn't mean, however, that nostalgia can't be used well and in authentic ways. Certain films, or emulations of those films, can add a layer of nostalgia over a story already well-told, creating more powerful photographs by tapping into the sense of "remember when." Cinematographers choose colour palettes this way, anchoring the telling of their story to a certain time. When done subtly, it's powerful, allowing us to access memories we forgot we have and the feelings we associate with them. The TV show *Stranger Things* is thematically rooted in the 1980s, and the colour grading used throughout that show creates a strong nostalgic connection for anyone, like me, who grew up in those years—or even for those who didn't but who want to feel that sense of nostalgia. The show doesn't rely on this nostalgia to succeed—it relies on great storytelling—but the nostalgic connection makes the story stronger, anchoring visual cues to memory and emotion.

Here's the second idea I want to explore in a chapter that is rapidly becoming a bit of an outlier but also perhaps a thoughtful diversion: some of your best photographs won't be very good at all, and that's okay. Is it possible that the pressure on photographers to create work that others will consider worthwhile, or in which they will find merit, is stopping you from making images that will eventually have the strongest and most authentic nostalgic connection for you?

Indulge me in a moment of melodrama: If your home was on fire, which photographs (assuming you print them at all) would you grab on the way out? If you knew you were in your final days and had a chance to look at the photographs that, when it's all winding down, meant the most to you, which ones would you look at? The perfectly sharp, the well-composed, the ones that got the most likes on social media or scored the best at the camera club? I doubt it.

I have a photograph of my father near me. He's sitting in his beloved but ancient Jeep. A car man his whole life, he was the most "Dad-like" when tinkering with, talking about, or driving one of his projects. I made this image several years ago. I planned to make another on my next visit, but my father died in November 2018, before that visit could happen. This photograph matters more to me than you can ever know, anchored as it is in a lifetime mixed with the memories and regrets of a boy and his father.

When push comes to shove, the most important photographs of our lives will be the casual snapshots. And I'd be remiss if I didn't acknowledge this and encourage you to take it to heart. Sometimes we get so focused on the perfect images, the clever images, the tack-sharp images, and the award-winners, that we forget photography can be so deeply human an activity, and we risk losing the profound and the poetic in pursuit of the perfect.

The question that suggests itself is a simple one: Are you photographing the moments and people most important to you? When is the last time you photographed your aging parents, your children, or Sunday lunches with the family? Will anyone capture those moments? Our memories are powerful, but we overestimate them. We credit them with greater abilities than they really have. They fail. They fade. We think we will always be able to say, "Remember when . . . " when, in fact, one day we will not.

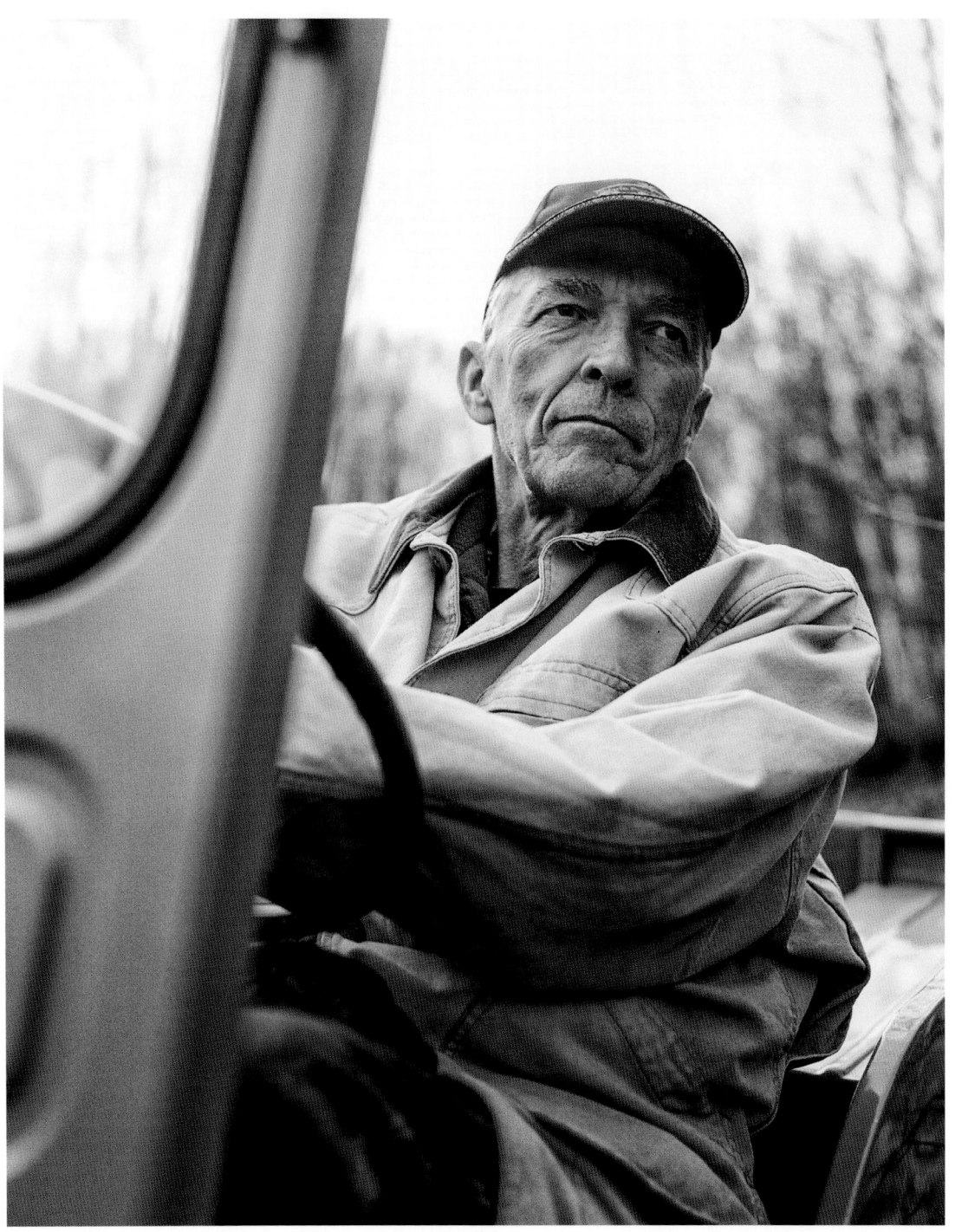

Richard Duchemin, 2011

Using symbols in our
photographs offers
us a good way to say
more with less.

25
Can I Use Symbols?

IN A PHOTOGRAPH, EVERYTHING MEANS SOMETHING, as all the words in a book mean something. Some mean more than others. Some are just necessary for holding it all together. And some carry impact on a level approaching the spiritual.

When an element in a photograph represents a larger idea or value, it's symbolic. And using symbols in our photographs offers us a good way to say more with less. When symbols are juxtaposed with contrasting ideas, they can stir deep emotion and imply certain perspectives. The flag is one such symbol in many countries. The crucifix is another. Combine the two, and depending on the rest of the image, you are making a potentially powerful statement, not just about the flag or about the crucifix, but about the values they represent.

What makes this challenging is that not all symbols represent the same values to everyone. One country's flag may mean one thing to its citizens and another thing entirely to the citizens of another country. Similarly, the cross, or any other religious symbol, is likely to have shades of meaning for many people, from comfort to its extreme opposite. Ask two people how they respond to the hammer and sickle symbol, and the reactions may be very different. This is, of course, true of any photograph as well, and I think this variety of interpretations of symbols is a strength, not a weakness. But it's something to be aware of.

Symbolism is not limited to the obvious, the nationalistic, or the specifically religious. As I prepared to write this chapter, I spent some time online researching symbolism in photographs, mostly just looking at a variety of symbols and what I inferred to be their intended meaning. Skeletons and skulls represent death. Barbed wire, bars, caged birds, and ropes represent captivity and entrapment. Other meanings were implied with butterflies, eyes, crowns, hearts, trees, mountains, waves, marionettes, masks, tears, wolves, lions, the moon and stars—not to mention certain colours and implied shapes. And that was just in the first couple minutes of searching. Some symbols were used powerfully and well, while others not only bordered on cliché, but crossed that border and camped out. It's not my place to say how you should use symbols, only to help make you more aware of them as visual tools and more able to perceive their presence.

Artists have been using symbols since early man painted figures on caves. Not only do we use them, we create them. While the list of established symbols is long, there is no reason the elements in your photograph cannot mean something more to you than what they are on the surface. It is your exploration of those elements and what they mean to you specifically that gives them power in your photographs.

In some of my photographs, sharks are just sharks. In others, they represent my fears. In some images, people are just people, but in others, they are silhouetted and abstracted, and symbolically, they represent me. They may never mean that to you, which is fine because I make my art first for myself. Making art gives you an opportunity to explore and experiment, and even if no one ever sees in it what you do, the symbol remains powerful. And, chances are, if it means something to you and you've wrestled with it to give it that meaning in the photograph, it will likely mean something to a viewer of your image. Here are a few questions to get you thinking about symbols in your photographs:

- What accepted or implied symbols might be present in this scene, and would including or excluding them allow me to say more about the subject?

- How can I juxtapose that symbol with contrasting ideas in order to say something unexpected or invite a reader of the photograph to explore an idea?

- What elements exist in my photograph that might function as symbols? Is a lone tree on a hill more than what it literally is? Could a rock symbolize stability?

Ultimately, there's got to be a reason why you point your lens at some things more than others. What do those things represent to you, and can you explore the importance and meaning of those things by investigating them as symbols in your photographs? On a very basic level, you're accepting and experimenting with the fact that certain things remind you of certain other things, and you're playing with those associations.

Is there a place for this kind of play in your photography? I suspect that, without you knowing it, there already is. Continue to explore it. The more you look for symbols, the more you will recognize them and use them to give different meanings to your subject.

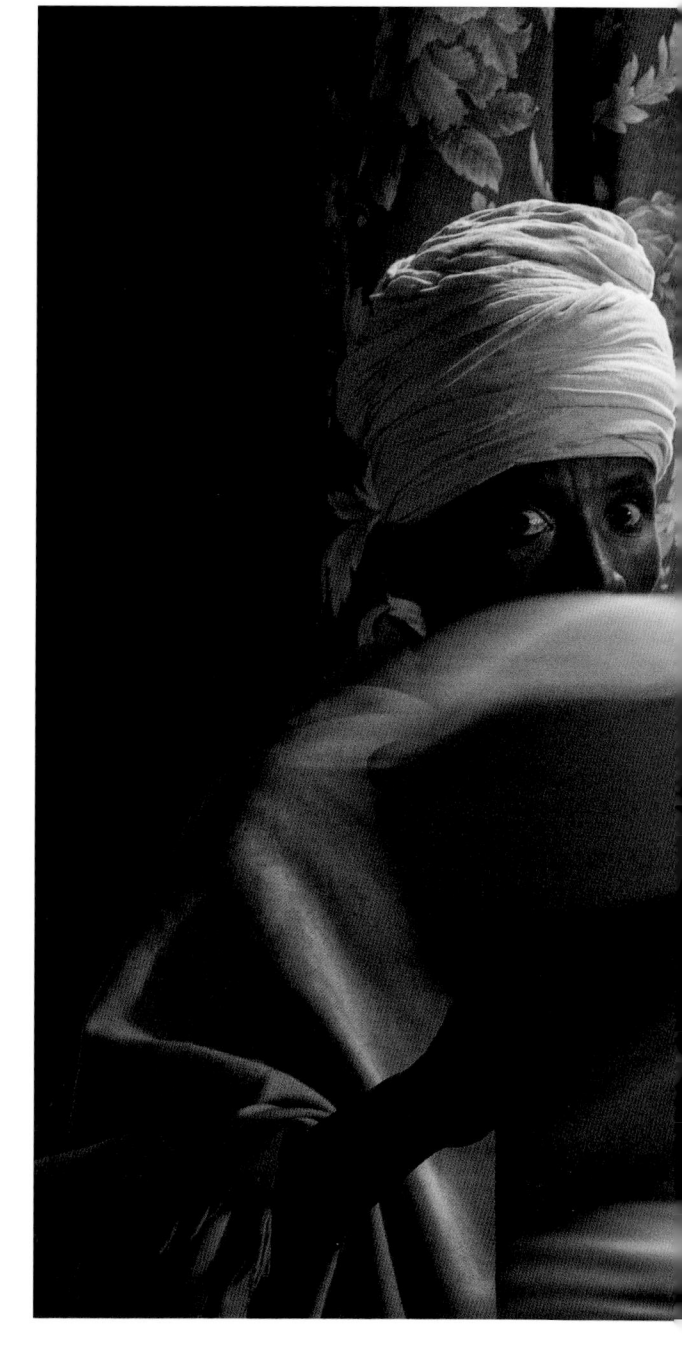

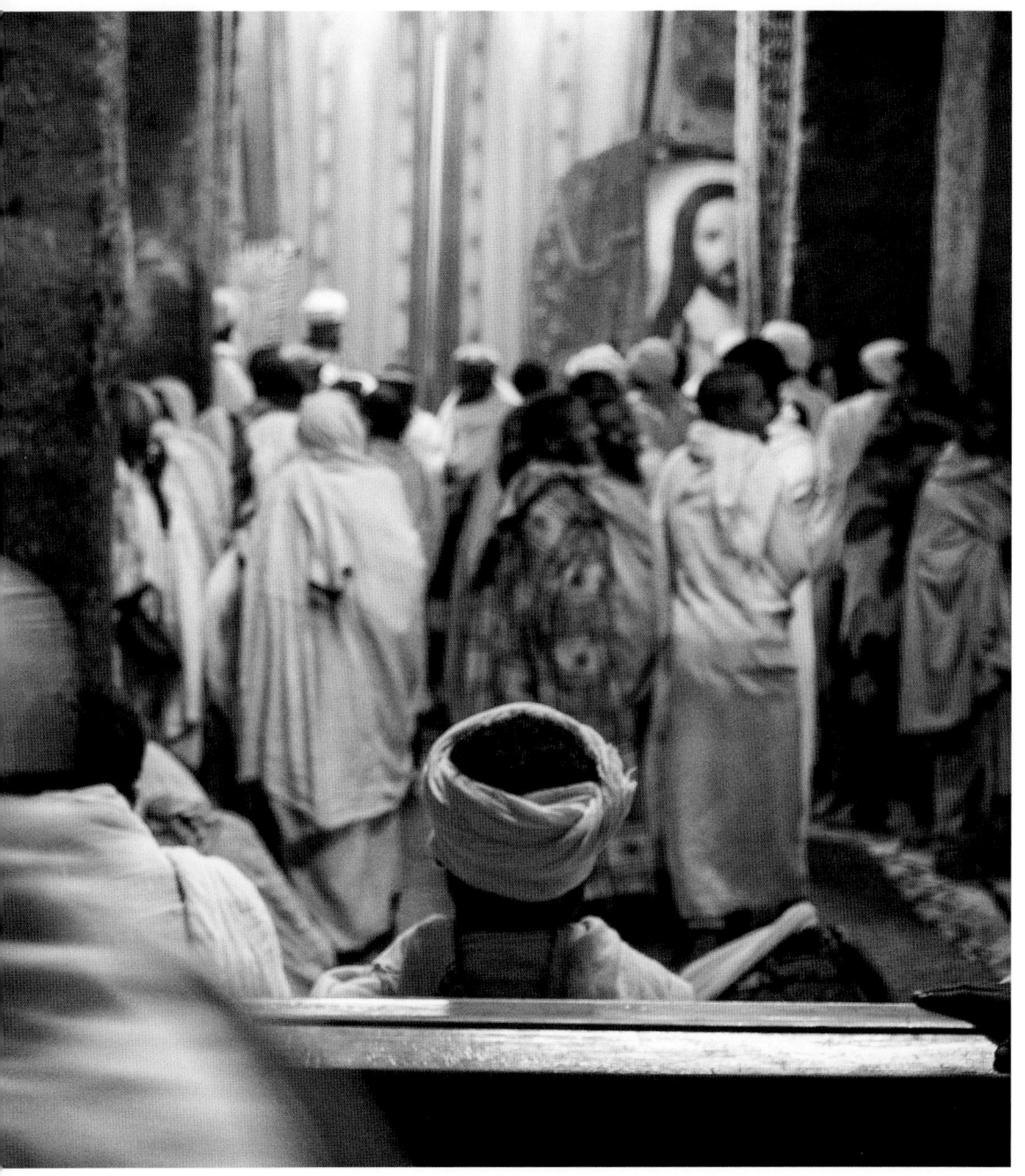

Lalibela, Ethiopia, 2017

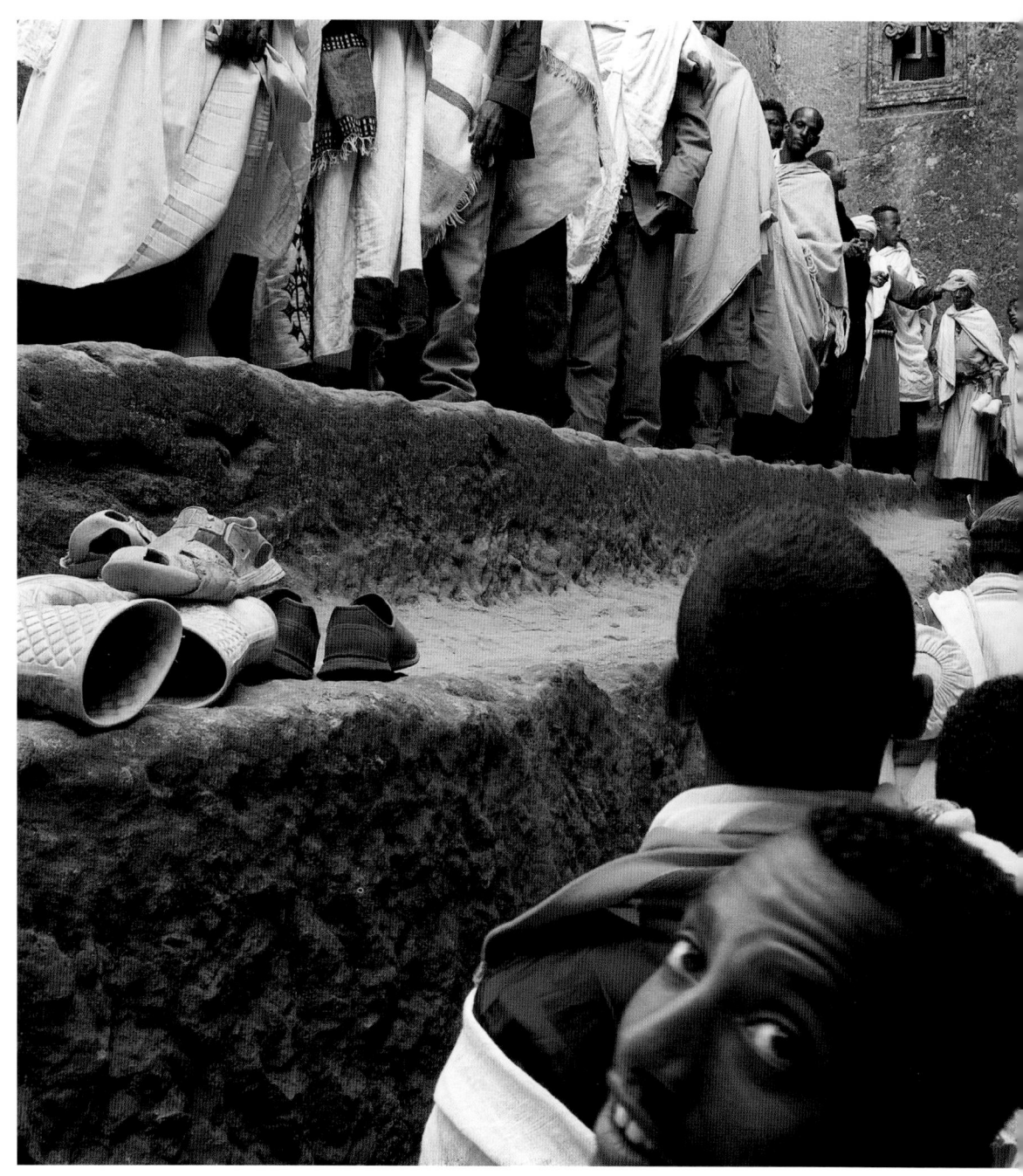

Lalibela, Ethiopia, 2017

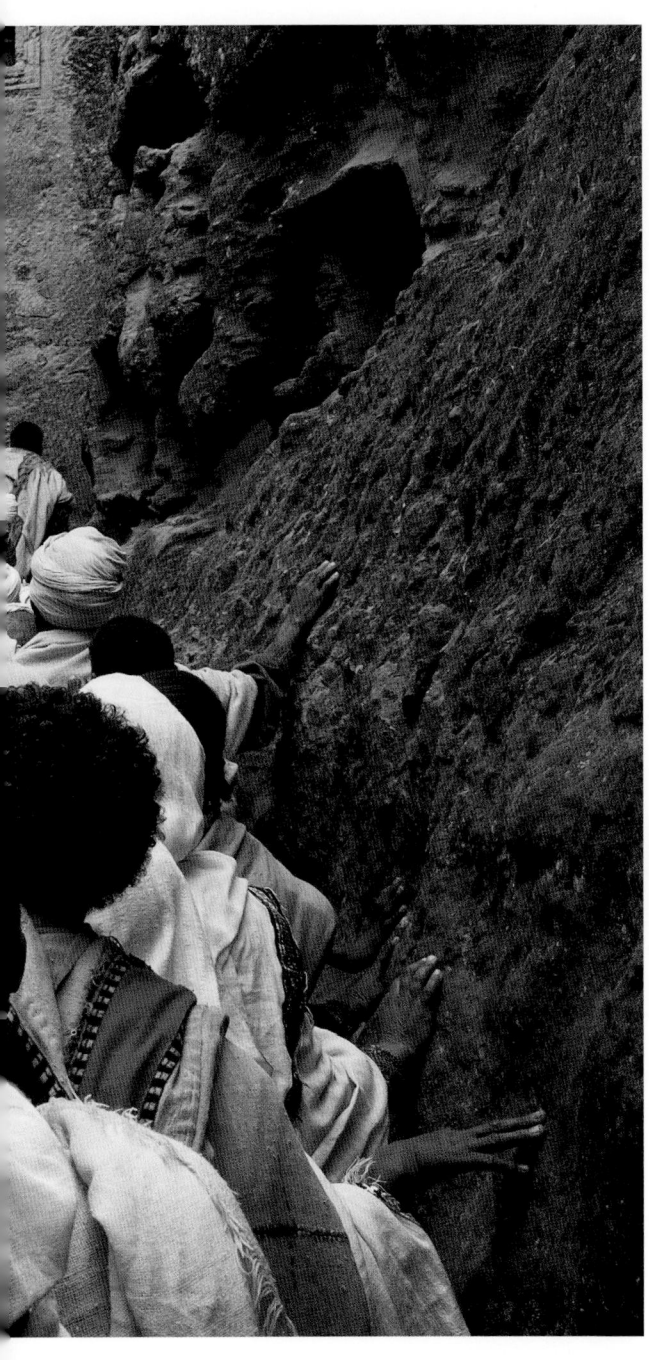

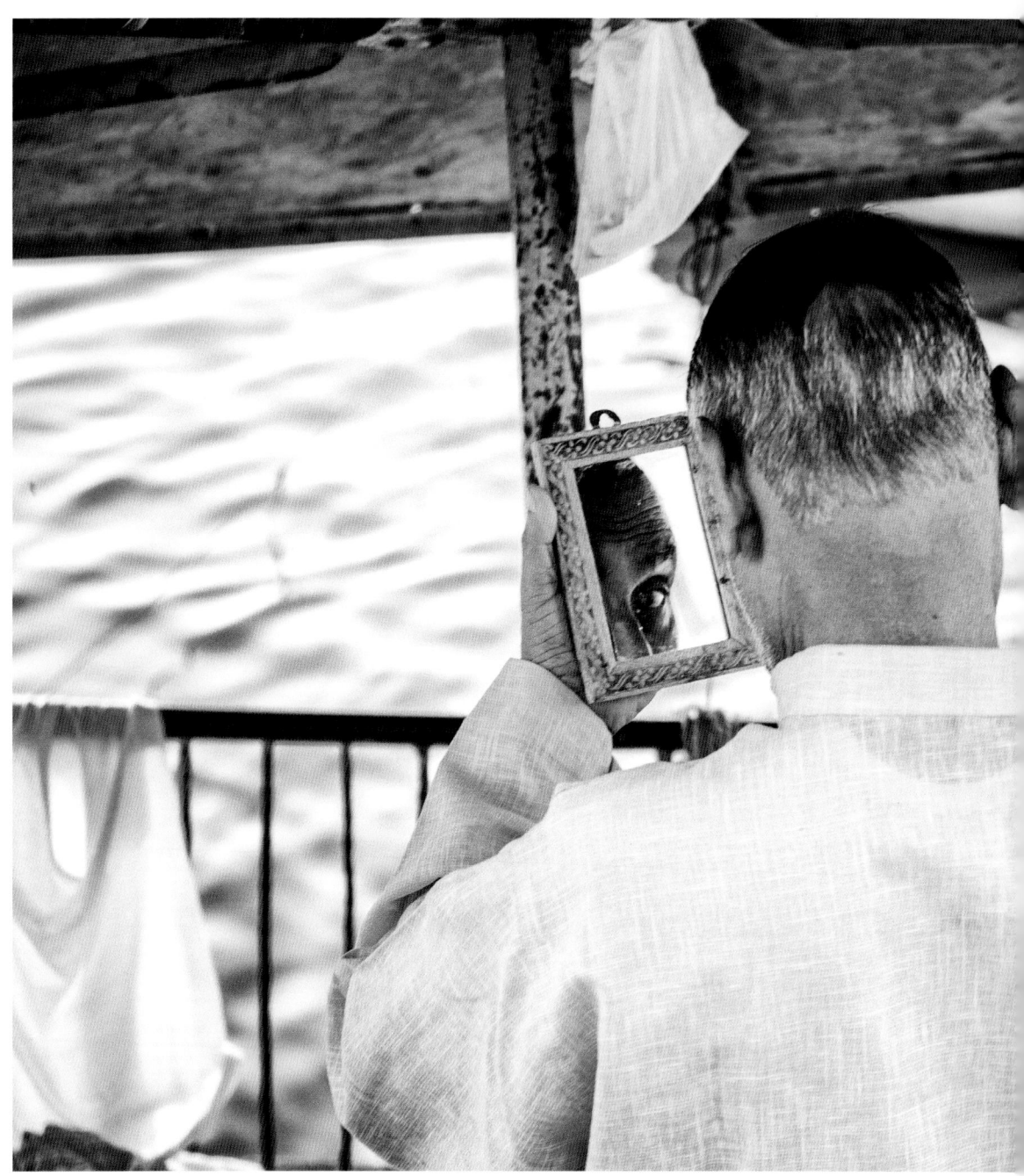

Varanasi, India, 2018

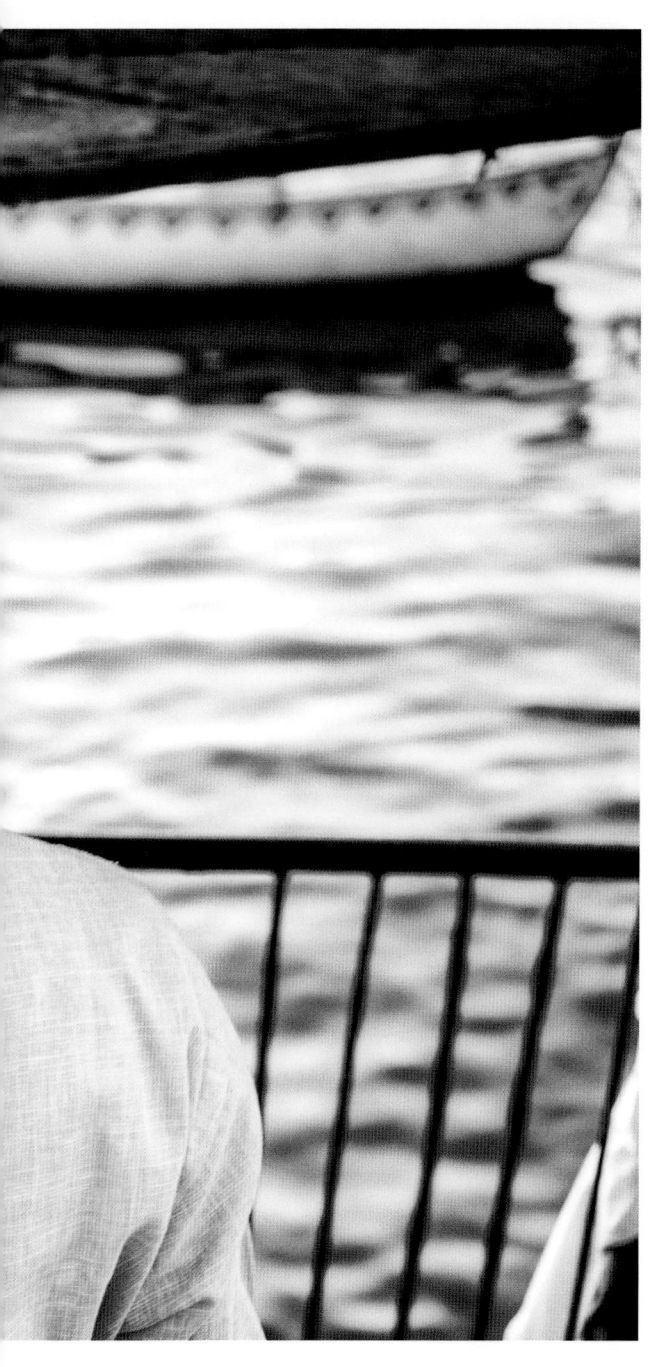

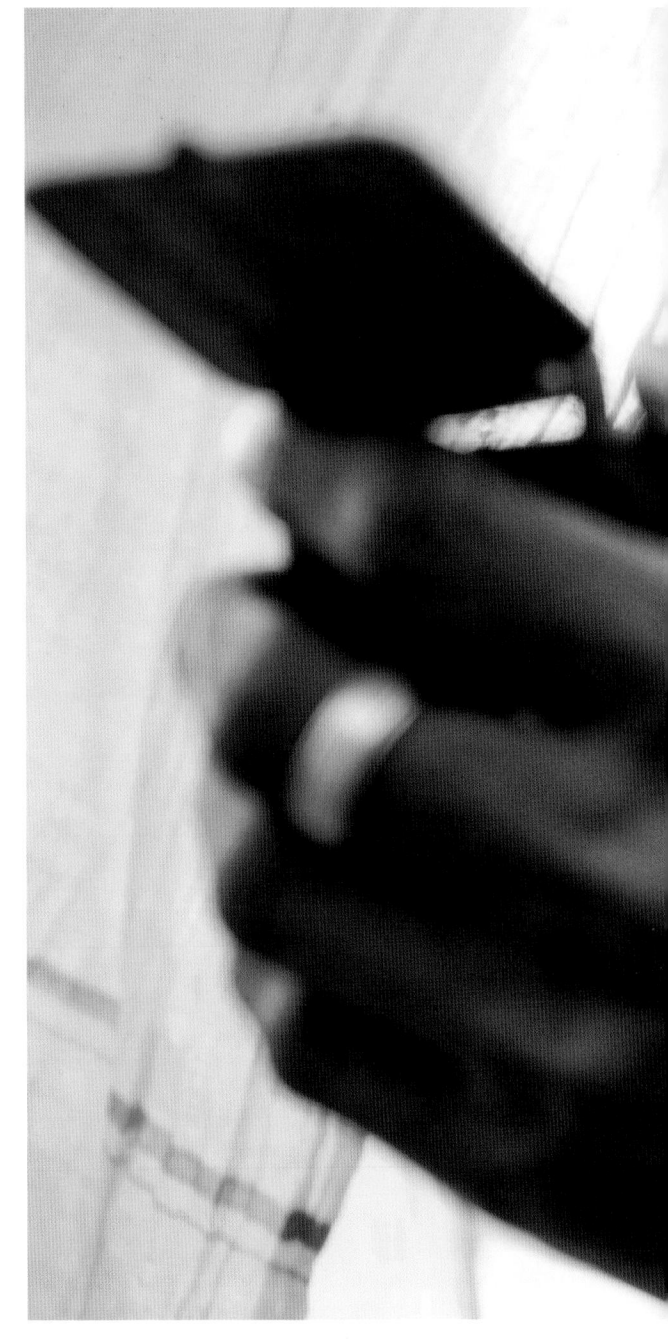

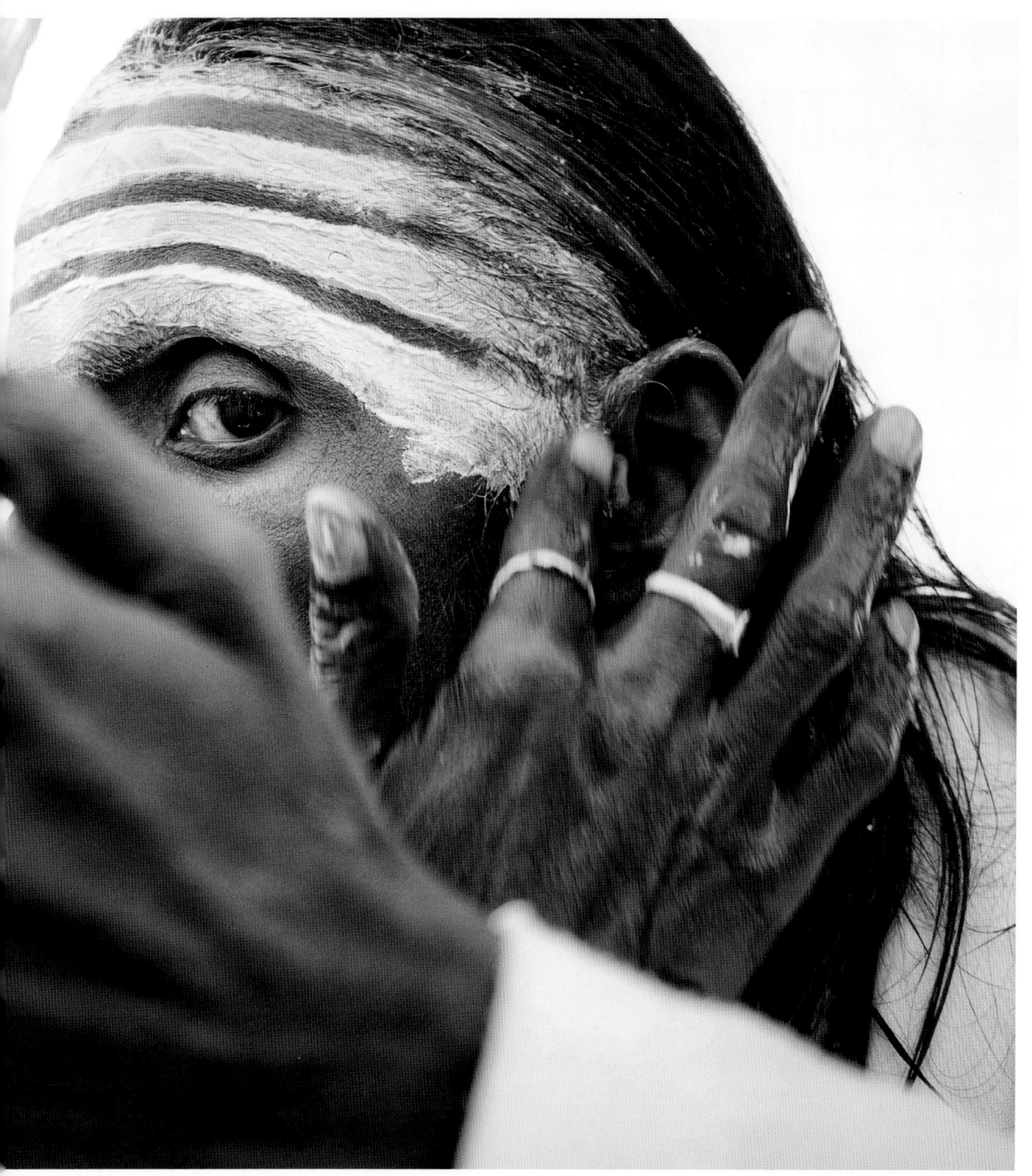

Varanasi, India, 2018

Sometimes we need
to bypass the mind
to draw the attention
of the heart.

26
Am I Being Too Literal?

NOT EVERY SUBJECT IS BEST EXPRESSED LITERALLY. The discussion of symbols in the previous chapter is an acknowledgement of that. Trying to fit a more abstract subject into forms that are only appropriate for literal subjects, or vice versa, will only lead to creative frustration and confusion. There are times when making the subject a symbol, asking it to represent something larger, is appropriate to your vision.

But there may be times when you ask it to be *less* specific. A symbol relies on an association with a known object: *this* means *that*. As we approach abstraction, we distance ourselves from identifiable objects and their meaning and ask instead, "What does this mean to you, if anything?" Abstraction is often interested in feeling and frequently relies on shape and colour that have no specific meaning in an image. The issue of meaning is left to others.

When did we all get so hung up on *understanding* and let it take precedence over *experiencing* and *feeling*?

I don't want this brief discussion to be about abstract photography (a movement all its own), but about using abstraction when more literal techniques just don't work, or when the image you want to make is about so much more than the actual thing you're photographing. I want to encourage you to make the occasional foray away from the literal.

Abstraction isn't the only way to do this. Impressionism, too, as it is explored by photographers, is incredibly liberating and offers creative options that more literal techniques do not. Spend an afternoon with the paintings of Monet, Cézanne, Van Gogh, or J.M.W. Turner, to name a few, and you will see the power of what came to be known rather spuriously as "Impressionism." Spend that same amount of time looking at Rothko, Picasso, or Pollock, and you will see the power of abstraction.

When I make this recommendation to photographers, I generally get one of three reactions. The first is that they just don't understand this kind of art, to which I ask what *understanding* that art has to do with *experiencing* it. Yes, a little context goes a long way. It's one reason to take the audio tour in museums and not only look at the art. But must you *understand* Turner to experience light the way he painted it? Not at all. Nor must you understand jazz to enjoy it, cuisine to appreciate it, or dance to feel its rhythm. When did we all get so hung up on understanding and let it take precedence over experiencing and feeling something with our guts and our hearts?

The second reaction I get is more serious. "But that's not the way the world looks," they say, as if the world really looks like any of the photographs we make: elements are pulled from their context by a frame, relationships are distorted and ordered by lenses and perspectives, time is misrepresented with shutter speeds, made to freeze forever. As if time ever stood still just once. The only thing I can say in reply is, "I guess that depends on how you choose to see," and hope they'll take me up on trying to see things a little more playfully.

The third reaction is my favourite: "Let me try that!" They are mesmerized by the possibilities and the unexpected. These photographers may never show another soul their efforts. They may never post them to Instagram, sell prints to a client, or include the images in their portfolio. But the play and the experimentation will help them understand their tools better and help them appreciate how their camera sees the world. They will begin to embrace play and experimentation, get more comfortable with failure, and take more delight in the play of line, shape, and colour when so-called realism isn't there to distract.

Assuming you have more in common with the third reaction than with the first two (though in my experience we usually slide from one to the other pretty quickly if we loosen up a little), here are some questions to help guide that exploration:

- Could I create abstraction through isolation by getting close enough, either physically or with my lens, to completely remove all visual clues about the identity of elements in my scene?

- Once I'm close, what lines and shapes can I find that hold my interest on their own merits?

- Could I create abstraction by defocusing my lens in order to render the scene in front of me into colour fields, and make a photograph about those colour relationships?

- Could I create abstraction or a sense of impression with my use of time and motion? Would a slow shutter and various camera movements introduce the feeling of motion and an impression of a scene, rather than a representation of it?

- Would multiple exposures, or even a combination of multiple exposures and intentional camera movement, create opportunities to make images about shape, colour, and motion?

- What possibilities exist in the darkroom or in Photoshop for combining images and finding new connections and interactions between them?

Above all, I want to encourage play and experimentation in your work. Yes, be intentional and figure out what gives your subject its strongest expression, but don't forget about delight. Don't forget that there is more than one way to tell a story or convey a thought, as poets and dancers and musicians have long known, using impressions and word pictures, relying on nothing more than sound and movement to move us deeply.

Sometimes we need to bypass the mind to draw the attention of the heart.

Photographers have a tendency to want to do it "right," to follow the rules, to run it all past the mind for approval. I suspect this is due to our strong connection to and reliance on the technical tools we use. Having the creative freedom to deny these rules their power and authority, to play with technique for the joy of it, will only spill into your other work, make it stronger, and allow you to become more comfortable with the nuance and ambiguity that have always accompanied art that speaks not only to our minds but to our hearts.

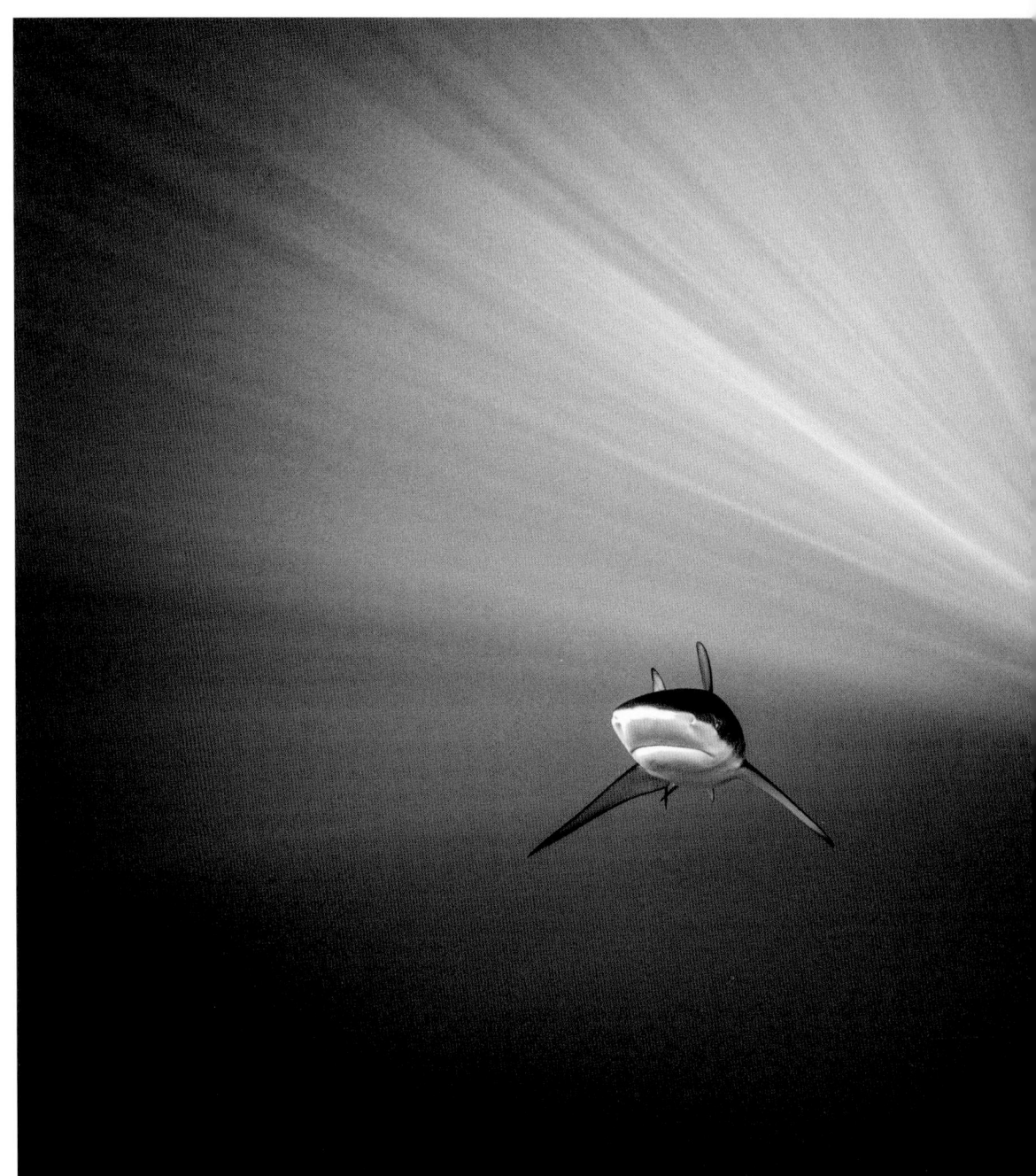

Revillagigedo Archipelago, Mexico, 2016

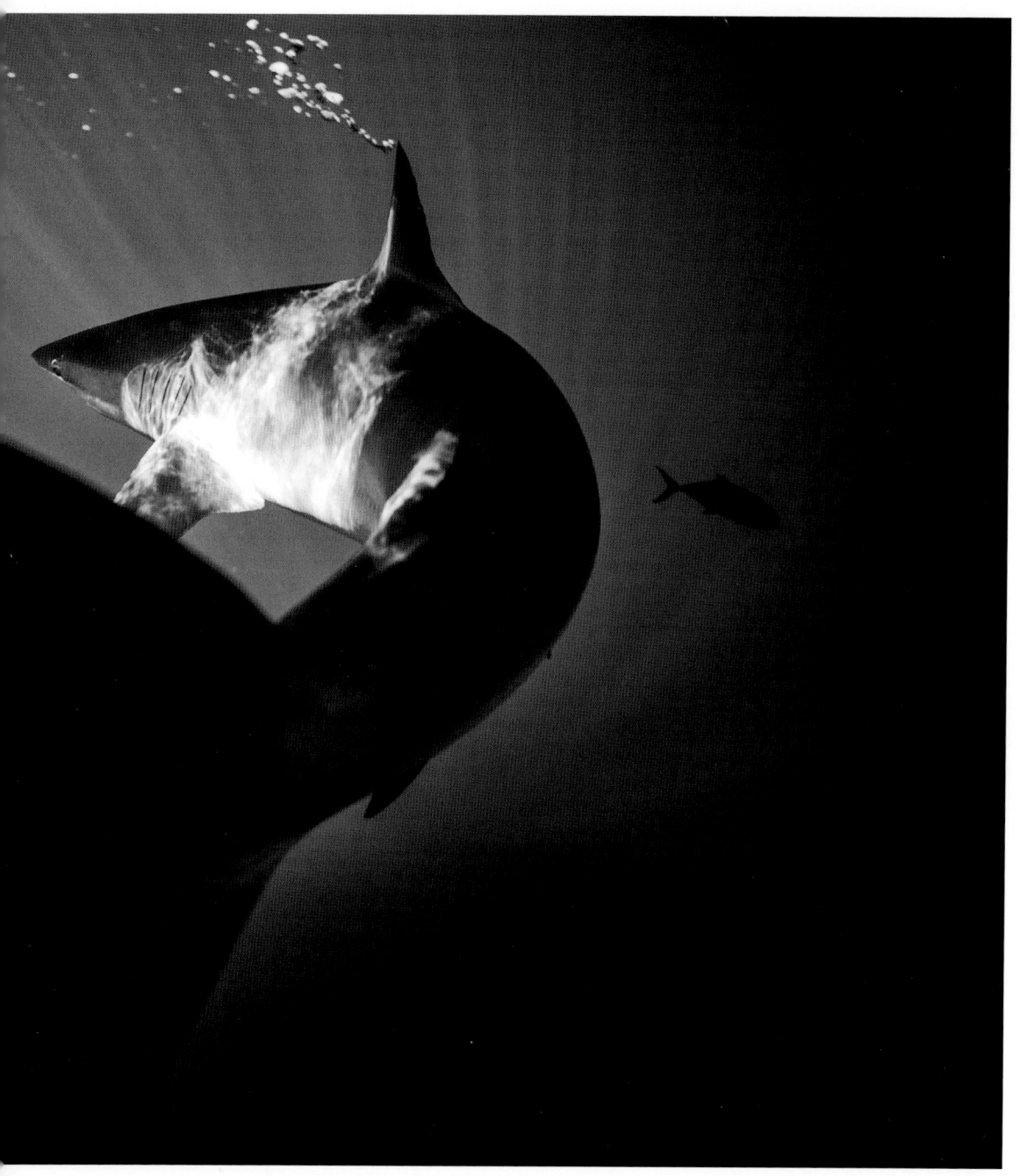

Revillagigedo Archipelago, Mexico, 2016

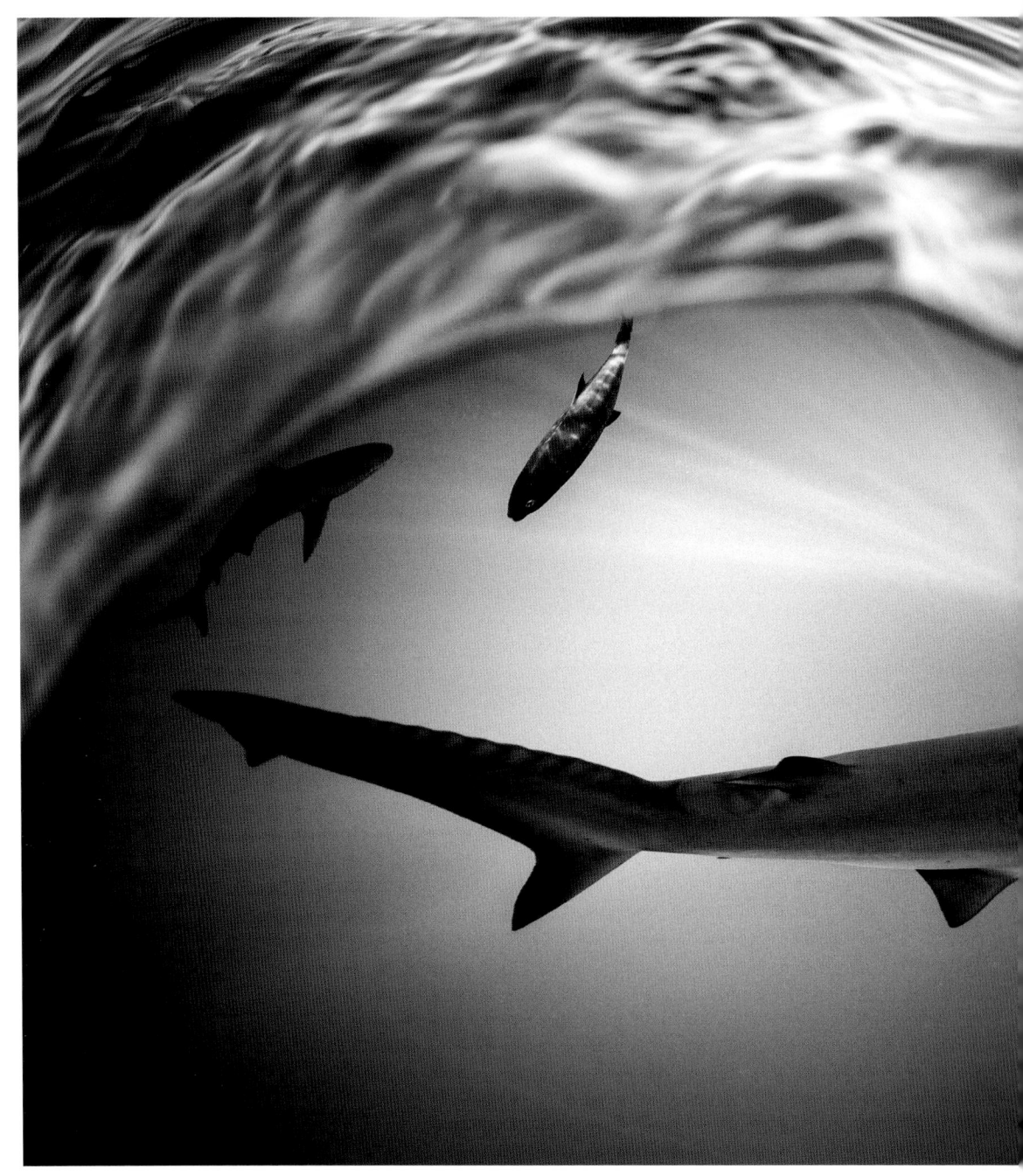

Revillagigedo Archipelago, Mexico, 2016

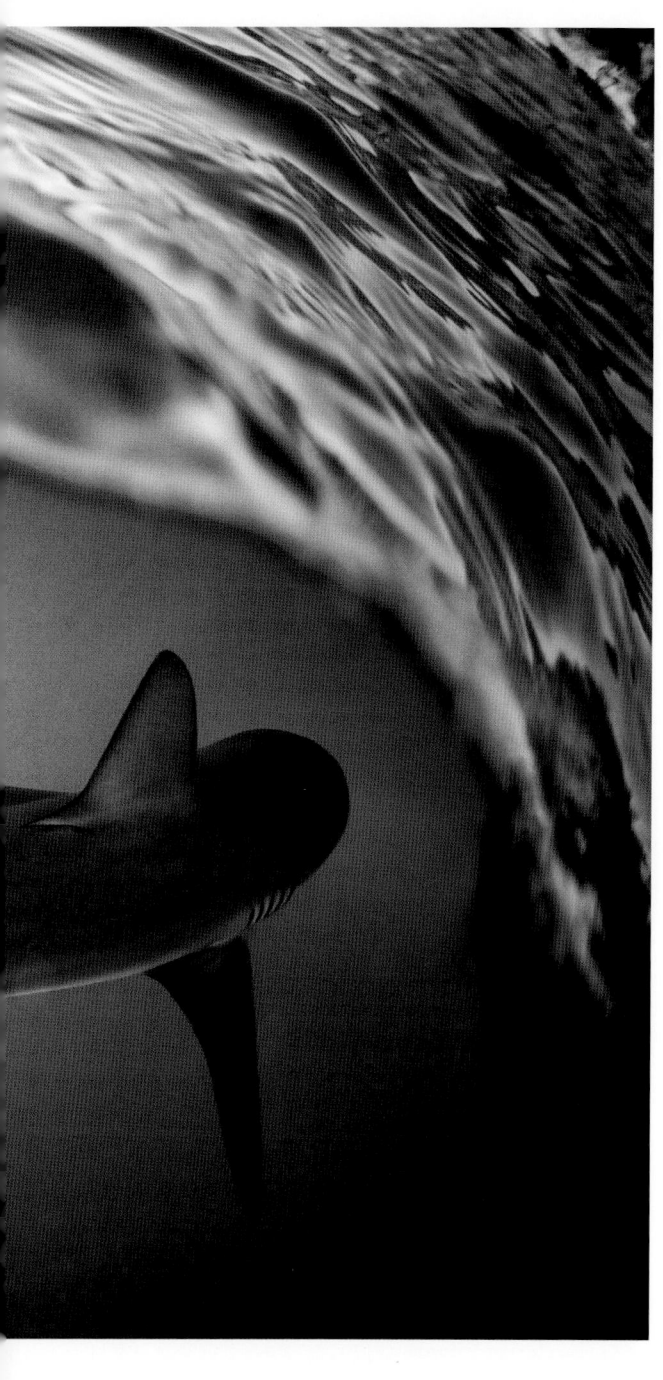

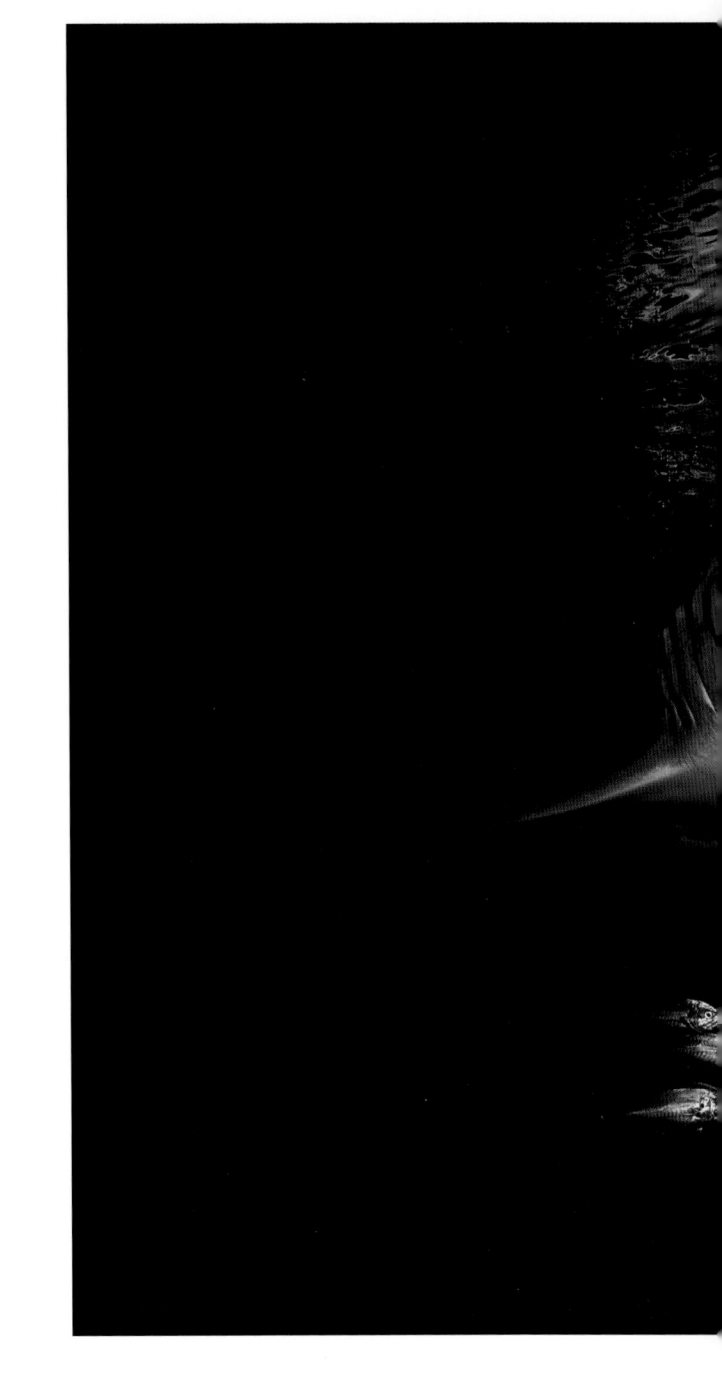

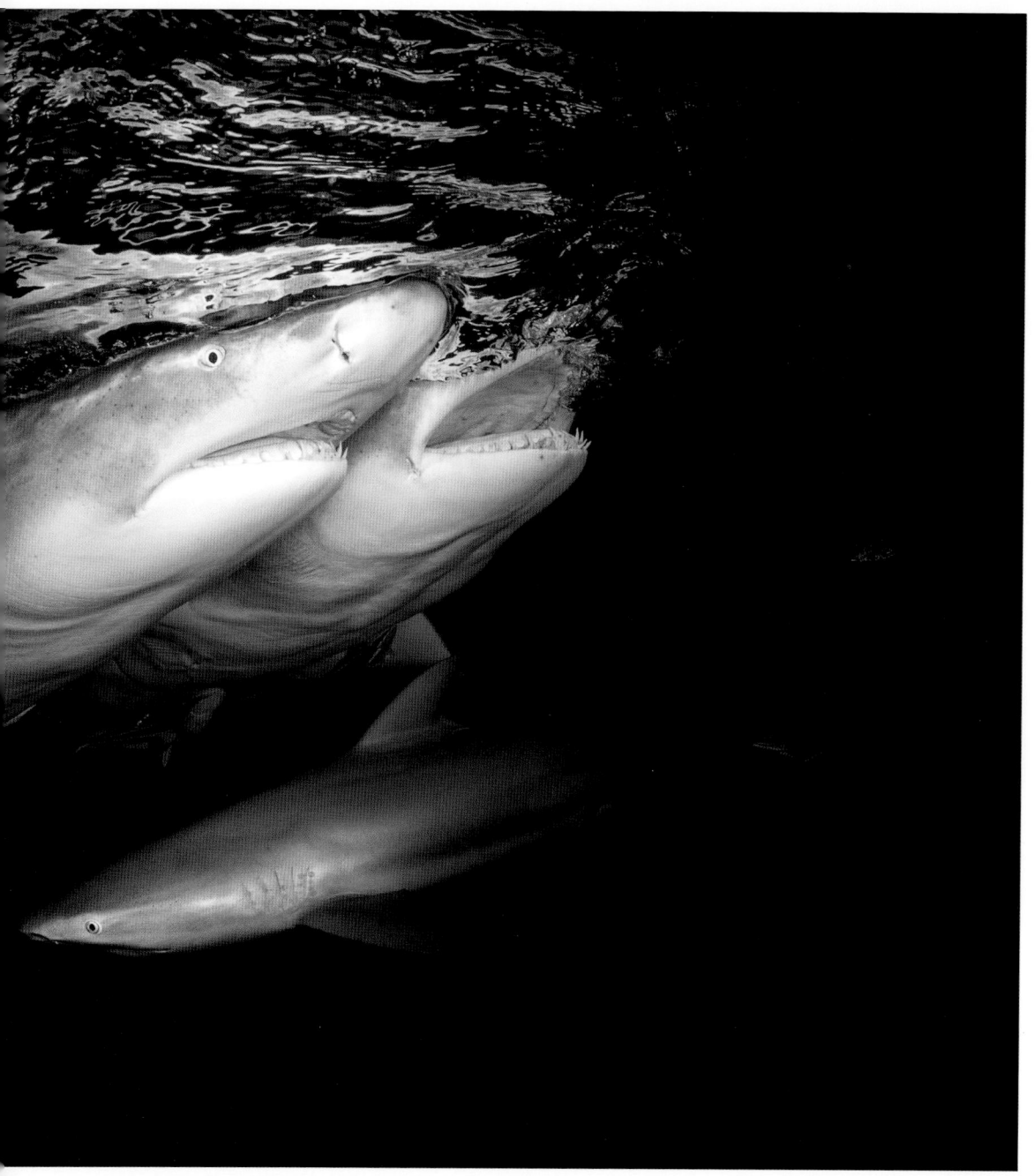

Tiger Beach, Bahamas, 2017

PART FOUR

Better Photographs

You are your own
first and most
important audience.

27

The Heart of the Photograph

THE HEART OF ANY PHOTOGRAPH will be as different from one image to the next as the infinite subjects and our thoughts and feelings about those subjects are from each other. What I have tried to do in this book is give you tools to explore those subjects more deeply, and to interpret them in your own way according to how you see them, how you feel about them, and what you want to say about them. I have tried to get you *thinking*.

I have tried hard *not* to give you formulas, rules, recipes, or platitudes. In giving you questions, I hope to nudge you away from the tendency of so many photographers to look for rules, to ask the one question I hope you will *never* ask:

"What *should* I do?"

There is no *should* in art. There is no one lens you should use for anything. There is no one setting, no single aperture, no rule of composition that will universally make a good photograph. There is only possibility. What lens *might* I use? What setting, aperture, shutter, or composition *might* I use? What can I try? What can I risk?

As I've written this book, in my mind I've treated this one idea as my north star: the heart of the photograph is the subject best expressed. But *best* is a meaning- less word unless we agree on who is determining that, for this one subject, in this moment, there is no better expression. So . . . *best* according to whom? You, and *you alone.*

Best according to how you see the subject and what you want to say. Best according to your tastes and preferences, the life you've lived, the emotions you feel, the opinions you have. Best according to your level of skill as you learn this craft. But never best in reference to the work of others. Art is not a competition, despite a photographic industry that makes it so. We do not make our best work looking at what others are doing, but rather by following whatever thread of curiosity is ours and ours alone.

We live in strange times. Never before has an artist been able to put his or her work into the world so broadly and so quickly. Never before has an artist been able to hear every voice that cares to praise, criticize, or issue feedback with neither context nor conversation. Most often, it's just a binary reaction: yes or no, a like or not, a heart or no heart. The subtle and complex shades of human reaction and emotion go out the window, replaced by comments like "Nice pic!" or worse, an emoji.

Not only can this suffocate our creativity, but it can lead us to misunderstand who our audience is. Surrounded by the metrics of social media or even the

There is no *should* in art. There is only possibility.

dozen people in your camera club, it's easy to begin thinking that they are your audience. They are not. Not at first. *You are.*

You are your own first and most important audience.

But how easily do we forget this when we put our work into the world and get mixed reactions, or no reaction at all? Or when we put it out there so soon after we make it and are still unsure about what we ourselves think and feel about what we've just made?

I think the biggest struggle of the artist is to know his or her own voice. To know it and trust it. To do that, it's helpful to understand who your audience is.

For whom do you make your art? If you don't know this, or mistakenly believe that it is anyone anywhere who looks at your photographs and has the means to tell you what they think about it, you will have a tough time ever discovering and taking responsibility for your own voice. Because voice is about authenticity, and you will not create authentic work when your first question is "What do they want?" instead of "What do I want?"

We all hope that the crowds will love both us and everything we make. They will not. Some will. Some people with whom your work resonates will eventually applaud, and that feels good. That audience might even grow. That feels even better. But it must never seduce you.

If you want to make art for your audience and have a chance at that audience loving your work and—best of all—discovering something of *you* in it, you must make it for yourself. That means not worrying how others will react to what you make. It means not putting your ego into your work so much that when the world out there doesn't so much as look sideways at your art, you don't mistake that rejection of your art for rejection of your self.

We live in a big, big world. The vast majority of our overpopulated planet will not applaud. They, like you, have other things on their minds. But rather than letting this fact deflate you, consider the freedom it brings to do things your way. To ask yourself the questions most important to you, and to answer them with your art.

And here is the miracle of art: when you create just for yourself and you do it in the truest way possible, your work possesses an authenticity that gives it its best chance to resonate with someone else. To be touched by your honesty. Your search for beauty. Your unflinching gaze. Your willingness to ask the hard questions. The astonishingly rare courage to be yourself. If you want to know what the world wants from your art, that's it right there. The world just doesn't know it yet.

Your art must be about you and for you. It's the meeting place of that honest soul and the place, time, and circumstances of life. Art is a mashup of you and life: a collaboration. And it can only be a gift to others if it begins not with them, but with you. Because you are all you really know. You are the source of your art. And you must be the first and most important audience for whom that art is made.

And it's in the making where you must find your joy. In the discovery. In getting your hands dirty and unearthing some new thing about yourself and the way you see the world. If you search for it there, you'll find it.

You are your own north star, your own demanding audience, and the only one who can make the art you most want or need to see in the world. Let that be

Here is the miracle of art: When you create just for yourself and you do it in the truest way possible, your work possesses an authenticity that gives it its best chance to resonate with someone else.

enough. Don't look over your shoulder at what others are doing. Don't cock your ear to one side to better hear the reactions of others. Make your photographs for you, and for now, only for you.

If you must seek feedback, as any earnest student of a craft must do to grow and learn, then do so from those few voices you yourself know, trust, and choose to listen to. Stop asking the internet and crowdsourcing your joy. It will dilute both your voice and the love of your craft.

Like the book that preceded this, *The Soul of the Camera*, it all comes back to you. You bring the humanity to your craft and your art. And it is your humanity that we so very badly need and which will be the source of not only your best photographs but your joy in making them.

Of all the questions in this book, each of them full of possibilities for new directions in your photography, the most important is this:

"Is it yours?"

Spend the rest of your photographic life seeking the answer to that question, and it will be hard to go wrong. Because ultimately, *you* are the heart of your photographs.

I wish you great light and unforgettable moments,

David duChemin
Vancouver Island, British Columbia, 2020

P.S. If this book has resonated with you, and you've found it helpful in taking needed next steps on your journey, I'd love to continue to accompany you on that journey. *The Soul of the Camera: The Photographer's Place in Picture-Making* would make an excellent follow-up to *The Heart of the Photograph* and can be found online or at your favourite local bookstore. If you would like to stay con-nected with me, you can download free resources, get access to the thousand articles about the photographic life and craft on my blog, or connect on social media channels at HeartofThePhotographBook.com. You can also find me and my work at DavidduChemin.com. If this book has made a difference to you, I'd be so grateful if you'd recommend it to others or leave a short review on Amazon or wherever you bought it. Thank you.

It is not the answer that enlightens, but the question.

—EUGÈNE IONESCO

Index